Strategic Questions in
Food and Beverage Management

Strategic Questions in Food and Beverage Management

Edited by Roy C. Wood

OXFORD AUCKLAND BOSTON JOHANNESBURG MELBOURNE NEW DELHI

Butterworth-Heinemann
Linacre House, Jordan Hill, Oxford OX2 8DP
225 Wildwood Avenue, Woburn, MA 01801-2041
A division of Reed Educational and Professional Publishing Ltd

ℛ A member of the Reed Elsevier plc group

First published 2000

British Library Cataloguing in Publication Data
Strategic questions in food and beverage management
   1. Food service management – Great Britain
   2. Food service – Social aspects – Great Britain
   I. Wood, Roy C. (Roy Christopher), 1959–
647.9'5'41

ISBN 0 7506 4480 X

Composition by Genesis Typesetting, Rochester, Kent
Printed and bound in Great Britain by
Biddles Ltd, www.biddles.co.uk

Contents

Hospitality, Leisure & Tourism Series

Acknowledgements

No matter how many times you do it, editing a book is never easy. In the case of this text, the task was made immeasurably easier, and indeed pleasurable, by my contributing colleagues whose enthusiasm for the project both motivated and sustained the editorial process. I am grateful to MCB University Press for permission to utilize some previously published work in Chapter 14 (cited there as Wood, 1996); the Controller of Her Majesty's Stationery Office for permission to reproduce Box 15.1; and to Tim Goodfellow of Butterworth-Heinemann who commissioned the text, and his colleague Sally North who saw it through the production process with great tact, style and expertise. With regard to the commissioning process it is a pleasure to acknowledge the linchpin role of Professor Conrad Lashley who saw the potential of the work. Last, but (in the words of an all-too-true cliché) by no means least, my largest debt of thanks is to my friend and colleague Leslie Mitchell who not only typed and composed the manuscript with great skill, speed, efficiency and good humour, but in the process learned more about food and beverage management than he ever wanted to know.

Professor Roy C. Wood
Glasgow
1999

Contributors

Matthew J. Alexander is Food and Beverage Manager at The Scottish Hotel School, University of Strathclyde.

Joseph E. Fattorini is a broadcaster and journalist. From 1996–1998 he was the Sir Hugh Wontner Lecturer in Hotel Management at The Scottish Hotel School, University of Strathclyde where he now holds an Honorary Lectureship. He is a regular contributor to *The Herald* newspaper, to various BBC radio programmes, and is the author of numerous academic articles and a book *Managing Wine and Wine Sales*.

Erwin Losekoot is currently the Sir Hugh Wontner Lecturer in Hotel Management at The Scottish Hotel School, University of Strathclyde. After graduating from Strathclyde University in hotel management and marketing, he took an MBA at Edinburgh University. He has worked for P&O Princess Cruises, Sheraton and Holiday Inn. A member of the Institute for Quality Assurance, his current research interests lie in the field of quality systems in the hospitality field.

Dr Dennis P. Nickson lectures in human resource management at The Scottish Hotel School, University of Strathclyde. He is the author of numerous articles on human resource aspects of the hospitality industry and co-author of a text, *Human Resource Management for Hospitality Services*. His current research focuses on aesthetic aspects of work and employment in hotels, restaurants and other service industries.

Professor John O'Connor is Professor Emeritus of Hotel Management at Oxford Brookes University and Visiting Professor, The Scottish Hotel School, University of Strathclyde. A distinguished educationalist, Professor O'Connor is the founding editor of the *International Journal of Hospitality Management*.

Sandie Randall is a lecturer in hospitality management at Queen Margaret University College, Edinburgh. Her recent research and publications have been concerned with media representations of food and hospitality. She is a main contributor to the new *Eyewitness Guide to Scotland*.

Professor Michael J Riley is at the School of Management Studies for the Service Sector at the University of Surrey. He is the author of several books and many articles on key areas of hospitality management including human resource management, food and beverage management and service quality issues in the hotel and restaurant industry.

Donald H. Sloan is Senior Lecturer in Human Resource Management in the School of Hotel and Restaurant Management at Oxford Brookes University. Previously a researcher on the Strathclyde Food Project where he undertook work on which his contribution to this book is based, he is also co-author of the text, *Human Resource Management for Hospitality Services*.

Stephen Taylor is Lecturer at The Scottish Hotel School, University of Strathclyde where he specializes in teaching strategic management. He has contributed to several journals and books on this and related topics, the latter including McDonaldization, and theory and method in hospitality management.

Professor Roy C. Wood holds the Chair in Hospitality Management at The Scottish Hotel School, University of Strathclyde. He is the author or co-author of seven books and numerous articles, principally in the areas of human resource management and food studies.

CHAPTER 1

Introduction: Is food and beverage management in a rut?

Roy C. Wood

Together, the management of accommodation, and of food and beverage services, constitute the defining features of hospitality *management*. That is, each represents a body of distinctive knowledge and knowledge applications which, though for the most part deriving from the generalized knowledge and techniques of other disciplines (business administration, accounting, engineering, information science), lend a specific character to the management of facilities directed towards the provision of hospitality.

On many courses in hospitality management at advanced (degree) level – at least in the UK – great emphasis is placed upon the operational aspects of food and beverage management. Students on such courses are (ideally) taught the principles underlying the management of food production and food services and typically engage in various extended role plays as part of this experience – actually preparing and serving food. The term 'ideally' is used advisedly in this context: there are still too many hospitality management courses where this supporting element of food and beverage management education actually becomes the central purpose of the educational experience, where operations management is subordinated to operations *training*. In a highly perceptive commentary, Mars, Bryant and Mitchell (1979) described this tendency in hospitality management education as part of the 'pre-entry socialisation' of students, 'pre-entry' referring to that training (including placements) prior to the careers that students would follow in the hospitality industry. In this view, the operational role play element of food and beverage 'management' education acts to instil a particular, traditional, view of management emphasizing the importance of day-to-day operational control, rather than the skills of long-term planning and any other of a number of techniques that today tend to fall under the heading of 'strategy'.

Mars, Bryant and Mitchell (1979) have a point. Yet at degree level, educators face any number of dilemmas of which the authors take no account. Most important of these is the vocational expectations of students and employers. It is frequently asserted by educators that operational skills in food and beverage are essential to the career progress of graduates once they enter the hospitality industry. There is some evidence to support this from studies of the career paths of successful general managers (see Wood, 1997 for a review). Equally, however, there are a number of reasons for viewing such assertions with suspicion. For example, it is generally accepted that graduate entrants to the industry accrue few, if any, advantages over non-graduate entrants who 'work their way up' (Riley and Turam, 1988). In other words, it is operational experience 'on the job' that counts and not formal education in terms of career progression. Successful managers, it appears, certainly do require operational food and beverage knowledge – but it is knowledge gained through employment experience that counts rather than formal education. Is it possible, then, for educators to abandon the operational simulation of food and beverage procedures in the educational environment without detriment to students' employment profiles? The answer, probably, is 'yes', but it would be a courageous (even reckless) and perhaps even foolish educator who would advocate complete abandonment of operational training in food and beverage management *in support* of operational education. This is simply because, irrespective of the realities of career progress in the hospitality industry, employers therein *expect* graduates in their field to possess some such experience (although employers perhaps look more to the experience of students gained on periods of industrial placement as part of their course rather than operational simulations that constitute a formal part of such courses).

There is, however, another reason why an emphasis on both operational education *and* operational training in food and beverage management is potentially limiting. This is because such an approach detracts from what was referred to above, in the most general terms, as the 'strategic' aspects of food and beverage management. If most degree courses in hospitality management are distinctive because of a core focus on activities such as food and beverage and accommodation management, then it is also the case that students are educated in broader management disciplines such as accounting and finance, marketing, law and human resource management. As any casual scrutiny of hotel school prospectuses reveals, there are a variety of approaches to such subjects within the curriculum. Three common models are:

1 General management disciplines are 'applied' directly to the hospitality industry using examplars drawn from research and practice in the sector.
2 General management disciplines are taught *as such*, and hospitality 'applications' and examples play a limited (and indeed sometimes negligible) role in the curriculum.
3 A combination of the above approaches, most typically exemplified by students taking a general introductory class or module in a subject before proceeding to more 'applied' study.

Whichever model is adopted by schools of hospitality management, there is intense pressure on the space available within a three- or four-year curriculum to accommodate these various subjects and this often leads to trade-offs and compromises in both time allocations to subjects, and in the construction of the curriculum itself in terms of the allocation of responsibility for teaching particular subjects.

Because of the operational emphasis given to food and beverage management education within the hospitality curriculum, it is not unusual to find that consideration of 'strategic' aspects of the subject are reserved to, and distributed among, subjects such as marketing, human resource management, law and so on. The risks of such an approach lie in the dislocation of consideration of these strategic aspects of food and beverage management from the operational dimensions of the subject. There is some irony in this, given that food and beverage is, as suggested earlier, one of the two distinctive subjects that characterizes, specifically, the nature of hospitality management.

At this point it is necessary to make clear that the argument here is not that such dislocation occurs in all courses in hospitality management. Nor is it the intention to take a particular, 'moral', stance about any specific educational approach to the hospitality curriculum. Rather, the position adopted, both here and throughout this book, is that the distinctiveness the study and understanding of food and beverage management lends to the wider field of hospitality management has not been fully exploited in terms of both:

- the development and synthesis of knowledge relating to the wider social, business and management aspects of food and beverage studies; and

- the integration of this 'strategic' knowledge with operational elements into a holistic perspective on hospitality businesses.

The term 'strategic' is used here in a very loose sense. Indeed, the word 'contextual' might be more appropriate to describe the wider social and business knowledge that hinges upon the operational aspects of food and beverage management. However, while 'strategy' and 'strategic management' have established specific and detailed connotations in the field of business studies, strategic management in the most general sense is concerned with the interactions between an organization and its environment and, more precisely, how such interactions are planned, maintained and utilized to the benefit of an organization. The emphasis placed upon operational aspects of food and beverage studies within the curriculum of hospitality management courses does not adequately reflect the academic progress that has been made in assessing strategic dimensions to food and beverage, evident, for example, in Davis and Lockwood's (1994) excellent collection of articles on the subject and the more recent and largely successful attempt by Waller (1996) to offer an integrated approach to the management of the food and beverage function. Nevertheless, with notable exceptions (see for example Houghton and Lennon on retailing applications to hospitality and Connell on branding in the Davis and Lockwood, 1994, collection) these efforts to offer a holistic, integrated strategic and operational perspective very much reflect a bias towards the former in terms of a focus upon the structural aspects of economic and financial performance in a corporate context (returning to the Davis and Lockwood collection, we find articles on quantitative decision making, the performance of corporate food and beverage, strategies for expansion, and restaurant company financial performance).

Clearly, all these subjects are important and pertinent to the successful management of food and beverage – even the simple operator in a small market town may derive much of value from the perspectives offered even though they have no interest in expansion. Similarly, in the light of the scholarly advances made in the *business* analysis of food and beverage management epitomized by the two sources cited thus far – Davis and Lockwood (1994) and Waller (1996) (to which we might add a third valuable source in the form of Jones and Merricks, 1994) it becomes increasingly obvious that the complexities of even the operational analysis and management of food and beverage are, conceptually, far more demanding and relevant than would be implied by the very limited notion of 'operations' that constitute the food and beverage mainspring on hospitality management courses, i.e. the processes of food production and service discussed earlier. Important, actually imperative, though financial and economic aspects of strategic management may be however, there are many factors which bear on organizational success.

Thus far there has been a scholarly tendency to focus not only on the economic/financial aspects of strategy but a bias (in the food and beverage context at least) towards examining the strategy process from the inside out, i.e. in terms of *developing* the food and beverage function or organization 'outwards' towards the macroeconomic, industry, environment. In this book, the main (though by no means exclusive) emphasis is on the 'outside in' aspects of strategy, that is, the effect of various elements in the external environment upon the operation of the food and beverage function whether this be in hotels, restaurants or other hospitality organizations. The adoption of this stance is beneficial in four principal ways. First, it allows exploration of how both social and economic processes and trends influence food and beverage provision and vice versa. Second, it permits discussion of topics which may influence all types of food and beverage organization, rather than assuming the definition of 'strategy' or 'strategic' more precisely associated with corporate organizational entities. Third, and relatedly, in adopting a looser definition of 'strategy' it is possible to focus upon certain pragmatic concerns that from time-to-time preoccupy food and beverage managers/operators but which are not ordinarily encompassed within the disciplinary boundaries of strategic management. Finally, the approach here allows a certain freedom to question key strategic *and* operational assumptions underlying the provision of food and beverage services (whatever their location) because the constraints imposed by the assumptions of a particular mind- or knowledge-set (e.g. strategic management) are absent.

Is it then the case that food and beverage management is in a rut? To satisfactorily answer this question we must return to the concepts of the 'operational' and 'operations management'. Where food and beverage *education* focuses mainly on a *training* model, emphasizing food production and service techniques to the exclusion or near-exclusion of all else other than a basic understanding of elements of the food and beverage cycle (e.g. purchasing, storage, see Chapter 5) then there is indeed an excellent case for arguing that food and beverage is trapped in a limiting paradigm or framework – it is in a rut. More generally, however, food and beverage management remains an exciting and fertile ground for research and analysis. Importantly, such research and analysis can have genuine implications for actual practice. In this book we seek to capture some of this excitement and to build on the existing research literature, but by adopting a somewhat different approach.

This approach is characterized by the posing of certain questions, as shown in the chapter titles. Pursuing our loose definition of strategy, the purpose of the book is to explore how issues in the business 'environment' bear on the operational practice of food and beverage management. The business environment is, inevitably, a social as well as economic phenomenon and each chapter draws on a variety of sources to explore issues which are often taken for granted in current academic scholarship on food and beverage management. Our purpose is not to be deliberately controversial, but to address those areas where acceptance of particular industry myths has practical consequences for business operations, and to examine what appear as especially persistent operational problems in the light of often ignored factors in the wider market environment. All the questions posed in this book have received (and continue to receive) attention in one form or another in the hospitality trade press and many have been similarly posed by individuals (in large and small hospitality organizations alike) who approach colleges and universities for advice. Interest in the topics reflects not only the centrality of food and beverage management within the hospitality industry but the efforts of both theoreticians and practitioners to come to terms with diverse forces that influence success in the sector.

In this regard, and finally here, the chapters in this collection draw on a wide range of other disciplinary sources including sociology, culture/media studies, philosophy, marketing, and economics. In recent years, there has been a huge growth of interest in food from these and other disciplines. The food and beverage element within hospitality management education has been largely left untouched by these developments, remaining trapped for the most part in a paradigm that emphasizes, as we have suggested, the narrowly practical. Social scientists on the other hand have indulged in a degree of apologetic self-flagellation in seeking to explain their recent interest in the cultural comparative of food. Thus Curtin (1992: 3) in full philosophical flow, writes:

> Philosophers in the dominant western tradition have been uninterested in those aspects of life that 'give colour to existence', those common, everyday experiences that, as we say, 'add spice to life'. Rather, they have confined their attention to those aspects they thought could be ordered by 'theories' (where theory-making is understood to be the activity of reducing temporal events to abstract, disembodied, atemporal schemata), and to those kinds of values that are defined as public, masculine, and universal. Our relations to aspects of life that can only be understood as concrete and embodied (primary among them our relations to food) have been marginalized. They have been pushed to the periphery of what is regarded as important.

Similarly, at the interface between philosophy and sociology Lupton (1996: 2–3) comments that:

> The practice of cooking has similarly received little serious scholarly attention because of its transitory nature and link with physical labour and the servicing of bodies rather than with 'science', 'art' or 'theory'. Cooking is identified as a practical activity, enmeshed in the physical temporal world. It is therefore regarded as base and inferior compared with intellectual or spiritual activities . . .[.] Philosophy is masculine and disembodied; food and eating are feminine and always embodied. To pay attention to such everyday banalities as food practices is to highlight the animality always lurking within the 'civilized' veneer of the human subject.

It would be perverse to suggest that those in the field of hospitality management, and food and beverage management in particular, have ignored the social dimensions to food and eating. It is, however, reasonable to suggest that such considerations have largely remained secondary to the models of pedagogic delivery discussed earlier. This book hopes to go some small way to correcting this imbalance by seeking to emphasize that what might seem abstract and tangential to food and beverage management is in fact central and critically relevant to reflective practitioners.

Thus, Chapters 2 and 3 examine two taken-for-granted issues, namely the nature of food and beverage markets and the meaning of the meal experience. In Chapter 4, Stephen Taylor examines the trend towards McDonaldization, something of relevance to the formation of operations and systems management and hence to customer 'meal experiences'. Donald Sloan examines the nature of the food and beverage supply chain in the hospitality industry in Chapter 5. Sandie Randall and Joseph Fattorini in Chapters 6 and 7 respectively explore the role of the media as an intervening force between the food and beverage operator and the consumer. Randall's article offers a forceful analysis of media influence on public taste while Fattorini tackles a frequently asked (but rarely answered) question about the impact of restaurant critics on the hospitality business. Fattorini pursues many of these issues further in Chapter 12 but in the context of the wine consumer. In Chapter 8, Michael Riley tackles the currently thorny question of the profitability of hotel restaurants. In an industry where there is a trend towards outsourcing hotel restaurant facilities, Riley offers a cautionary analysis. Following this, in Chapter 9, Riley focuses on the issue of food and beverage productivity. In an industry in which interest in productivity is once again resurgent, this chapter offers refreshing insights into some of the key areas for action. Chapters 10 and 11 return to more 'qualitative' questions in food and beverage management and in particular the role of the chef in hospitality enterprises and recurrent debates about the artistry of food.

Chapter 13, by Riley again, explores the central significance of food and beverage provision to the tourism product. Whether tourists or not, restaurateurs and their diners will be at least passingly familiar with debates about dress codes (Alexander and Losekoot, Chapter 14) and smoking (Nickson, Chapter 15) in restaurants. The collection concludes with an overview of the recent history of food and beverage management and its implication for current trends in an incisive account by John O'Connor (Chapter 16).

The nature of this book militates against any particular structure of logic: the book can be dipped into at will or read cover-to-cover. The provision of food and drink for public consumption is an exciting business but it too often lacks a certain logic: customers can be fickle; their tastes and desires uncertain; restaurateurs can be eccentric. This book seeks to capture some of this exciting pluralism.

References

Curtin, D. W. (1992) Food/Body/Person, in D. W. Curtin and L. M. Heldke (Eds) *Cooking, Eating, Thinking: Transformative Philosophies of Food*, Bloomington and Indianapolis: Indiana University Press, 2–15.

Davis, B. and Lockwood, A. (Eds) (1994) *Food and Beverage Management: A Selection of Readings*, Oxford: Butterworth-Heinemann.

Jones, P. and Merricks, P. (1994) *The Management of Foodservice Operations*, London: Cassell.

Lupton, D. (1996) *Food, the Body and the Self*, London: Sage.

Mars, G., Bryant, D. and Mitchell, P. (1979) *Manpower Problems in the Hotel and Catering Industry*, Farnborough: Saxon House.

Riley, M. and Turam, K. (1988) The career paths of hotel managers: a developmental approach. Paper given at the International Association of Hotel Management Schools Symposium, Leeds, November.

Waller, K. (1996) *Improving Food and Beverage Performance*, Oxford: Butterworth-Heinemann.

Wood, R. C. (1997) *Working in Hotels and Catering*, London: International Thomson Business Press, 2nd edition.

What do we really know about the requirements of food and beverage consumers? Food and beverage markets in the modern age

Roy C. Wood

Introduction

Any modestly systematic scrutiny of the hospitality trade press, lifestyle magazines and the more literate newspapers over a relatively short period of time would lead one to believe that the food and beverage consumer was a fickle creature. In the last twenty years or so we have had prophecies of doom about the decline of traditional mealtaking, both in the domestic and public spheres of dining; we have seen and believed countless 'informed' commentaries about how the food and beverage consumer has shifted to 'grazing' (and as a corollary, several different definitions of what grazing might be – here we will employ the concept of eating little, frequently); or more recently the growing preferences for 'street foods' (whatever they may be). The continuing, often seemingly exponential, growth of media coverage of all matters concerning food and eating has (among those who work in the media and a relative minority of slavish would-be trendsetting followers) created confusion, complexity – indeed one might say a 'feeding frenzy' – and a stew of often contradictory information that makes it difficult to see beyond the froth to what is actually happening, if anything, to consumer tastes and requirements. Perhaps all we need to know is that people eat out a lot. If only it were so simple. Current conceptions of food and beverage management are beset by myths, half-truths and the downright spurious when it comes to 'facts' about consumers. In this and the next chapter we concentrate on some of these issues in an effort to uncover some of the realities of dining out.

The importance of a square meal

There is some measure of agreement among serious scholars of food and eating that since the beginnings of mass industrialization in the nineteenth century, there has been a trend towards the 'interpenetration' of private and public dining (Mennell, 1985) a process which has probably accelerated in the last thirty years or so (Driver, 1983; Wood, 1995). Stripped of its sociological pretentiousness, the term 'interpenetration' means that there has been a growing alignment between what we eat at home and what we eat when we dine out – each has influenced, and continues to influence, the other. This process has been supported by refinements in agricultural production; improved transportation; the development of technology; the opening-up or broad democratization of markets so that more people eat out because they can afford to; a growing acceptance and diffusion of the idea of eating out as a leisure activity; and changes in the patterns of work and hence consumption.

At the heart of all this is, as the earlier introduction implied, how people eat, what it is that they eat, and why they eat as they do – particularly when dining out. This chapter is mainly concerned with the first two – the 'how' and 'what' questions, and any consideration of how people eat must begin in the home, with the 'family' meal.

How people eat

Is the traditional 'family' meal in decline? With monotonous regularity some freelance journalist trots out this thesis and it is published as a feature in a respectable broadsheet newspaper. Before we know it, such information is absorbed into everyday culture and discourse, it becomes a fact. A somewhat better version of the usual kind of 'isn't it dreadful' piece is exemplified by Quigley (1996) in an article for the well-regarded Scottish broadsheet *Scotland on Sunday*. Supported with results from a poll undertaken by Market Research Scotland based on 1022 inter-views, Quigley's article focuses on the supposedly pernicious influence of television on the decline in family meal taking. Two of the samples' responses are of particular interest and we can compare the results as shown in Table 2.1.

Average number of times per week family sit down to eat together		How many times per week do you watch TV while eating a meal?	
	(per cent)		(per cent)
Never	3	Never	15
Less than once per week	4	Less than once per week	7
Once a week	6	Once a week	9
2–3 days a week	14	2–3 days a week	18
4–6 days a week	17	4–6 days a week	9
Everyday	55	Everyday	42

Table 2.1

This is the kind of survey that can get research a bad name. Who was asked these questions? How was a meal defined (it is, as we shall see, a problematic concept)? Why are (a) the family sitting together for a meal and (b) watching television mutually exclusive categories? To turn to anecdote, as a child many of the families in my working class/lower-middle class neighbourhood would eat their evening meal upon the breadwinner's return home from work. Small houses with few rooms often meant that the television was in the same room as the dining table. If the television was on, it might form the focus point for shared discussion of the early evening news, it might just be background noise. One could proceed to extrapolate from this a whole series of (documented) cases and variations in the role of television in family meals. One thing is clear from the survey noted above, however, and that is that 92 per cent of the respondents dined with their family at least once a week, 86 per cent 2–7 days per week, and 72 per cent 4–7 days per week – hardly evidence of the decline of family meal taking. Nor is the data on watching television while eating a meal commensurate with the first set. Who is to say that the meals eaten watching television are the same as the ones self-identified by the sample in response to the first question (for example, breakfast is much less likely to be taken as a 'family' meal but may be accompanied by the television)? There is a reasonable amount of good quality evidence to suggest that domestic meal-taking is as routine a part of household life as it ever was. Warde (1997: 149) refers to speculation about the rise of grazing and the decline of the family meal. In his survey, 85 per cent of households recorded a daily family meal with 13 per cent having several per week. Dickinson and Leader (1998: 126) cite a 1994 study that showed that many low income households eat together because it was more economical to do so. Their own survey of 233 children aged 11–18 showed that 52 per cent shared meals with their whole family every day and 55 per cent said their family usually ate around the table at evening mealtimes: only 15 per cent said they ate alone (Dickinson and Leader, 1998: 127). Murcott (1997) also cites market research reports broadly supportive of these findings.

We can add further to the above observations by speculating as to whether the tone of moral panic in Quigley's article would have been the same had the radio (or stereo) been playing. Characteristic of these shock horror pieces is the marshalling of comment from various interested parties. In Quigley's piece, one notable remark comes from Dr Annie Anderson of the Department of Human Nutrition at Glasgow University. Anderson is quoted as stating: 'Do people really notice what they are eating if they are watching television at the same time? Food needs time and space.' Sadly (for Dr Anderson) people often do notice what they are eating under such circumstances. The kinds of values expressed in Anderson's comment are worth noting. At one level they suggest (a no doubt proper) concern with the joys or hedonism involved in eating but they also cast a middle-class world view – why does eating need 'time and space' – what about these people who have one but not the other? Or neither? What about the people who cannot afford to eat complex meals because they are poor?

Nutrition is, of course, in scientific terms the witchcraft of the modern age which is why repeated surveys show extensive and justifiable scepticism among the public as to official nutritional advice. At a second level, Anderson's comments reflect the nutritionists concern with 'watching what we eat'. The Scottish diet has a notorious reputation (Glasgow is credited in culinary mythology as the home of the deep-fried, battered, Mars bar) and dietary-related ill-health, broadly defined, is a significant hazard in the central belt of Scotland. Nevertheless in the survey supporting Quigley's work, 66 per cent of respondents thought their diet fairly healthy and 20 per cent very healthy. But as nutritionists know through their extensive interaction with sociologists (see, for example, Fieldhouse, 1995: 36–37 and Wood, 1995: 59–63), what people *regard* as 'healthy' may not compare with nutritional concepts of healthiness.

Now, a reasonable objection to at least some of the above would be that not all people live in families: statistical evidence suggests that the number of single person households has increased dramatically in recent years, at all points in the age spectrum. Then there are multiple-person households that do not conform to the pattern of the conventional nuclear family, notably single parent households. All true, but most people learn how to eat, and what is appropriate and available to eat in family or quasi-family situations at the start of their lives and research is at least suggestive of the view that the ideal of domestic dining remains with most people throughout their lives. At the same time, good academics are always cautious and we can agree at least to some extent with Murcott (1997: 46) when she says 'There is . . . a good deal more steady investigation to be undertaken before any conclusion about family meals can be confidently . . . drawn'.

None of the concerns discussed thus far have escaped the modern foodservice industry. Here we can see a rich tapestry of concerns in a state of almost constant tension. The very concept of the restaurant is predicated on the notion of sociability – that is, eating is a social activity shared by people. Historically, of course, food and beverage provision has been highly stratified by class, by gender (separate dining facilities for women in hotels and restaurants; the control of women's access to public houses – see Mazurkiewicz's 1983 landmark study for further details) but there has been a process of growing democratization, as noted earlier, which has led in the 1990s to concerns about the extent to which the industry meets the needs of niche or hitherto largely ignored markets – single travellers/diners; children (Buck, 1995; Webster, 1994); older customers; women – not all mutually exclusive categories, of course. To illustrate this point we will take a brief detour and focus on two core groups – single diners and women.

Lyons (1995: 62–63) notes the traditionally negative welcome given to single diners in restaurants despite (at that time) some six million people in the UK living alone (some 11 per cent of the population) with, according to English Tourist Board estimates for 1993, some 90 million solo trips taken in the UK per annum. Some of the interviews with restaurateurs conducted by Lyon for her piece indicate a generally positive attitude towards single diners, particularly regular customers who provide a predictable stream of income. One, however, raised the point that despite marketing his chain to young singles, it was not on the basis of them dining on their own, it making no sense to fill a restaurant with single diners.

The intensely social nature of the act of eating is addressed by Lukanuski (1998) in the context of dining alone. She begins by noting that eating alone is solitary but never isolated, because a diner alone is aware of the intense tapestry of values associated with shared dining experiences. The problem for the solo diner is that there is no sense of what constitutes 'correct' eating behaviour when dining alone. Lukansuki marshals evidence to show that solo diners eat differently to when they share their eating occasions. Thus obese people eat more and the non-obese less; older men and women who live alone prepare fewer meals at home; solo diners take less time to eat (Lukanuski 1998: 155). She goes on to point out that single diners are often regarded as social misfits, the victim of some tragedy, or unwanted. We must be careful not to exaggerate this point as Lukanuski (1998: 116) gets a little carried away, but her observations resonate with the findings of other studies, for example, Coxon's (1983) study of an all-male cookery class where participants' motivations were rooted in the absence of women to cook for them (as a result, largely, of divorce, separation or the death of the female spouse or partner). But Lukanuski (1998: 117) is surely correct when she points out how certain forms of the promotion and advertising of foods centre on the concept of eating as a shared experience, often in the family context. Thus, cookbooks designed with the solo diner in mind are not only few and far between but 'filled with simplistic recipes and a hollow cheeriness that barely marks a tone of disdain and pity'. Certain prepared foods, in contrast, are marketed towards the solitary eater whereas others, such as pizzas or french fries, are usually advertised in the context of consumption by families or large groupings. At odds with this is Dickinson and Leader's (1998: 128) finding from an analysis of peak-time television viewing that eating is presented as something people do alone. However, one important qualification to these authors' findings is, that, though some 60 per cent of all eating scenes viewed entailed a lone diner, in more than half of cases the food being consumed could be classed as a snack rather than a meal.

Until the 1980s women constituted a hitherto largely ignored market, despite comprising half of the population. Yet findings from research into domestic dining consistently suggest that women are substantially disadvantaged in the domestic food system. They often subordinate their own tastes to those of their male partner and/or children. In poorer families they eat less than other family members. Women also remain the principal purchasers and prepares of food. Talk of greater democracy in the sharing of domestic duties is just that – talk (see Wood, 1995: 55–62; 65–70 for a review of several sources in this regard). Women also have less economic independence than men overall, although to some degree this may be changing, particularly among younger women. Nevertheless, the hospitality industry has had to make a real effort to begin to overcome its traditions of indifference, or even hostility, to women customers. Consider, for example, research as recent as the 1970s and 1980s which showed that women customers tend to be stereotyped by hospitality organizations' employees as fussy, demanding, low spenders, and poor tippers (Bowey, 1976; Mars and Nicod, 1984). Of course, this may well reflect greater directness and 'correct-ness' on the part of female customers, though as often as not, such behaviour is as much a reflection of women's economic disadvantage when dining out. Reflect also upon the observation that as consumers in restaurants and other public places, women have traditionally been carefully controlled, or policed, and the stereotypes of female restaurant customers that abound in the hospitality industry are as much an aspect of the rhetoric of this control as they are a marketing judgement (Mazurkiewicz, 1983; see also Finkelstein, 1989 and Wood, 1994). In an industry where the majority of those engaged in food service are women, women as customers, as a market, tend to be marginalized and treated as an appendage to male clients or as part of a family unit. Women customers are unlikely to receive more sympathy from women workers in the industry and are often regarded as being fussy, or poor tippers, or making a coffee and a cake last all afternoon. When a man and woman dine together, it is still often the case that the man is presented with the bill at the end of the meal, even if he is not paying. Similarly, if beef and chicken are ordered, assumptions about gendered taste will often lead to the woman receiving the chicken, the man the beef. These factors serve to treat women customers as 'different' and undermine their credibility as independent consumers.

That women are treated differently by the hospitality industry can, perhaps, be seen more clearly in the variety of initiatives, most from the 1970s onwards, that have been introduced to secure female custom. These range from (in hotels) female executive rooms to (in restaurants) the general concession to 'light' eating in restaurant menus (women are still regarded as more health and figure conscious than men) and (in pubs and bars) to creating a more welcoming environment for women. The trade literature over the last twenty years or so is littered with news items that reflect operators' views of women as a distinct and different market to be incorporated into the mainstream. One typical of the genre is a report by Sargent (1995) who examines elements in the selection of pubs among women. Traditionally an area of the hospitality industry that has excluded women, this has started to change since the 1980s as the pubs sector has sought to extend its markets. Whereas women were once unwelcome in pubs unless accompanied by a male (still the case in many instances); or confined to a particular room; and lone women could be made to feel uncomfortable or even prohibited by landlords (Mazurkiewicz, 1983) some parts of the industry have sought to rectify this. Reporting on research undertaken for the Brewers and Licensed Retailers' Association, Sargent (1995: 58) notes that the greatest increase in frequent pub-going is among women aged 18–34 and that a lone women is more likely to go in a pub if she is known there, obtains instant recognition from staff, if there are newspapers or magazines for her to read whilst drinking, and if the environment is clearly women friendly (e.g. no pin-up calendars). Sargent (1995: 60) also notes that measures particularly attractive to female customers include high(er) standards of decor, furnishings, comfort and cleanliness; good levels of service; good food, generally available; wide drinks choice, including wine, cider and soft drinks; and a welcome and facilities for children. Despite the efforts of the hospitality industry to render itself more welcoming to women unaccompanied by men, doubts remain as to how successful these efforts have been. A survey in London reported by Golding (1998: 18) find that lone businesswomen claimed to frequently 'experience leering waiters and patronising managers with more than 70 per cent feeling that service was "secondary" purely because of their gender'. Also, when dining with a male companion 74 per cent said waiters assumed the man to be settling the bill and selecting wine. Some 41 per cent claimed to feel uncomfortable dining alone and 62 per cent chose to eat in their rooms, thus avoiding public areas.

The case of single diners and women, two different but not (as we have seen in the case of lone businesswomen) mutually exclusive groups remind us that eating out is a far from sociable activity for many people. More important, perhaps, is the way in which we see an 'interpenetration' of circumstances between domestic and public dining, disadvantage in the former being mirrored in disadvantage in the latter. Food and beverage markets are not homogeneous nor are they structured alone by considerations of economic access or personal tastes. Yet in realizing this, the hospitality industry has some way to go before it is able to fully exploit, in an economic sense, customer groups who do not feel 'included'.

What people eat

Before examining what people eat when they eat out, we have to briefly square the circle of 'how' people eat outside the home. In respect of the propensity to eat out, Warde (1997: 149) and Warde and Martens (1998a: 147) note that a great many eating events now take place outside households, and that restaurant, pubs, cafes and takeaways absorb a significant proportion of total household expenditure on food, some 3.6 per cent of total household expenditure being spent on meals out in 1991. The Family Expenditure Survey showing that the proportion of food expenditure devoted to food eaten away from home rising from 10 per cent to 21 per cent in the period 1960–1993. Warde's research showed that nearly everyone in his sample ate out at some point but few ate out very regularly (Warde, 1997: 149–150). Warde and Martens, 1998b: 119–120) note that in their survey:

- 21 per cent ate out once a week; 7 per cent claimed to never eat out.

- 48 per cent had never eaten in ethnic restaurants in the previous year; 27 per cent said they had never eaten an ethnic take-away. Customers of ethnic restaurants were likely to have higher incomes; live in London; have qualifications from higher educational institutions; have attended private school; have a professional/managerial occupation; and a middle-class father. Warde and Martens (1998b: 119) note that: 'Familiarly with ethnic cuisine seems to be a contemporary mark of refinement', a view supported by James (1997).

- There was a definite metropolitan mode of eating – in London people dined out more frequently with the range of venues more diverse such that the authors are moved to note (Warde and Martens, 120) that '. . . the peculiarity of the metropolitan mode is sufficient to justify a warning – beware of the generalizations of food journalists based in London!'

An NOP poll for the *Caterer and Hotelkeeper* (Anon, 1998: 60–62) interviewed a representative sample of 1000 people aged over 15 between December 1997 and February 1998 (the dates are significant because of Christmas and New Year festivities which are likely to exaggerate the value of some variables – for example, the frequency of eating out). The key findings of the study were:

- 77 per cent of all British adults had at least one proper meal (sandwiches and snacks were excluded from the research) in a restaurant, pub or bar during the 3 months in question and 70 per cent had had more than one meal out, 60 per cent more than two.

- Young people aged 15–24 are most likely to eat out – the survey showed that 90 per cent had at least one meal out in the study period.

- Social class is closely related to the likelihood and frequency of dining out, 15 per cent of ABC1s had not eaten out in the period compared to 20 per cent of C2s and 36 per cent of DEs – the survey suggests that although ABC1s make up 46 per cent of the adult population they contribute 60 per cent of frequent diners.

- Gender remains an influence on dining out, men being slightly more likely to have eaten out than women but considerably more likely to eat out frequently – men are more likely than women to eat out with friends or on business occasions; women tend to be greater participants in family meals and those with children.

- 70 per cent of all diners have had a meal out with their family, the same proportion as have eaten out with friends: however family meals were a much larger proportion of dining out occasions among the over 35s, whereas for the 15–24 group dining out with friends was more common.

- The types of restaurant used during the period included independents (64 per cent); independent pubs (62 per cent); Chinese, Oriental and Indian (52 per cent); pub chains (44 per cent) hamburger restaurants (36 per cent); pizza and pasta restaurants (36 per cent); and steakhouses (22 per cent); 32 per cent of respondents had dined in at least two of those restaurant types/categories; 43 per cent in three or four; and 19 per cent in five or more.

- The most influential factor in selecting where to eat out was prior experience: 84 per cent of the sample had bought a meal from a place where they had dined before: 75 per cent acted on personal recommendation from acquaintances; 25 per cent chose a restaurant they had seen advertised in a local newspaper (see also Chapter 7).

These two relatively comprehensive and contemporaneous sources of information evince echoes of several of the themes already raised in this chapter but also contain some minor surprises. Principal among the latter is the finding of Warde and Martens (1988a) and *Caterer and Hotelkeeper's* NOP poll that around half of the dining-out public seem averse to eating in ethnic restaurants. Given that the data in both cases must be treated with a degree of tentativeness, it is nevertheless interesting to speculate that references to the ubiquity of ethnic restaurants in popular culture, as well as to their integration to British 'culinary culture' appear to have been somewhat exaggerated. It is also worth adding that a propensity to eat out in a particular type of 'ethnic' restaurant is a distinct phenomenon from enjoying the foods conventionally provided therein but in a different context. Indeed, the term 'ethnic restaurant' is a wholly unsatisfactory one when, as is typically the case in British food writing of all genres, it is employed to refer to diverse Asian and Oriental cuisines. After all, any system of food that can make legitimate claims to distinctiveness on the basis of regional or cultural traditions has some quality of 'ethnicity'. As a case in point, and following the arguments of social scientists and others (see for example, Driver, 1983, for a useful journalistic insight relevant to this discussion) about the 'interpenetration' and integration of diverse food styles into 'host' cultures, many dishes of overseas origin are now incorporated into the menus of 'mainstream' restaurants: it is not necessary to dine in a Chinese restaurant to enjoy spring rolls; or an Indian restaurant to obtain curry, nor an Italian restaurant to obtain pizza and pasta dishes. One slightly (perhaps askew) perspective on this is the Sutcliffe Catering Group's review of favourite lunches in their staff restaurants, comparing 1994 to

	1968	1994
1	Roast meats	Curry
2	Battered Fish and Chips	Roast meats
3	Steak and Kidney Pie	Lasagne
4	Braised Steak	Battered Fish and Chips
5	Brown Stew and Dumplings	Home-made Meat Pies
6	Mixed Grill	Roast Beef
7	Cottage Pie	Steak and Kidney Pie/Pudding
8	Home-made Faggots and Peas	Cottage/Shepherd's Pie
9	Curry	Other pasta dishes
10	Salads	Chilli Con Carne

Table 2.2

Hospitality, Leisure & Tourism Series

1968 (reported in *Caterer and Hotelkeeper*, 27 October 1994: 18). The results are shown in Table 2.2.

Although the 1994 menu is still dominated by 'traditional' British dishes, the popularity of Curry and the presence of Lasagne, other pasta dishes and Chilli Con Carne gives some small insight into the extent of the interpretation of so-called ethnic foods in the British diet.

Other findings from the two sources discussed at the beginning of this section worthy of passing comment relate to the persistence of social class as a core indicator of the likelihood and frequency of dining out: both present a serious qualification to the claims of those who would have us believe that culinary culture is essentially classless. The *Caterer and Hotelkeeper*'s NOP findings are broadly supported by other research (e.g. Tomlinson, 1994). In the light of the concluding discussion of the previous section of this chapter, the same survey's findings concerning women diners are significant.

Turning, at last, to the issue of what people eat when they eat out, we should begin by noting that if sociologists are to be believed, the traditional staple diet of the British urban working-class has, and largely remains, the 'cooked dinner' of typically roast meat, potatoes, other vegetables and gravy. Middle-class diet, though held to be more varied in the range of ingredients employed, is also centred on a cooked dinner. In the last section we saw how claims about the 'death of the meal' are, at best, somewhat exaggerated. But what are we to make of these claims about the foods we consume? Again, the evidence is not favourable to those who argue for fundamental shifts in our eating habits. Most empirical research suggests that although there may have been a growth in the use of convenience foods and in the variety of foods eaten, the 'cooked dinner' model still occupies a privileged position in the British dietary system (see Wood, 1995, for a review of the evidence to that point; and Beardsworth and Keil, 1997 and Warde, 1997, for more recent reviews). Surely however, in dining-out markets, we must find some change? Are we not constantly subjected to academic pronouncements and market research that tells us of the diversity of customer tastes and preferences? Well, yes we are and, for the most part, these assertions are, simply, wrong. Indeed, one of the most remarkable features of food and beverage provision and food and beverage consumption in the UK over the last twenty years is its consistency.

The public provision of food is very closely linked to domestic family food systems. Although the hospitality industry is relatively heterogeneous in terms of the varieties of foods provided, the dining out market is, generally, one of small extremes and a large centre. At one extreme are restaurants that provide various forms of *haute cuisine* and specialist foods and styles for which there is a limited market. At the other extreme are the street-corner take-away food shops offering the most basic foodstuffs. In the middle, popular catering covers a multitude of establishments including everything from steak houses, carveries and most Chinese and Indian restaurants, to fast-food restaurants and chain restaurants offering speciality cuisines such as pizza and pasta.

The National Catering Inquiry of the 1960s produced a number of reports exploring the continuity between domestic and public food provision (National Catering Inquiry 1966; McKenzie, 1967). In the most important of these (for dining out) seven population centres were surveyed using questionnaire techniques, with respondents asked to select on the basis of personal preferences, a number of courses from a list provided. The list comprised the most popular dishes served by restaurants at the time of the research and caterers were asked to estimate customer preferences for the dishes on the list. The results of this exercise are summarized in Table 2.3. Some of the disparities between consumers' choices and caterers' beliefs about consumer prefer-

		Consumers	Caterers
Starters	Soup	71	46
	Melon	4	17
	Fruit Juice	3	14
Main Courses	Meat	60	42
	Poultry	10	26
	Mixed Grill	12	21
Vegetables	Potatoes	63	78
	Peas	50	29
	Sprouts	19	26
*Desserts**	Fruit Salad	Pies/Tarts	
	Pies/Tarts	Ice Cream	
	Cheese		
	Ice Cream		

*Rankings only are given in source

Source: National Catering Inquiry, 1966: 13–17.

Table 2.3 Comparison of consumers' menu preferences and caterers' perception of consumers' preferences (per cent of those responding)

Hospitality, Leisure & Tourism Series

ences are striking. The second, supplementary report published a year later (McKenzie, 1967) focused on a group of 420 people (half the sample from London, half from Leeds). Each respondent eating out at least once a month was asked to nominate one of three prices which most reflected their likely spending behaviour – five shillings (25 pence), twelve shillings and sixpence (62.5

	5/- (25p)		12/6 (62.5p)		£1.00
First course					
Soup	76		43		20
Fruit juice	19		14		4
Prawn/Shrimp Cocktail	N/A		24		25
% of choices accounted for by top three selections	95		81		49
Main course					
Steak and Kidney Pudding	24	Fillet Steak	29		23
Roast Lamb	17	Roast Beef	11	Duck	17
Roast Beef	15	Chicken	10		14
% of choices accounted for by top three selections	56		50		54
Potatoes					
Roast	38		35		21
Mashed	24		19		15
Sauté	N/A		14		21
Chipped	17		14		21
% of choices accounted for by top three selections	79		82		78
Other vegetables					
Brussel Sprouts	22		29		21
Peas	29		22		19
Cauliflower	17		8		9
% of choices accounted for by top three selections	68		59		49
Dessert					
Steamed pudding	24	Cheeses	18	Fresh fruit salad	28
Fruit pie	23		18	Cheese	21
Tinned peaches/fruit salad	21	Fresh fruit	17	Melba peach/pear	14
% of choices accounted for by top three selections	68		53		63

Source: After McKenzie (1967)

Table 2.4 Restaurant menu choices by consumers at different prices (per cent response)

pence) and one pound – and were then presented with a menu within that price range and asked to choose a meal from it. For the most part, McKenzie concentrates on the twelve shillings and sixpence menu on the grounds that it matched most clearly the average price paid at that time for a meal (of thirteen shillings and two pence – around 66 pence in decimal coinage). In Table 2.4, however, the top three items for each course across all three price ranges are shown.

Two points can be made about McKenzie's findings. First, as the price range increases, then so, in the main, does the percentage of choices accounted for by the top three dishes diminish, suggesting perhaps (and assuming a class-income relationship) the greater flexibility of middle class tastes. Second, within individual food categories there is some evidence – along the lines offered by Bourdieu (1984) in his observations on French domestic dining – that class-based tastes do exist. The preferences for soup, steak and kidney pudding, peas and steamed pudding on the five shilling menu when compared to the prawn cocktail, fillet steak, sprouts and fresh fruit salad of the one pound menu are suggestive.

By the 1980s, the range of public catering provision had expanded dramatically. Between 1983 and 1989, the trade magazine *Caterer and Hotelkeeper* carried an annual Gallup survey of trends in consumption. The popularity of dishes was again established by what caterers provided on their menus. For most of the period of the surveys, the cooked dinner type meal prevailed, often in the form of prawn cocktail, steak and chips and Black Forest gateau. The 1989 survey was fairly typical of trends during this period (Wood, 1989). Covering twelve different sub-sectors of the hospitality industry including continental restaurants, burger joints, Chinese and Indian restaurants, and pizza operations, the 1989 survey did notice a minor change in trends – Black Forest gateau had suddenly become less popular! The typical lunch meal was soup of the day followed by fish and chips and then ice cream. For dinner, it was prawn cocktail, steak and chips and ice cream (Wood, 1989: 49).

Fast forward to the 1990s and probably the most reliable study of eating out habits of the decade conducted by Professor Alan Warde. Comparing a sample of 1001 people in three centres – London, Bristol and Preston – the most popular dinner menu when dining out was – you guessed it – prawn cocktail; roast meat, peas, carrots and chips; with gateau to follow (Warde and Martens, 1998b: 121–122). The ubiquity of this type of meal was celebrated on the occasion of the launch of a biography of Sir Reo Stakis, the doyen of the Scottish hotel industry where the meal (Anon, 1999: 25):

... mirrored the dishes made famous at his early Glasgow restaurants; prawn cocktail, gammon steak with pineapple, followed by Black Forest gateau. The only complaint appeared to be that the gateau was a modern version and not the traditional wedge. Mess with hallowed memories at your peril.

Conclusions

What, then, do we *really* know about the requirements of food and beverage consumers in the modern age? The answer is by way of a paradox. At any one point the answer must be 'not very much'. Yet there appear to be certain relatively unchanging, if not quite eternal, verities. In summary:

- The death of meal-taking has been greatly exaggerated: people still think in terms of meals when dining in both domestic and public environments.

- The concept of the 'proper meal' consisting of meat, potatoes and other vegetables is carried over into dining out where the parallel structure of meal content remains the preference of the majority of consumers.

- Access to food and beverage provision outside the home is highly stratified by such general social variables as class and gender, and the supply of food and beverage is subject to the efforts of providers to segment a variety of markets in order to increase market penetration.

- The proportion of household expenditure spent on eating out has risen dramatically in the years since 1960 though there is some evidence that few people eat out on a regular basis.

Trend data is valuable in tracking changes over time (see John O'Connor's review of post-war trends in dining out contained in Chapter 16). The preoccupation that we all have with 'now', however, means that it is easy to take too readily at face value the many, often conflicting, statements advanced about the current state of our food habits, especially as they appear in popular media. Sensitivity to social nuance is required, as is a certain scepticism about the many agendas that inform pronouncements about why we eat what we eat. This is not to say that consumer markets for dining out are static and unchanging, but rather that such change is rarely radical, often incremental and always in need of careful, factual verification.

References

Anon (1998) Dining by numbers, *Caterer and Hotelkeeper*, 26 March: 60–62.

Anon (1999) Book launch was a piece of cake, *Caterer and Hotelkeeper*, 8 July: 25.

Beardsworth, A. and Keil, T. (1997) *Sociology on the Menu: An Invitation to the Study of Food and Society*, London: Routledge.

Bourdieu, P. (1984) *Distinction: A Social Critique of the Judegement of Taste*, London: Routledge and Kegan Paul.

Bowey, A. (1976) *The Sociology of Organisations*, London: Hodder and Stoughton.

Buck, A. (1995) How to sell to children, *Food Service Management*, September: 47–48.

Coxon, A. (1983) Men in the kitchen: notes from a cookery class, in A. Murcott (Ed) *The Sociology of Food and Eating*, Farnborough: Gower, 172–177.

Dickinson, R. and Leader, S. (1998) Ask the family, in S. Griffiths and J. Wallace (Eds) *Consuming Passions: Food in the Age of Anxiety*, Manchester: Mandolin, 122–129.

Driver, C. (1983) *The British at Table 1940–1980*, London: Chatto and Windus.

Fieldhouse, P. (1995) *Food and Nutrition: Customs and Culture*, London: Chapman and Hall, 2nd edition.

Finkelstein, J. (1989) *Dining Out: A Sociology of Modern Manners*, Cambridge: Polity Press.

Golding, C. (1998) Hotels must update attitudes to women, *Caterer and Hotelkeeper*, 10 September: 18.

James, A. (1997) How British is British Food?, in P. Caplan (Ed) *Food, Health and Identity*, London: Routledge, 71–78.

Lukanuski, M. (1998) A place at the counter: the onus of oneness, in R. Scapp and B. Seitz (Eds) *Eating Culture*, New York: State University of New York, 112–120.

Lyons, V. (1995) The power of one, *Caterer and Hotelkeeper*, 2 March: 62–63.

Mars, G. and Nicod, M. (1984) *The World of Waiters*, London: George Allen and Unwin.

Mazurkiewicz, R. (1983) Gender and social consumption, *The Service Industries Journal*, **3**(1): 49–62.

McKenzie, J. (1967) *Food Choice and Price: A Supplementary Report to The British Eating Out*, Glasgow: National Catering Inquiry.

Mennell, S. (1985) *All Manners of Food: Eating and Taste in England and France from the Middle Ages to the Present*, Oxford: Basil Blackwell.

Murcott, A. (1997) Family meals – a thing of the past?, in P. Caplan (Ed) *Food, Health and Identity*, London: Routledge, 32–49.

National Catering Inquiry (1966) *The British Eating Out*, Glasgow: National Catering Inquiry.

Quigley, E. (1996) Families make a meal of the telly, *Scotland on Sunday*, 4 August: 9.

Sargent, M. (1995) Drinking partners, *Caterer and Hotelkeeper*, 16 November: 58–60.

Tomlinson, M. (1994) Do distinct class preferences for food exist? An analysis of class-based tastes, *British Food Journal*, **96**(7): 11–17.

Warde, A. (1997) *Consumption, Food and Taste: Culinary Antinomies and Commodity Culture*, London: Sage.

Warde, A. and Martens, L. (1998a) Eating out and the commercialisation of mental life, *British Food Journal*, **100**(3): 147–153.

Warde, A. and Martens, L. (1998b) The prawn cocktail ritual, in S. Griffiths and J. Wallace (Eds) *Consuming Passions: Food in the Age of Anxiety*, Manchester: Mandolin, 118–122.

Webster, J. (1994) Child benefit, *Caterer and Hotelkeeper*, 7 April: 36–40.

Wood, A. (1989) Lager clout, *Caterer and Hotelkeeper*, 14 September: 49–55.

Wood, R. C. (1994) Hotel culture and social control, *Annals of Tourism Research*, **21**(1): 65–80.

Wood, R. C. (1995) *The Sociology of the Meal*, Edinburgh: Edinburgh University Press.

How important is the meal experience? Choices, menus and dining environments

Roy C. Wood

Introduction

The concept of the meal experience is central to the development of the western concept of hospitality management and has been particularly influential, through the subjects of operations and marketing, in the rhetoric of UK hospitality and hospitality education. In part, this is no doubt due to the influence of Campbell-Smith's (1967) seminal work, *The Marketing of the Meal Experience*. This book was among the first serious hospitality management texts to appear in the UK but more than that, it was an essential publication in the field of marketing. Campbell-Smith articulated the quite explicit view that when dining out, the customer's concerns and their experiences were a function of a much wider range of factors than the quality of food and drink alone. Indeed, a central theme of his work is that the quality of food and drink itself is perceived within a network of other considerations, for example quality of service, ambience of the restaurant and so on. While this may seem blindingly obvious now, at a time of more complex and sophisticated knowledge about marketing and consumer behaviour, and while it may have seemed to many at the time as articulation of mere common sense, Campbell-Smith's achievement was to cement the concept of the meal experience into the lexicon of hospitality marketing. Further, it was the 'marketing' element that was important, because the implication of conceiving of a meal as an 'experience' was that hospitality industry operators could manipulate elements of that experience to improve customers' reactions to the kind and nature of provision (and by the same token, inattention to this process of manipulation could create negative responses in customers).

Campbell-Smith (1967) set a hare running, a search for the Holy Grail of the most important set of elements in the meal experience that has preoccupied hospitality researchers to the present day such that thirty years later, Johns, Tyas, Ingold and Hopkinson (1996: 15) write:

> It is generally held that the 'product' of a foodservice outlet is a 'meal experience' consisting (like other hospitality 'products') of an amalgam of tangible and intangible components . . .[.] Authors have identified three broad categories of factors which make up the meal experience: those concerned with customer traits and preferences, those which are directly important in terms of managing a foodservice outlet, and those which seem intuitively to be attributes or benefits of eating outside the home.

These authors undertook a complex study of factors active in forming the 'meal experience' using a SERVQUAL methodology and as a general conclusion, observed that 'it was impossible to identify clearly the factors which make up the meal experience' although suggestive associations in their data seemed to indicate that 'food was the most important element of the majority of meal experiences . . .' (1996: 23), a view supported by Clark and Wood (1998) and several other studies to have reached similar conclusions. Could it be, shock, horror, that the idea of the meal experience is not such an amalgam of tangibles and intangibles? That in eating a meal in a restaurant it is the food (and drink) which is most important – the tangibles?

In the last chapter, we focused on 'how' people eat (with an emphasis on the importance of food consumption as a social and normally shared experience) and 'what' they eat in terms of the relative narrowness of preferences. In this chapter we explore more 'why' people eat as they do, and more specifically examine the scope for consumer choices, and the impact of such choices upon the meal experience (and indeed the effects of this 'impact' in turn upon consumer choice behaviour). To this end it is necessary to briefly consider the nature of the concept of 'choice' itself.

Choice or selection

The concept of choice is at the very heart of individual and social identity in Western liberal democracies. We all believe we can make choices and choice is associated with other desirable social states, notably 'freedom', such that 'freedom of choice' is not only prized by individuals but has become a central tenet in the philosophies of political parties. But what if we are mistaken about the nature of, and scope for, choice in our lives? What if choice is largely illusory? Or as Warde and Martens (1998: 130) put it, in the context of UK political rhetoric of the 1980s which equated freedom of choice with Thatcherite policies of the supremacy of the market and private ownership, there is a tendency for the 'exaggeration of the scope of the freedom implied by the concept of consumer choice'.

Warde and Martens go on to identify four shades of meaning associated with the term 'choice', these being to select; to pick in preference; to consider fit or suitable; and to will or to determine. In a fascinating discussion, they propose that in the field of consumption – including food consumption – there has been a tendency to conflate the first two meanings – to select and to pick in preference – with the fourth. The point is simpler than at first might appear. It is that in most fields, consumers do not enter into a 'pure' state of choice characterized by their absolute freedom to select and pick in preference something of their choice. Rather, choice is always pre-structured such that what is presented to the consumer, from which they select/pick, is determined by other usually powerful, influences – principally 'providers'.

Now this in itself may seem a far from stunning revelation but it repays considered reflection. Straughan (1995) examines some of the practical implications of philosophical concepts of choice. He argues that total freedom, in the sense of 'freedom to choose' is unattainable. In shopping for food, for example, there are always constraints. These can be physical/geographical (access to outlets selling food may be restricted because of the limitations of transport options); economic (freedom is limited by consumers' income); availability (as a result of natural disasters or the operations of the market); and certain marketing techniques. In respect of the latter, Straughan (1995: 14) points to the 'sinister' ways in which the behaviour of customers in supermarkets can be manipulated by the use of music, physical product placement; and the use of lighting. Finally, there are those constraints on freedom of choice that consumers might place on themselves, for example by ethical selection (becoming a vegetarian; eating meat reared in 'humane' conditions); perceptions of risk (BSE and its effect on beef sales would be a reasonable example); and matters of individual or collective preference. Writing in a similar vein, Wrigley (1998: 112) notes that by the early 1990s, food choice was 'exercised within budget constraints in a food distribution system which, when viewed in international terms, had developed a series of quite distinct characteristics'. One of the most important of these, according to Wrigley (1998: 113–114) was the diminution in the number of sources from which one could choose to buy food. By 1990, he notes, five retail grocery chains controlled 60 per cent of the market (both Straughan and Wrigley offer fairly summary discussions of these issues: readers interested in the more complex aspects of those arguments could do worst than consult the excellent account of Warde and Martens, 1998: 129–144).

One possible counter to the above line of argument is to observe that certain benefits have flowed from food production and retail arrangements. For example, it might be argued that together with advances in technology, such arrangements have increased the range of foodstuffs available to the consumer. Warde (1997: 166–170) considers this and related arguments in some detail. He argues that while the British shopper in the 1990s faced a greater variety of foodstuffs than at any time in the twentieth century, this reflected less an absolute increase in ingredients for sale and more the wider availability of the same foodstuffs because of the growth of large supermarket chains. He goes on (Warde, 1997: 167):

> Supermarkets have given the opportunity for variety to a much wider section of the population. To be sure, some of the appearance of increased variation is illusory. Some of that variety is created by offering alternative forms of packaging (brands) or storing (frozen, tinned, fresh) the same item; some by having many versions of the same item, as with different fruit flavours for yoghurt or sauces for chicken.

One of the difficulties with this line of argument is that even if the variety of foods on offer is largely illusory as a result of the tricksiness of food retailers (i.e. choice is less real than it seems) then the presence of foods in multiple brands, modes of storage, or different versions still constitutes a (pre-structured) choice, i.e. choice *could* be perceived as just as real as it seems. The apparent tension here derives to a large extent, one suspects, from the idealized notion of choice represented by Warde and Marten's (1998) fourth definition noted earlier – to will or to determine. It is perhaps best if, following Straughan, we abandon such notions altogether. Also following Straughan, it would be a mistake to assume that the existence of a greater variety of foodstuffs means that all people have access to, or if they have access, choose to eat across this range. Many constraints face consumers in this regard and as we saw in the last chapter, what people eat in actuality is, in aggregate terms, probably fairly narrow in terms of the number and variety of foodstuffs. Warde (1997: 167) also makes the point that as new tastes develop, older tastes often decline. An important implication of this view is that in a system of apparent variety there is a form of internal regulation engendered by external forces such that the rate of change within the system is greater than the rate of growth of the system itself. Whatever the case, the concept of 'choice' cannot be taken for granted, no less in food and eating, and dining out, as in any other area of consumption.

Commercial food and beverage provision and consumer choice

We can clearly see how several of the issues raised in the previous section apply to commercial hospitality by abandoning simplistic notions of consumer sovereignty and adopting a supply-side perspective. The first thing to note is that despite the diversity of the foodservice sector, large corporations with multiple brands operating in specific market niches coexist with individual owner-managed units. There remains, as we saw in the previous chapter, a substantial 'middle ground' of provision. Research on restaurant selection has tended to focus on eliciting the role of key variables in the choice of restaurant given a number of alternative scenarios. For example, June and Smith (1987) in their survey used conjoint analysis on a sample of fifty affluent upper middle-class professionals. Conjoint analysis involves a complex ranking of attributes set against the chosen hypothetical contexts (for notes on the method see Ryan, 1995, who offers a useful introduction). For four such contexts, June and Smith derived the results shown in Table 3.1.

	Intimate dinner	Birthday celebration	Business lunch	Family dinner
1	Liquor availability	Liquor availability	Service	Service
2	Service	Service	Price	Price
3	Food quality	Price	Liquor availability	Liquor availability
4	Atmosphere	Food quality	Food quality	Food quality
5	Price	Atmosphere	Atmosphere	Atmosphere

Table 3.1 Ranking and key variables influencing restaurant chosen in four hypothetical circumstances after June and Smith, 1987

Given that this survey drew on data from affluent diners the results are fascinating insofar as food quality is, in all but one case, relegated to fourth position, and atmosphere to fifth position. This raises questions about the significance of 'intangible' factors other than service in restaurant selection, a point central to the work of Lewis (1981) and Auty (1992).

Lewis (1981) considered five factors: food quality; menu variety; price; atmosphere; and convenience factors. The importance of these attributes varied according to the type of restaurant which in Lewis' case was a category united with food type: family/popular; atmosphere; and gourmet. In all three instances, however, food quality was found to be the most important consideration influencing restaurant selection by consumers. Auty's study more closely follows the distinct pattern set out by June and Smith (1987). From a pilot questionnaire ($n = 40$) conducted in the centre of a northern English city, a variety of choice factors in the restaurant decision process were collected and then collapsed into ten categories: food type; food quality; value for money; image and atmosphere; location; speed of service; recommended; new experience; opening hours; and facilities for children. To see if the type of restaurant chosen varied according to dining occasion, Auty also elicited four such occasions from the pilot: a celebration (e.g. birthday); a social occasion; convenience/need for a quick meal; and business meal. The inclusion of the latter is a little of a mystery since Auty (1992: 326) states her focus to be restaurants serving evening meals, and the inference must logically be that meal selection and the timing of meals are regarded by the author as distinct from this.

Auty's findings are based on 155 subsequent house-to-house interviews conducted on a random sample of four electoral wards in the same city having the highest population of social class ABC residents, a sample she claims as being representative,

85 per cent of these falling into social classes ABC, and 42 per cent having annual incomes in excess of £15,000. Her key results are as follows. First, the percentage of respondents ranking each of the ten variables in the top three yielded the following results (Auty, 1992: 328): food type (71); food quality (59); value for money (46); image and atmosphere (33); location (32); speed of service (15); recommended (11); new experience (9); and opening hours, and child facilities, eight (8) each. Secondly, Auty found that restaurant type influenced the order of choice criteria. Only four restaurants out of 22 were chosen more for image than value for money and food type and food quality generally always ranked higher than image and atmosphere. Thirdly, the occasion for dining out affected the ranking of variables although image and atmosphere still did not appear among the most important factors (see Table 3.2). Auty's conclusions are straightforward enough. Food type and food quality are the most frequently cited choice variables for dining out in restaurants, regardless of occasion. After food type, quality and price, atmosphere then becomes the main way of making distinctions between alternatives although this is mediated by the occasion for, as Auty (1992: 337) notes, only in one case did the same restaurant appeal to those in search of a social night out and those wanting a quick, convenient meal.

Clark and Wood (1998) in a study of customer loyalty to restaurants, asked respondents to rate ten aspects of their preferred restaurant on a five-point scale. The ten aspects are as in Table 3.3. The five-point scale was (1) very satisfactory; (2) satisfactory; (3) neither satisfactory nor unsatisfactory; (4) unsatisfactory; (5) very unsatisfactory. Figures after the parentheses in Table 3.3 show the percentage of respondents scoring in the (1) 'very satisfactory' category. The most significant of these values is for 'quality of food', the only value other than 'friendliness of

	Social		Celebration		Speed/convenience
1	Food type	1	Food quality	1	Food type
2	Food quality	2	Food type	2	Food quality
3	Value	3	Value	3	Value
4	Image/Atmosphere	4	Location	3	Speed
5	Location	5	Image/Atmosphere	4	Location
6	Recommended	6	Recommended	5	Image/Alternative
				6	Opening hours

Table 3.2 Attributes ranking for three occasions after Auty (1992: 329)

	People indicating that aspect (%)	Very satisfactory (%)
Price of food	(90)	35
Price of drink	(80)	13
Speed of service	(84)	45
Quality of food	(84)	61
Atmosphere	(84)	48
Friendliness of staff	(87)	52
Parking facilities	(55)	21
Lavatory/washroom facilities	(66)	13
Range of food choice	(84)	32
Opening hours	(83)	43

Table 3.3 Respondents ratings of ten aspects of preferred restaurant (Clark and Wood, 1998)

staff' where more than 50 per cent of respondents rated a factor 'very satisfactory'. All the 'very loyal' respondents rated quality of food first in overall importance and quality of food was the most important factor in brasseries and independent restaurants. This last result is interesting for generic reasons of restaurant choice. Respondents were asked to select five of the above factors and rank them in terms of their general importance in choosing a restaurant. Of the 31 respondents, only 20 provided usable responses to this question, of whom 19 ranked food quality as the most important variable in restaurant choice. The five factors most commonly included in respondent's rankings were:

(1) Range of food   20
(2) Quality of food   19
(3) Price of food   14
(4) Atmosphere   14
(5) Speed of service   14

In general then there is indicative evidence from all these studies to suggest that it is relatively concrete factors that are important in consumers' choice of restaurant. The interesting point about Table 3.2 is that even in the context of 'speed/convenience' where the ranking of attributes might be regarded as wholly predictable, they constitute little variation from the pattern for other social occasions. Clues as to why this might be the case are to be found in economic studies of restaurant choice amongst the affluent middle-class. For example, Frisbee and Madeira (1986: 173) hypothesized that, in the case of two-earner middle-class households 'as time becomes more valuable to household members, the total cost of home-prepared meals (food costs plus time costs) increases relative to the total cost of restaurant meals (which are generally less time-intensive)'. The authors' Canadian evidence suggests their hypothesis is correct and that restaurant meals are perceived as inferior goods by such households. Partially in confirmation of this view, Pavesic (1989: 45) introduces the familiar distinction between eating out and dining out. He writes:

> Customers will evaluate a restaurant as a place to *eat-out* or as a place to *dine-out*. If a restaurant is considered an *eat-out* operation during the week (a substitute for cooking at home), customers will be more price conscious. If a restaurant is considered a *dine-out* operation, the visit is regarded more as a social occasion or entertainment and price is not as much of a factor.

Pavesic's observations are a useful reminder that caution is necessary before we abandon entirely the concept of the 'meal experience'. The evidence reviewed here does not suggest that less tangible factors in the dining experience are unimportant – only less so. The motivations to take food away from the home are important stratifying devices that may even influence restaurant choice ('eating out' may lead to the selection of one type of restaurant, 'dining out' another, in Pavesic's terms), and the relative importance of elements of the 'meal experience', thus influencing the experience of the meal experience, so to speak, because of the (self) conditioning of expectations.

We should also note that underlying the research alluded to above is an important assumption, namely that restaurant selection is generally an individualized action. Yet there is good indicative evidence that friends and peer group influence are extremely important in selecting a *particular* restaurant. Jolson and Bushman (1978: 69 and see Chapter 7) found that in deciding whether to dine at a restaurant for the first time, consumers depend primarily on personal recommendations and remarks by critics in contrast to restaurant advertising. Similarly, Barrows, Lattuca and Busselman (1989: 90) found that, collectively, a friend or friend's recommendation was the most valued factor in determining whether to go to a restaurant for the first time. These were US studies. In the UK context, a Mintel survey for the *Caterer and Hotelkeeper* (Anon, 1992: 14) found that:

- 90 per cent of people listed recommendation by a friend as most important in choosing a *new* place to eat ('a happy customer is the best salesperson').

- Only 25 per cent said they took note of reviews in newspapers or magazines.

- Good reviews were 'more important' (the term is not defined) by those in the 45–54 age group, the AB socio-economic group and Londoners.

- Only 10 per cent said they read guides like *Egon Ronay* or entertainment guides.

- Promotional literature through the door swayed only 16 per cent of respondents and had greatest effect on 15–19 year olds, attributable to the fact that such literature is normally from the fast-food sector.

- Spontaneous entry to a restaurant from the street was most influenced by a good, varied menu (58 per cent); cheap prices (29 per cent) and a no smoking area sign (28 per cent).

- The biggest put off to returning to a restaurant was poor quality food.

Finally, here, it is worth noting one further gap in our knowledge. Having explored some of the evidence concerning the selection of restaurants, and the factors involved in such selection, it is significant that there is a relative paucity of research on what customers, once inside the restaurant, 'look for' in terms of the significance of elements likely to contribute to a positive meal experience. Disparate reports have suggested that: 'Diners are more concerned with hygiene than anything else in a restaurant ... [.] ... among the first things guests look for in restaurants are clean crockery, cutlery and glassware; presentable staff; clean lavatories; and no flies' (Anon, 1997: 12). In a study of the American 'grey' market, Harris and West (1995) examined the expectations of mature restaurant diners (aged 55 and over) and found a preference among this group for full-service restaurants. Beyond this, factors considered most important when dining out were service by waiting staff (39 per cent); clean bathrooms (28 per cent); a menu offering a wide variety of choices (20 per cent); a quiet dining area (20 per cent); and being greeted and seated by a host or hostess (16 per cent) (Harris and West, 1995: 43). The authors also probed the behavioural dimensions of their sample. Some 95 per cent dined out at least once a week and a significant proportion preferred no-smoking sections (89 per cent); and separate areas from families with children (63 per cent). Asked to indicate the worst mistakes made by restaurant management and/or staff, first in line was poor service (38 per cent), followed by poor food (24 per cent) and poor sanitation (21 per cent). Only

5 per cent cited 'poor atmosphere' in this category though, interestingly, in terms of behavioural preferences, only 56 per cent desired music during their meal (Harris and West, 1995: 43–44).

To briefly summarize the discussion thus far, we have seen that the concept of 'consumer choice' in general must be treated with some caution as the scope for choice is always structured by factors that both enable and constrain such choice. Extending this view into the realm of eating, and especially eating out, we know a little about reasons for selecting a restaurant and a little less about what customers look for once inside a restaurant. In general, what some social anthropologists term 'material' factors seem to be more important to consumers – things like food type and quality, monetary value and 'service' (by which we must assume the relatively tangible aspects of service). More abstract categories, such as 'atmosphere' appear to be less important. Within the totality of the meal experience, therefore, some elements are seemingly more important than others. What more, then, do we know about the meal experience?

Meal experience or meal dystopia?

Meal experiences can be good or bad. Following from the earlier discussion, the most important tangible element guiding the meal experience is the menu. The menu is a supply-side device. As Mooney (1994) notes, the menu is traditionally depicted as a marketing communications device, listing what the customer is offered. In a rare (for the conventional approach to food and beverage management offered up in textbooks) insight, however, Mooney (1994: 45) also states that 'In reality, more often than not, the menu also serves as a limit on what a foodservice operation is willing and able to prepare and serve'. Invariably presented as the vehicle of customer choice, the menu serves thus as an illusory device: its real purpose is exactly the opposite – to state at its simplest what the vendor is willing to offer. In other words, the menu is a limiting device, pre-selecting dishes that the vendor is willing to provide. It may of course be fairly objected that no restaurant could offer an unlimited range of dishes from which customers may select. This, however, is only partially true. Two objections to this view can be raised, one conceptual, the other evidential.

Conceptually, any restaurant that is not locked into offering pre-purchased and processed regenerative cuisines is technically in a position to offer a very large selection of 'knowable' dishes.

That is, except in those very small number of cases where customer knowledges and preferences are truly extensive and their requests idiosyncratic, the presence of a range of basic ingredients and half-competent cook can combine to offer pretty much anything that customers are *likely* to ask for. Thus it is that regular customers in 'traditional' restaurants can (and do) ask for their particular preference even though it may not appear on the menu. Relatedly, and at an empirical level, in the era of relatively élitist public dining, lengthy (if not quite exhaustive) menus were the norm, a restaurant prided itself on the variety of dishes on offer. Such restaurants are an increasing rarity in the contemporary world for at all levels of public gastronomy, the trend has been to shorter menus. The simplification of the menu in a generic sense aids the supplier because it reduces the range of choice (through, paradoxically, not necessarily the act of making a choice). The use of tempting dish descriptions or the emphasis given to particular items as special offers (either on the menu or on clip-ons or boards within the restaurant premises) may be used to guide customers towards profitable items.

That menu design has enjoyed a growth in importance in recent years is beyond doubt. Yet, at the same time, choice and manipulation of menu content is perhaps less important than internal 'massage' of that content. There is some evidence to suggest that restaurateurs rarely employ external 'scanning' techniques other than in a rudimentary sense, in determining their menu content. For example, Easton and Auty (1989) (reported in Auty, 1992: 325) found that:

> The main finding of relevance to the present study was that restaurateurs suited their own inclinations in running their restaurants rather than taking note of the competition in the area. If their style did not suit a regular set of diners, they went out of business rather than making dramatic changes. Changes tended to be in small increments, like adding garlic bread to the menu. Proprietors on the whole denied being competitive, though they admitted keeping an eye on what similar restaurants were doing. None could remember changing their way of doing business in response to a competitor's action, but at the same time they were quite sure that any innovative action of theirs would be copied. In short, each respondent was sure that he/she had a unique and winning style that appealed to a specific set of customers. In a sense they are selling their own personalities rather than plates of food.

Similarly, in their study of the menu as a marketing tool, Cattet and Smith (1994: 161) noted:

> The description of menu items seems to be an area of growing importance and research among certain restaurateurs. Indeed, this is a challenge that all the hotel food and beverage managers interviewed found difficult to face. They put a lot of effort and time into it, on the grounds that it was worthwhile. However, they found it even more difficult for their 'light' menus, as they wanted to find words that created a notion of freshness, at the same time as being informative. Moreover, they did not want their customers to feel frustrated because the calories are counted, so the description of the dish becomes the field where the notion of creativity is really important.

> The situation is different for independent restaurateurs, especially those belonging to the mid-range category. The impression resulting from the survey is that they did not pay any attention to it. Following the rule 'keep it simple', most of the time they used a limited description as they said that they would rather explain the dish verbally to the customer. Higher up the scale, the restaurateurs interviewed said they did devote quite a lot of time and attention to it, trying to avoid pompous words, as the time of pretentious and flamboyant descriptions is over.

This small but worthwhile detour into the social psychology of the menu yields some mixed messages. Nevertheless, if the type, perceived quality and value of food are uppermost in customers' minds then the menu is a device that whatever else it conditions, conditions customers as to the likely tone, tenor and content of their meal experience.

In the view of some academic writers those meal experiences can rarely be anything other than desultory, empty affairs. Such a view is proposed by Finkelstein (1989) in a landmark book. Her argument runs something as follows. According to Finkelstein (1989: 3), contemporary dining out has much to do with self-presentation and 'the mediation of social relations through images of what is currently valued, accepted and fashionable'. Restaurants are depicted in culture as places of excitement and pleasure and these and other images, such as wealth and luxury, are represented iconically within restaurants through such means as ambience, décor, furnishings, lighting and tableware. Following Campbell-Smith's (1967) lead, Finkelstein argues that so important are these iconic representations of people's emotional expectations that the 'physical appearance of the restaurant, its ambience and décor, are as important to the event of dining out as are the comestibles'. Restaurants are places which constitute the loci of certain emotions which the restaurants themselves are instrumental in producing, for example, a sense of romance might be found in an exclusive and atmospheric bistro. Restaurants also allow expression of the individual's private world: people who visit restaurants demonstrate the value they attach to activities and aesthetic forms that are deemed by society as worthy of pleasurable response.

Now, Finkelstein argues, in this sense the individual who dines out acts in an automatic way, seeking to realize desires that are actually 'programmed' by society. Individuals believe themselves to be acting from choice when they dine out and they have expectations that restaurants will help them realize both 'objective' desires – for good food and service – and deeper emotional desires for status and belongingness. In this way, the 'emotional desires' themselves become commodities in which restaurants trade. Eat at this restaurant and you will be seen as part of the *beau monde*, eat at another restaurant and you will be seen as 'cool', or at yet a third where you will be regarded as conventional.

Finkelstein's argument is that to a large degree, the desires of individuals are distorted by the marketplace. Some people have a desire for romance: some types of restaurant by their nature imply that they can satisfy elements of that desire, through there is no natural association between romance and restaurants. For a family 'meal', with children, McDonald's is an obvious choice as the chain embraces the concept of family fun and togetherness. But Finkelstein goes further, suggesting that dining out is not a wholly individual act but one instance of 'uncivilized sociality', whereby restaurants encourage styles of interaction that make dining out a mannered act. These styles of interaction are imitative – of the behaviour of others, of prevailing images and fashions – and are actions of habit, without the need on the part of the consumer for thought, self-scrutiny or 'an examined life'. In other words, when dining out, Finkelstein argues, people behave within an almost automatic framework of interaction already laid down for them, where they have little need to engage meaningfully with others (Finkelstein, 1989: 5). People act 'from habit or in response to the anonymous edicts of conventions' (1989: 12).

Finkelstein (1989: 12) does offer the caveat that only if individuals accept 'the fashions, regimentation and artifice of dining out as being legitimate and attractive features of the event' does 'uncivilized sociality' as a form of behaviour stand as adequate description of consumers' responses to their circum-

Hospitality, Leisure & Tourism Series

stances. She also introduces a rather subtle distinction between individuals as responsible for their actions and individuals not fully conscious of such responsibility (Finkelstein, 1989: 183), thus allowing that individual action on the part of consumers to avoid 'playing the game' represented by the challenge of uncivilized sociality is possible. She writes:

> Having asserted that individuals can rightly be thought of as responsible for their actions, it is necessary to point out that this is not the same as claiming they are fully conscious of that responsibility . . . For example, I know full well that I am responsible for choosing to dine in a bistro *mondain* rather than a local ethnic cafe. I have not been compelled or driven to do so, I simply choose to act in this way. However, if I am asked the question why I chose this restaurant and not that, and all I can offer as an answer is that I prefer the food here not there, or my companions suggested this one and not that, then I am only offering a personal idiosyncrasy as reason. I am not acknowledging any responsibility for the social status that dining out has as a source of personal pleasure, nor for the growing popularity of the practice, which of course would not occur unless I was willing to comply with the fashion . . . [.]If the ability to articulate reasons for actions is a good basis from which to judge the development of an individual's consciousness, then it becomes reasonable to see inarticulateness in these matters as an equally good indication of the absence of full consciousness.

Finkelstein's message is that many consumers subordinate themselves to the priorities of the restaurant – emotions become commodities to be manipulated in the same way as other elements of the 'meal experience'. Moreover, consumers come to expect that these behaviours are legitimate aspects of the act of dining out. Finkelstein's views are controversial but have not gone unchallenged. Lupton (1996: 99) notes that the idea of a 'true self' constrained through the dining experience is a fixed rather than dynamic concept. Adopting the jargon of post-modernism, Lupton prefers 'to adopt the poststructuralist notion of subjectivity as being highly dynamic and contextual rather than fixed' and the 'self' is 'constructed in and through the dining experience, and is highly contextual upon that setting in time and space'. Stripped of its pretentiousness, what Lupton is saying is that how we feel about the dining-out experience depends on our state of mind at the time, and how much we do or do not enjoy ourselves, and our dining environment. Very original.

Warde and Martens (1999: 128–130) offer a far more detailed and empirically based interrogation of Finkelstein's arguments. Far from being unreflective 'dupes' submissive to the imperatives of the restaurants, Warde and Martens' respondents clearly gave considerable thought to the dining-out experience and 47 per cent 'agreed strongly' with the proposition that 'I always enjoy myself when I eat out' with a further 35 per cent 'agreeing slightly'. Further, some 82 per cent had 'liked a lot' their last experience of eating out. Dissecting the elements of the meal experience most enjoyed by respondents, Warde and Martens found aspects of sociability (those very aspects of the meal experience that Finkelstein suggests are at best artificial and at worst acted-out without any 'real' enthusiasm) likely to be most pleasing, nearly 97 per cent saying they liked the company and the conversation. However, 94 per cent said they enjoyed the food and 87 per cent the service and value for money. In seeking to explain such levels of customer satisfaction, Warde and Martens suggest that people guard against uncongenial experiences by revisiting restaurants where they have had positive experiences – some 62 per cent of their respondents having before eaten out at the venue of their last dining-out experience. More fundamental reasons include dining out as a regular, reliable source of pleasure; and the fact that dining out involves freedom from meal preparation (women gave more affirmative replies than men to the question 'Would you like to eat out more often?').

In terms of acquiescence to the norms of the restaurant by customers envisaged by Finkelstein, Warde and Martens (1999: 127–128) are at pains to point out that few of their respondents appeared intimidated by waiting staff or experienced any significant manipulation of their experience in emotions. One possible reason for this is that avoidance techniques operate, with people not revisiting restaurants that make them uncomfortable. Also, Warde and Martens detect among their sample a strong view of dining out as 'special' which, one supposes, may predispose people to reinforce positive prior experiences. Perhaps the most telling evidence against Finkelstein presented by Warde and Martens is that the role of companions is critical to the enjoyment of the meal experience, unsurprising in itself but a firm indicator that Finkelstein's notion of passive clients acting out social scripts supplied by others is not, perhaps, persuasive. Elsewhere, but focusing on the same issues, Martens and Warde (1997: 146) conclude with this observation, relative to Finkelstein's claims:

> The various sources of pleasure reported imply that diners are discerning people, who actively participate in

and shape the event, rather than being confused, blinded or de-sensitised by the regime of the establishment in which they find themselves.

Despite this, one can retain a sympathy with certain elements of Finkelstein's arguments. In some contexts, dining out is a heavily rationalized experience, not only in terms of the 'hardware' of that experience (the food, the physical environment) but also the software, the emotional rationalization of eating out, the control of pleasure by the dictates of the restaurant. This is to some extent reflected in the process of 'McDonaldization', a concept developed by Ritzer (1993, see also Chapter 4) which applies no less to the fine dining end of the market as it does the eponymous fast-food chain and its competitors. Kelly (1997: 9) is but one journalistic source to alight on this trend, pointing to the tendency of many so-called 'quality' restaurants in London to insist that their customers eat in shifts or sittings, two sittings per night being usual with customers at the first often being required to 'eat and complete' within two hours so as to clear the restaurant for the next sitting. To what extent this trend is conducive to anything other than a cursory 'meal experience' is unclear but it hardly suggests a happy prognosis. On the other hand, we cannot dismiss the observation that the growth in number of design-led restaurants suggests that the eating environment is becoming more important or critical to the wider meal experience. As Chaudhuri (1999: 14) notes of some of London's best designer restaurants, 'It is now more likely that you are eating a dish dreamed up in a corporate kitchen after intense market research. The result of all this focus group activity seems to be that the architecture – the mysterious ambience – is more important than the food.' What then are we to believe?

Conclusions

In answer to the closing question of the last section, we can say that the meal experience is alive and well – up to a point. The key messages to arise from the review of evidence contained in this chapter suggest that:

- The concept of choice in dining out is more problematic than is usually thought: food and beverage management research and teaching has often failed to examine in sufficient detail supply-side perspectives, analysing the extent to which those who provide meal experiences control and constrain consumer choice.

- Following from the preceding point, once inside the restaurant of their choice, the menu remains the principal means by which the provider influences consumer choice: the menu is not a catalogue of customer choices but a directory of pre-selected provider choices.

- Such as it is, available research evidence suggests that while relatively intangible elements of the meal experience (for example, décor, atmosphere and ambience) are important to consumers in selecting where to dine, food type, quality, range and price remain pre-eminent factors in the decision-making process.

- While the meal experience has acquired a degree of sterility as a result of standardization of products and services, tangible and non-tangible elements of that experience are important: recent research has interestingly pointed to the role of the customer in creating their own atmosphere and ambience in the form of interaction with their co-diners.

It is, perhaps, time to revisit the whole concept of the meal experience in a systematic manner. It is no longer safe to assume that the meal experience consists simply of a combination of tangible and intangible elements centred on the physicality of the restaurant. In the age of the restaurant as fashion statement and accessory, much of that which forms the quality of the meal experience from the consumer point of view is located in status-driven systems of fashionability and social exclusiveness. Arguably, it was ever so. The danger lies in generalizing the atypical restaurant choice-as-fashion-statement to all dining out. For the serious consumer (and what is the consumer who chooses a restaurant for reasons of fashion if not trivial?) the heartening prospect is that all of the concern for the joys of food, of eating that food, of enjoying the company of others sharing that food, is one experiencing a renaissance, if it ever really went into decline. Designer restaurants and designer meal experiences, together with celebrity chefs and the other vulgar paraphernalia of the hospitality industry which command so much of the media's attention, do not appear to be able to dent most consumers' desire for good food and good company. It would appear that a need for traditional hospitality lives!

References

Anon (1992) Report finds word of mouth sells covers, *Caterer and Hotelkeeper*, 30 April: 14.

Anon (1997) Study shows diners focusing on hygiene, *Caterer and Hotelkeeper*, 5 June: 12.

Auty, S. (1992) Consumer choice and segmentation in the restaurant industry, *The Service Industries Journal*, **12**(3): 324–339.

Barrows, C. W., Lattuca, F. P. and Busselman, R. H. (1989) Influence of restaurant reviews upon consumers', *FIU Hospitality Review*, **7**(2): 84–92.

Campbell-Smith, G. (1967) *The Marketing of the Meal Experience*, Guildford: University of Surrey Press.

Cattet, A. and Smith, C. (1994) The menu as a marketing tool, in C. P. Cooper and A. Lockwood (Eds) *Progress in Tourism, Recreation and Hospitality Management, Volume 6*, Chichester: John Wiley and Sons Inc, 149–163.

Chaudhuri, A. (1999) Choice is off the menu, *Independent on Sunday*, 29 August: 14.

Clark, M. A. and Wood, R. C. (1998) Consumer loyalty in the restaurant industry: a preliminary exploration of the issues, *International Journal of Contemporary Hospitality Management*, **10**(4): 139–144.

Finkelstein, J. (1989) *Dining Out: A Sociology of Modern Manners*, Cambridge: Polity Press.

Frisbee, W. R. and Madeira, K. (1986) Restaurant meals – convenience goods or luxuries?, *The Service Industries Journal*, **6**(2): 172–192.

Harris, K. J. and West, J. J. (1995) Senior savvy: mature diners' restaurant service expectations, *FIU Hospitality Review*, **13**(2): 35–44.

Johns, N., Tyas, P., Ingold, T. and Hopkinson, S. (1996) Investigation of the perceived components of the meal experience using perceptual gap methodology, *Progress in Tourism and Hospitality Research*, **2**: 15–26.

Jolson, M. A. and Bushman, F. A. (1978) Third-party consumer information systems: the case of the food critic, *Journal of Retailing*, **54**(4): 63–79.

June, L. and Smith, S. L. J. (1987) Service attributes and situational effects on customer preferences for restaurant dining, *Journal of Travel Research*, **26**(2): 20–27.

Kelly, A. (1997) No lingering over the linguine, please, *Independent on Sunday*, 9 November: 9.

Lewis, R. (1981) Restaurant advertising: appeals and consumers' intentions, *Journal of Advertising Research*, **21**(5): 69–74.

Lupton, D. (1996) *Food, the Body and the Self*, London: Sage.

Martens, L. and Warde, A. (1997) Urban pleasure: on the meaning of eating out in a northern city in P. Caplan (Ed) *Food, Health and Identity*, London: Routledge, 131–150.

Mooney, S. (1994) Planning and developing the menu, in P. Jones and P. Merricks (Eds) *The Management of Foodservice Operations*, London: Cassell, 45–58.

Pavesic, D. V. (1989) Psychological aspects of menu pricing, *International Journal of Hospitality Management*, **8**(1): 43–49.

Ritzer, G. (1993) *The McDonaldization of Society*, Thousand Oaks: Pine Forge Press.

Ryan, C. (1995) *Measuring Tourist Satisfaction: Issues, Concepts, Problems*, London: Routledge.

Straughan, R. (1995) What's your poison? The freedom to choose our food and drink, *British Food Journal*, **97**(11): 13–20.

Warde, A. (1997) *Consumption, Food and Taste: Culinary Antinomies and Commodity Culture*, London: Sage.

Warde, A. and Martens, L. (1998) A sociological approach to food choice: the case of eating out, in A. Murcott (Ed) *The Nation's Diet: The Social Science of Food Choice*, Harlow: Addison Wesley Longman, 129–144.

Warde, A. and Martens, L. (1999) Eating out: Reflections on the experience of consumers in England, in J. Germov and L. Williams (Eds) *A Sociology of Food and Nutrition: The Social Appetite*, Oxford: Oxford University Press, 116–134.

Wrigley, N. (1998) How British retailers have shaped food choice, in A. Murcott (Ed) *The Nation's Diet: The Social Science of Food Choice*, Harlow: Addison Wesley Longman, 112–128.

Is McDonaldization inevitable? Standardization and differentiation in food and beverage organizations

Stephen Taylor

Hold the pickles, hold the lettuce
Special orders don't upset us
All we ask is that you let us serve it your way

(Advertising jingle used by Burger King Corporation in the 1970s)

Introduction

The industrialization of services is not a new phenomenon, nor are academic explorations of its various manifestations and implications. In an early and influential contribution, Harvard academic Theodore

Levitt (1972) commented upon the 'Production-line approach to service' which drew heavily on the practices of the McDonald's Corporation. In 1976, Levitt wrote a further article entitled 'The industrialization of service' where he extolled the virtues of service organizations embracing a manufacturing approach to their activities. More recently, there has been renewed interest in the industrialization of services. This time the extensive standardization inherent in the many modern service firms which have adopted and adapted manufacturing thinking and practices is being generally viewed in a considerably less positive light. This chapter explores this theme in the context of likely future developments in food and beverage organizations.

In talking about industrialization (standardization) in food and beverage operations, we would say that the service delivery system (Sasser, Olsen and Wyckoff, 1978) is regulated by established routines and processes which provide the intended uniform outputs in a consistent fashion. A particular feature of these processes is typically the substitution of human skill by 'technology' in the widest sense of this term. Thus, here we would include in our definition of technology the division of labour (task specialization) as well as the more tangible examples that typically accompany it such as machinery. Accordingly, the Escofferian revolution of the nineteenth century (Wood, 1998), which established the template for the classical organization of the commercial kitchen (in the form of the *partie* system) and restaurant, and the codification of recipe materials, is an excellent early example of the introduction of both technology and standardization.

As noted above, there has been a tendency in the latter part of the twentieth century to imbue the term standardization with a somewhat negative connotation. This, however, misrepresents and distorts the true nature of this particular phenomenon that is simply a manifestation of a much larger economic process that began in the early nineteenth century – industrialization. Consequently, our central concerns surround the issues of both production and consumption within the economic system that we have come to refer to as capitalism. This has been fertile ground for economic and social thinkers, most notably Karl Marx and Max Weber who each provided critical explorations of various aspects of the capitalist system. More recently, writers such as Braverman (1974), and Ritzer (1993), have revisited the original contributions of these two theorists. Ritzer has provided an extensive critique of the increasing spread of Weberian rationalization in service organizations, a process which he has called 'McDonaldization'.

What is 'McDonaldization'?

The term 'McDonaldization' was coined by American sociology professor George Ritzer in his book *The McDonaldization of Society* (1993: 1) to describe 'the process by which the principles of the fast-food restaurant are coming to dominate more and more sectors of American society as well as of the rest of the world'. In this first book and its subsequent variants (Ritzer, 1995; 1999; forthcoming), Ritzer expounds a doom-laden prognosis for life as we know it, whereby our daily existence will become increasingly dominated by McDonaldized systems (eating, health care, education, banking, media and so on) and by the handful of individuals who control these systems. These systems are characterized as transferring the logic of the mass production factory to the service context, '. . . notably homogeneous products, rigid technologies, standardized work routines, deskilling, homogenization of labour (and customer), the mass worker, and homogenization of consumption' (Ritzer, 1993: 155). It is claimed that the objective of such systems is to achieve 'efficiency, calculability (or quantification), predictability [and] increased control through substitution of non-human for human technology' (Ritzer, 1993: 34). Concern is expressed that this 'inexorable process' is dehumanizing and that it is in effect 'an iron cage' as it imposes control on not only those who work within a McDonaldized system but also its customers who '. . . are placed on a kind of assembly line; [of which] the drive-through window is the most obvious example' (Ritzer, 1993: 26).

It could be argued that the industrialization of services described by Ritzer is treated as something of a 'straw man' and that there is a failure to engage in any substantive understanding of the phenomenon which it purports to critique. As has been argued elsewhere (see Wood, 1998) Ritzer's work can perhaps, at best, be viewed as a populist restatement of Weber's thoughts on rationalization and at worst, it could be viewed as a selected and exaggerated representation of reality that fails to withstand any serious scrutiny as a piece of academic work (Gilling, 1996). This said, the McDonaldization thesis has become, in the USA at least, extremely popular (the original book is, in academic terms, a major best seller) and highly influential in the teaching of introductory sociology. Indeed, so ubiquitous is Ritzer's book that it has become, somewhat ironically, a 'McText', a force for standardization just like its subject matter (Wood, 1998; O'Neill, 1999).

However, it is not intended in this chapter to critique *per se* what has become known as the 'McDonaldization Thesis' (Ritzer, 1998). This task has been adequately performed in two recent edited volumes of essays by academics (see Alfino, Caputo and Wynyard, 1998; Smart, 1999). In addition, there has been some limited debate within hospitality as to the merits of Ritzer's thesis (see Lyon, Taylor and Smith, 1994, 1995; Taylor and Lyon, 1995; Wood, 1995 and Silverstone, 1995). The most recent and comprehensive treatments from a hospitality perspective are probably Taylor, Smith and Lyon (1998) and Wood (1998), the latter being of particular note. In this chapter our central concern is to assess the extent to which standardization (as exemplified by McDonaldization) threatens to remove (or perpetuate the lack of, depending on your viewpoint) differentiation in food and beverage organizations.

What do we mean by standardization and differentiation?

At the outset it is important to explore the meanings to be ascribed here to the terms standardization and differentiation respectively. These terms can be problematic as ultimately it is not simply a case of standard versus non-standard (i.e. differentiated), but rather one of *degrees of difference*. For our purposes we take standardization to refer to the situation where uniformity is achieved either in outputs (products or services) and/or in the processes that produce such outputs. Note that we have not assumed that standardized outputs *must* be produced by standardized processes, certainly at least, not in the sense that Ritzer means. For example, two skilled chefs can produce the same classical dish (for example, Chicken Kiev) and could in theory do so *ad infinitum*. Thus we would achieve a standardized output, but have not standardized the production process . . . or have we?

A moment's reflection on the above example would suggest that we have indeed used a type of standardized production process, or rather, a series of processes. In this instance our chefs have almost certainly resorted to a recipe and this is a clear form of standardization in that it embraces the actual ingredients to be used, their quantities, how they should be combined and what, if any, cooking process (another form of standardization based upon technology) to which they should be subjected. In addition, the chefs will probably have undergone a formalized training programme to provide them with their requisite craft skills. Thus a craftsperson (in this instance, a chef) can be viewed as being a standardized output (from a professional training programme/apprenticeship) who subsequently becomes a standardized input as part of a production process. Clearly, one needs to use caution when attempting to establish what does and what does not constitute standardization. Our example is, of course, a highly stylized one and smacks somewhat of sophistry, but it does make the point. It also leaves us with something of a problem, namely, what then is differentiation?

Taking Ritzer's key characteristics of McDonaldization, we might suggest that differentiation involves those processes and outputs where efficiency, calculability, predictability, control and substitution of human labour by non-human labour are absent. Unfortunately, it is hard to think of even Michelin starred restaurants (for some the epitome of differentiation in the food and beverage context) operating in the absence of *any* of these characteristics. For even in this rarefied environment, standardization will be evident in staff skills (in both the kitchen and restaurant), the work routines followed, the level of service provided and so on. One can be certain that standardization (that is the 'standards of the house') will be embodied in everything from the table settings, the service of food and drink, the pace of service, the desired ambience (controlled by the interior design, lighting, music) the types of customers, the employees and so on.

This begins to take us closer to a serviceable definition of differentiation and suggests its existence is dependent upon a form of process and output relativity. That is, there is an absence – to a certain degree – of *external* replication of either processes and/or outputs. Of the two, we typically give greater weight to the latter when we think of differentiation, in that we tend to define differentiation from the consumption perspective (i.e. output in the form of menu items, quality, price) rather than the production (i.e. process) side of the equation (although Ritzer and some others would take issue with this view). On this basis, differentiation will be intimately related to the amount of flexibility inherent in a foodservice operation in terms of its ability to service a wide variety of customer needs. Nonetheless, it would be erroneous to see processes and outputs as unconnected given that the former begets the latter. Additionally, it could be possible that operators employing, cook-chill, cook-freeze and 'traditional' production processes respectively, produce largely undifferentiated outputs from one another (although purists might vehemently disagree!).

The rise of standardization

In the case of food and beverage organizations, the point of origin of industrialization is widely recognized as being the innovative production methods originally developed in the late 1940s by the

McDonald brothers (the so called 'Speedee Service System') which were later refined by the founder of the McDonald's Corporation, Ray Kroc. It was under Kroc's direction that the standardization for which McDonald's is noted was aligned to a strategy of business format franchising. This was to provide the catalyst for the rapid diffusion of the McDonald's production system and its outputs. Today (in mid-1999), the McDonald's Corporation has twenty-five thousand units operating across one hundred and seventeen countries which serve in excess of forty million customers every single day. Its annual sales are thirty-six billion dollars and 60 per cent of these sales originate outside the United States. In economic terms it would be difficult to dispute the success of the McDonald's organization and this success resides primarily in its ability to replicate its highly standardized operating procedures and practices across both temporal and spatial dimensions.

The story of the founding and creation of the McDonald's empire is generally well known. However, it is a story worth revisiting in order to understand the innovative nature of the standardization process, which has been widely adopted across food and beverage organizations, particularly in the quick-service restaurant (fast-food) sector. The official company history (i.e. the firm's own version) goes something like this. Two brothers, Richard and Maurice McDonald, started a restaurant in 1940 located in San Bernardino, California. In 1947, in response to increasing local competition they decided to make some changes to their operation. This involved reducing menu items from twenty-five to nine (i.e. narrowing product scope); focusing on take-away and self service by removing car hop service (mainly used by teenagers); and the removal of cutlery and plates, using instead paper bags and cups. Aligned to the changes to the customer offer, the brothers standardized the processes required to produce these outputs. Together, these changes facilitated uniform food quality, quicker service, attracted more families (due to the absence of teenagers), reduced staffing levels and enabled the McDonald brothers to sell menu items at a lower price than competitors while still making a profit. Importantly, it was from these modifications that the four principles of quality, service, cleanliness and value (QSC & V) that were to become the bywords of the McDonald's Corporation originated.

At the heart of these changes was the application of the Taylorist scientific management principles which had been refined and deployed to such telling effect by Henry Ford in the production of the Model T automobile. For the McDonald brothers this entailed task specialization for staff (division of labour); laying out the kitchen for maximum efficiency; the development of specially designed kitchen equipment; and the standardization of key labour routines (cf. Nelson and Winter, 1982). This was necessary to facilitate and support the new kitchen system which required a reduced labour component (a major source of operating costs) consisting of a maximum staffing complement of twelve. Each staff member's tasks were documented in detail and this enabled the McDonald brothers to employ cheaper untrained cooks. This produced a service delivery system that was cheaper (i.e. more efficient) and had a 'better quality' output (i.e. greater effectiveness) than those employed by the competition. Such was the success of this innovation that in 1951 the McDonald brothers licensed it as the 'Speedee Service System' and sold it to businessmen who, for the sum of $1000, could then open their own restaurant using both this system and the name 'McDonald's'. It was around this point that milkshake mixer salesman Ray Kroc's attention was caught (his first visit was in July 1954) and the rest, as they say, is history.

These relatively simple innovations at McDonald's were ultimately to change the 'rules of the game' within this particular sector of the restaurant business (although, as Emerson, 1990, points out, and for the sake of accuracy, the origins of the fast-food industry can be traced back to a number of earlier developments such as Bob Wian's 'Bob's, Home of the Big Boy' which was granting franchises in the 1940s). The McDonald brothers were, through their relatively simple changes (in essence, the creation of a highly efficient and effective delivery system, i.e. operating processes/routines), able to offer superior customer benefits (a higher speed of service, a consistent standard of quality, cleanliness, and value for money) relative to competitor outlets. Furthermore, at the outset, this service delivery system was sufficiently innovative and causally ambiguous that (1) it could not be readily imitated by competitors and (2) consequently the tacit knowledge embodied in this system could be licensed and sold to others. Ironically, this implies that McDonald's early success can be attributed to the fact that it was a *highly differentiated foodservice organization*, in so far as the product offer provided unrivalled price/value in the chosen market segment, albeit this differentiation resided in its extensive standardization. Later, with the subsequent development of a detailed operations manual and the commitment to the associated training (as epitomized in the creation of its very own Hamburger University) McDonald's was able to codify and articulate its know-how and to transfer this to franchisees. In this way the food delivery system was to be replicated thousands of times with only small variations to account for relatively minor differences in consumer tastes in different national markets.

Hospitality, Leisure & Tourism Series

In the forty-five years since its founding the McDonald's standardized system has been highly influential, not just in the hospitality sector, but as Ritzer's first book testifies, for the service sector more generally. What is perhaps not widely appreciated is that in creating their food production system, McDonald's were also responsible for radical changes in the US food processing and food distribution industries. Indeed, the modern shape of both these industries can be largely attributed to the demands of the McDonald's system for standardized inputs in the form of the frozen French fries (the first frozen fries were developed in conjunction with McDonald's) frozen hamburgers, chicken and so on that make up the basic raw materials of the system. The scale of demand for these raw ingredients by a single organization has perhaps been the source of some of the more negative attention heaped on the McDonald's Corporation over the years, most notably the highly embarrassing 'McLibel' trial in the 1990s (Vidal, 1997). However, any large-scale entity as economically powerful and successful as McDonald's is certain to attract attention and raise the sort of fears in people upon which Ritzer so effectively plays. Critics denounce the standardization inherent in its processes and products not because of their failure but because of their success. Professional restaurateurs view with considerable disdain the 'plastic' food purveyed by fast-food restaurants and point to the intrinsically superior merits of their own 'craft-based' establishments. Accordingly, consumers need to be 'saved from themselves' and to 'rediscover' the joys of fine dining. Of course, this assumes that: (1) consumers do not wish to eat standardized foods, and (2) that they can afford to eat the very much more expensive differentiated offers of the traditional restaurant sector.

The issue of consumer demand

The rise of standardized food and beverage operations, which includes not only fast-food restaurants, but also mid-scale chains such as Beefeater, TGI Fridays, Pierre Victoire (all of which are standardized in terms of both processes and products to varying degrees), can be attributed to a number of demand factors. First and foremost has been the social changes that have originated from the rise in the standard of living in many countries due to economic growth, largely driven, note, by the spread of mass production. The expansion of the middle classes in many nations has led to generally increased demand for products and services in these economies. The expansion of eating out is but one example of the effects of increased levels of disposable income. Aligned to this economic factor, which has led to the rise of what we know as 'consumerism', are increased demands from people for new experiences and a general trend towards more extrinsically oriented lifestyles (partially fuelled by exposure to alternative cultures and foods) among those individuals who frequently have more money than they have time to actually spend it. Thus, we have seen the rise of 'designer brands' and indeed 'designer' or 'signature' restaurants with the obligatory 'superchef'. In this environment, differentiation is very much the name of the game. To be successful, at least for an initial period, restaurants must provide something unique if they are to attract the experience-hungry (*sic*) restaurant patron. Clearly, however, this describes a relatively small élite in most societies, for the majority of people eating out (fast-food consumption aside) is, and will probably continue to remain, an irregular pastime. Again, it is a simple case of economics.

Of course, consumer demand is but one half of the equation. The other side is the issue of supply. A sophisticated understanding of this in the modern market economy has to recognize that supply can and is shaped by suppliers (as Ritzer contends), but also that it can be shaped by the demands of consumers. Accordingly, the rise of standardization in food and beverage organizations can partially be attributed to consumer demand for (or alternatively, acceptance of) a uniform quality of food at an affordable price. Inherent in this situation is the need for some form of trade-off, and that trade-off is the range of food choice (variation) that a given operation can accommodate. It is this situation that has led to the successful proliferation of fast-food formats that offer standardized outputs through utilizing standardized processes. Consumer choice is limited in the sense that although they have access to an increasingly wide range of food types (hamburgers, chicken, pizza, Mexican and so on), ultimately they have to avail themselves of a standardized food production system (i.e. a McDonaldized one). Here we have differentiation, but this is simply between the various fast-food systems (e.g. Burger King versus Pizza Hut) and for some critics such as Ritzer, this is no differentiation at all.

This last point underlines the discussion above regarding the definition of standardization and differentiation in food and beverage organizations. That is, the issue of delineating the two concepts is dependent upon degrees of differences rather than clear and sharp distinctions. Once again, applying the terms standardization and differentiation, demands that we have recourse to some sense of relativeness if we are to operationalize their meanings. Another issue, and perhaps this might be the most germane one, is whether it really matters to consumers that suppliers have adopted standardization as a means of yielding an economic return from their endeavours. In the absence of such practices would consumers be happy to endure higher prices and variable quality all in the name of some notion of differentiation? Alternatively, is there another possible future for food and beverage organizations where they can achieve the efficiencies they prize (as these are in the highly competitive mass eating-out sector, the source of their economic gain) yet move towards treating customers as individuals and providing them with greater choice at prices they can still afford? Such a win-win situation may on the face of it seem somewhat fanciful, but there are indications that a scenario like this *might* just be possible. Perhaps somewhat ironically, the source of this possibility is the very same source that provided the inspiration and techniques that facilitated service industrialization, that is the manufacturing sector.

Combining standardization and differentiation

In the late 1970s and early 1980s manufacturers became increasingly aware that their traditional approach to production was ceasing to deliver the success that they had enjoyed through the 1950s and 1960s. That mass production was failing can be attributed to two key factors according to Pine (1993). First, there were the inherent limits to the process itself due to input stability. For example, how low can labour costs go and how high its productivity? Second, was the fact that the market homogeneity (i.e. undifferentiated demand) required by mass production had disappeared as markets became fragmented. Additionally, mass production requires growth markets, but its very success had led to market saturation. This coupled with increasing change in economic and social environments had removed the stable conditions necessary for mass production systems. The challenge for manufacturers was to find some means of maintaining competitive cost structures through standardization, but produce a greater variety of products to meet increasingly diverse customer needs, that is differentiated outputs.

Intuitively, the idea of combining standardization and differentiation is something of a contradiction. How can we take two opposites and hope to reconcile them? This, however, is exactly what leading-edge manufacturers have achieved as a means of coping with the inherent limitations of the mass production system. In effect, this has been attained by little less than a paradigm shift that was necessary to address the increasing levels of consumer diversity that confronted manufacturers. This revolution is termed 'mass customization' which represents a shift away from the standardized outputs of mass production to an emphasis upon variety and customization through flexibility and quick responsiveness. As Pine (1993: 44) notes, '. . . this is the controlling focus of . . . mass customization . . . [which shares] . . . the goal of developing, producing, marketing and delivering affordable goods and services with enough variety and customization that nearly everyone finds exactly what they want'. In effect this process entails a move away from the emphasis of mass production upon inducing sales volume through a lowering of unit costs and instead the placing of greater emphasis on stimulating sales through meeting customer needs.

The critical difference between the mass production and mass customization paradigms is a reversal on the importance of outputs and processes. In mass production the product is the starting point and the processes are then configured to produce the desired output in a uniform manner. In doing this the output and the production process become permanently coupled together. Any variety in output requires a different product process and this traditionally could only be achieved through extensive retooling. In mass customization the starting point is the process not the products. Unlike mass production whereby economies of scale (quantity) are used to lower costs, mass customization uses economies of scope (variety) to lower costs. Cyberneticists recognize this phenomenon in their law of requisite variety which states that market fragmentation requires flexibility in production and an increased diversity of output (Ashby, 1956). Recent advances in manufacturing such as *kanban* ('just-in-time' raw material delivery) and lean production are some of the building blocks upon which this shift is achieved. The obvious question is, can such approaches be adopted by food and beverage organizations?

Mass customization in food and beverage organizations

The market changes discussed above which had confronted the mass manufacturers soon began to also affect their foodservice cousins. In the USA the 1980s saw increasing market saturation (particularly in the fast-food sector) which led to significant pressures being placed on operators to compete more aggressively with one another. One result of this was a redoubled effort to provide a greater variety of outputs (i.e. differentiation) in order to retain existing customers. All the major players in the US fast-food sector introduced (and continue to introduce) new product ranges in an effort to halt declining market shares and profit margins. This as Crawford-Welch (1994: 169) notes: '[W]as, in essence, a response by corporations to the plurality of the marketplace and the diverse price/value needs of multiple market segments. In today's hospitality industry there is no such thing as a mass market. Mass markets are a vestige of the past.'

Even the hitherto exemplar of service industrialization, McDonald's, has reacted with an aggressive expansion of its menu items. Thus it now offers '. . . pizza, chicken fajitas, breakfast burritos, submarine sandwiches, spaghetti and meatballs, bone-in chicken, a grilled chicken sandwich, carrot and celery sticks, fresh-ground coffee and even bottled water' (Scarpa, 1991: 112). As one might imagine, such a shift has not been an easy matter given the rigidity that McDonald's had developed to sustain its fabled uniformity. In the early stages of this change the creation of an increased variety of output within a standardized production environment was not without its difficulties: 'It was a big mistake. Our stores are small. They didn't have space for the new equipment that was needed. It [the menu item] was really popular with our customers, but started to mess up the rest of our operation' (quoted in Langeard, Bateson, Lovelock and Eiglier 1981: 89).

A key difficulty for standardized foodservice firms is the need to abandon their historical belief in the 'absolutism of scale economy' that places efficiency above all other considerations (Yasamuro, 1993: 210). This will only happen when these organizations realize that they cannot continue to tackle the challenges they confront while continuing to subscribe to 'production-line thinking'. However there is limited evidence that some firms are making the necessary fundamental changes.

Perhaps the best documented example of a foodservice organization that has apparently made real progress to embracing the mass customization approach and to transfer the new manufacturing logic to foodservice is Taco Bell. Schlesinger and Heskett (1991) give an account of the radical transformations undertaken at Taco Bell to facilitate a shift away from a production-line approach to what they term the 'service-driven service company'. This entailed a radical rethinking of how the restaurants actually operated and what customers actually wanted. Perhaps one of the most tangible effects of this change programme was an inversion of the restaurant space from 70 per cent kitchen, 30 per cent seating, to 30 per cent kitchen, 70 per cent seating. This resulted from adopting just-in-time (JIT) deliveries and radically reducing the amount of food preparation carried out in the restaurant. Instead, the emphasis was placed on performing at the restaurant only those food preparation activities that added the most value from the customer's perspective. Anything else was contracted-out to suppliers or centralized production facilities. By applying the new manu-facturing logic embodied in JIT, value-chain analysis and placing an increased emphasis on customer contact, Taco Bell has, it is claimed, gone a long way towards resolving the tension that historically resided between having an efficient low-cost operation and providing a flexible output (Bowen and Youngdahl, 1998). Or did they?

The Taco Bell story does not quite have the happy ending the preceding paragraph implies. In the early stages, the perform-ance of the reengineered Taco Bell was encouraging with positive responses from both its employees and customers. However, by late 1996 the organization had experienced six quarters of very indifferent sales that, ultimately, cost John Martin (the then, Taco Bell CEO and architect of the radical restructuring programme) his job. As Durnford (1997) indicates, in the final analysis Taco Bell's sole source of differentiation resided in its low prices. Consequently, when competitors retaliated with their own price cutting initiatives, customer volume dropped dramatically. Taco Bell's failure was routed in its confusion of price differentiation with true differentiation of its foodservice output (i.e. variety). While Martin's initiatives did make Taco Bell more efficient, they failed to make it a more effective and truly differentiated restaurant organization capable of providing real value from a customer's perspective.

Conclusions

The changes described above suggest the beginning of a new phase in the industrialization of services. Consequently, one might be moved to suggest that McDonaldization, the produc-tion-line approach to food and beverage organization, is far from inevitable. The new paradigm of mass customization will allow restaurant organizations to continue to standardize their produc-tion processes and thus gain access to desired efficiencies, but this will be allied to an improved ability to meet the needs of individual customers. Given an increased variety of output, capable of meeting a wider diversity of customer needs, the paradox of standardization versus differentiation would appear to be capable of resolution. Nonetheless, as Wood (1998: 96) has argued: 'Adapting menus to incorporate vegetarian foods and local specialities are merely examples of the methods by which organizations like McDonald's seek to incorporate opposition and conflict in a manner intended to pacify and neutralize hostility to their activities'. In a somewhat similar vein, Ritzer (1996) argues that nothing has changed, and rationalism is still to the fore. Ritzer sees mass customization simply as a process of 'sneakerization' that continues to restrict and shape consumer choice as it has done in the past.

In we fall in line with the preceding comments, it would appear to take us to something of an impasse. For it suggests that regardless of the amount of variety offered by foodservice organizations, they will continue for some critics to represent a standardized provider of food and beverage. This, it would appear, is because they continue to adopt an industrialized process (albeit in an updated form) approach to food production. Clearly, this view is predicated upon defining foodservice standardization/differentiation from a supply or process perspective not a demand or product one. However, it is from this latter perspective that restaurant customers typically approach the determination of the degree of differentiation of a food and beverage organization. For them the means are considerably less important than the ends that are achieved. They are less concerned with how restaurants produce the food and are more concerned with what the food is that is actually produced in terms of choice, quality and price. Accordingly, one might be moved to suggest that the emphasis critics give to process standardization is something of a 'red herring' that chooses to ignore what really matters – the degree of customer choice that is actually achieved.

Earlier, in attempting to define differentiation, we suggested that the level, or degree of external replication, particularly of product output, was of some importance. This emphasizes the point that differentiation needs to be viewed from a demand side perspective and related to the output variety (i.e. food choice) of one restaurant relative to another. If we accept this definition of differentiation it suggests that a chain restaurant cannot be considered to be truly differentiated for the simple reason it externally replicates itself. Regardless of the differences between one restaurant chain and another, the very scale of modern chains would appear to ensure that despite the increased level of consumer choice they may provide, they will continue to be regarded as being standardized. This, however, is the nature of the beast. Without a high degree of standardization these organizations would cease to have access to the operational and financial benefits of the chain form of organization. This leads us to two concluding points.

First, is that the mass production as embodied in McDonaldization is almost certainly not inevitable, since it is increasingly incapable of delivering the output variety desired by an increasingly fragmented marketplace and, consequently, the economic returns sought by producers. Following from this, a second conclusion is that McDonaldization will evolve towards the modern variant of mass customization since this would appear to be capable of delivering the efficiencies required by producers coupled with the variety increasingly demanded by customers. Ultimately these changes would mean that, in the mass eating-out market, customers *will* have a greater choice than they experienced in the past, but this will continue to be provided by restaurant chains based upon standardized operating processes. Nonetheless, given the economics of restaurant chains and their resultant ubiquitous nature, one must ultimately conclude that they will never be perceived as truly differentiated providers of food and beverage regardless of the level of choice they aspire to provide individual customers.

References

Alfino, M., Caputo, J. S. and Wynyard, R. (1998) (Eds) *McDonaldization Revisited: Critical Essays on Consumer Culture*, Westport, CN: Praeger.

Ashby, W. (1956) *An Introduction to Cybernetics*, New York: John Wiley.

Bowen, D. E. and Youngdahl, W. E. (1998) 'Lean' service: in defence of a production-line approach, *International Journal of Service Industry Management*, **9**(3): 207–225.

Braverman, H. (1974) *Labor and Monopoly Capital*, New York: Monthly Review Press.

Crawford-Welch, S. (1994) Product development in the hospitality industry, in R. Teare, J. Manazec, S. Crawford-Welch and S. Calver (Eds) *Marketing in Hospitality and Tourism: A Consumer Focus*, London: Cassell.

Durnford, T. (1997) Redefining quality: for whom the Taco Bell tolls, *Cornell Hotel and Restaurant Administration Quarterly*, June: 74–80.

Emerson, R. L. (1990) *The New Economics of Fast Food*, London: Van Nostrand Rinehold.

Gilling, A. (1996) Review of G. Ritzer *The McDonaldization of Society* (revised edition), *The Times Higher Education Supplement*, 16 August: 24.

Langeard, E., Bateson, J., Lovelock, C. and Eiglier, P. (1981) *Services Marketing: New Insights from Consumers and Managers*. Cambridge, MA: Marketing Science Institute.

Levitt, T. (1972) The production-line approach to service, *Harvard Business Review*, **50**(5): 41–52.

Levitt, T. (1976) The industrialization of service, *Harvard Business Review*, **56**(5): 63–74.

Lyon, P., Taylor, S. and Smith, S. (1994) McDonaldization: a reply to Ritzer's thesis, *International Journal of Hospitality Management*, **13**(2): 95–99.

Lyon, P., Taylor, S. and Smith, S. (1995) Is Big Mac the big threat?, *International Journal of Hospitality Management*, **14**(2): 119–122.

Nelson, R. R. and Winter, S. G. (1982) *An Evolutionary Theory of Economic Change*, Cambridge, MA: Belknap Press.

O'Neill, J. (1999) Have you had your theory today?, in B. Smart (Ed), *Resisting McDonaldization*, London: Sage, 41–56.

Pine, B. J. (1993) *Mass Customization: The New Frontier in Business Competition*, New York: Harvard Business Press.

Ritzer, G. (1993) *The McDonaldization of Society.* Thousand Oaks, CA: Pine Forge Press.

Ritzer, G. (1995) *Expressing America: A Critique of the Global Credit Card Society*, Thousand Oaks, CA: Pine Forge Press.

Ritzer, G. (1996) *The McDonaldization of Society*, Thousand Oaks, CA: Pine Forge Press, revised edition.

Ritzer, G. (1998) *The McDonaldization Thesis: Explorations and Extensions*, London: Sage.

Ritzer, G. (1999) *Enchanting a Disenchanted World: Revolutionizing the Means of Consumption*, Thousand Oaks, CA: Pine Forge Press.

Ritzer, G. (forthcoming) *Cathedrals of Consumption*. London: Sage.

Sasser, W. E., Olsen, R. P. and Wyckoff, D. D. (1978) *Management of Service Operations*, Boston: Allyn and Bacon.

Scarpa, J. (1991) McDonald's menu mission, *Restaurant Business*, 1 July: 110–117.

Schlesinger, L. A. and Heskett, J. A. (1991) The service-driven service company, *Harvard Business Review*, **69**(5): 71–81.

Silverstone, R. (1995) A response to Lyon, Taylor and Smith, *International Journal of Hospitality Management*, **14**(2): 111–115.

Smart, B. (Ed) (1999) *Resisting McDonaldization*, London: Sage.

Taylor, S. and Lyon, P. (1995) Paradigm lost: the rise and fall of McDonaldization, *International Journal of Contemporary Hospitality Management*, **7**(2/3): 64–68.

Taylor, S., Smith, S. and Lyon, P. (1998) Consumer choice in the future: an illusion or the next marketing revolution?, in M. Alfino, J. S. Caputo and R. Wynyard (Eds) *McDonaldization Revisited: Critical essays on Consumer Culture*, Westport, CN: Praeger, 105–120.

Vidal, J. (1997) *McLibel: Burger Culture on Trial*, London: Macmillan.

Wood, R. C. (1995) Misunderstanding and misinterpreting McDonaldization: a comment on Lyon, Taylor and Smith, *International Journal of Hospitality Management*, **13**(4): 293–295.

Wood, R. C. (1998) Old wine in new bottles: critical limitations of the McDonaldization thesis – the case of hospitality services, in M. Alfino, J. S. Caputo and R. Wynyard (Eds) *McDonaldization Revisited: Critical Essays on Consumer Culture*, Westport, CN: Praeger, 85–104.

Yasamuro, K. (1993) Conceptualising an adaptable marketing system: the end of mass marketing, in R. Tedlow and G. Jones (Eds), *The Rise and Fall of Mass Marketing*, London and New York: Routledge, 205–235.

CHAPTER 5

Strategic purchasing policy. Reality or chimera in the foodservice sector?

Donald H. Sloan

Introduction

The broad aim of this chapter is to examine the extent to which foodservice operators have integrated the food purchasing function into strategic management. Management rhetoric would suggest that the role of food purchasers has changed from being purely administrative and reactive to being integrated with other business functions and supportive of corporate strategy. If this is so, it would be in line with the generic development of the purchasing function that can be tracked in management literature from the 1970s onwards.

Competitive pressures are continually increasing in most industries. In the manufacturing sector (to which most of the literature on purchasing relates) this is largely due to technological innovation, periods of economic recession and the emergence of new competitors. Competition is also intensifying in the foodservice industry due to the increasing number of operators, the changing composition of the customer base, the increased sophistication of customers and the concentration of unit ownership. As competition grows, organizations attempt to increase productivity, often by implementing new production methods; encouraging greater labour efficiency; implementing cost containment policies; and introducing up-to-date technological systems. Less attention has been paid to the purchasing function (Baily, Farmer, Jessop and Jones, 1994: 61). Recent research (e.g. Reck and Long, 1988; Rajagopal and Bernard, 1993; Watts, Kim and Hahn, 1995) suggests evidence of a realization amongst progressive corporate strategists of the importance of developing the purchasing function. Commentators often distinguish between strategies that are designed to improve operational effectiveness within purchasing departments, and the role of the purchasing function in supporting wider corporate strategy. Indeed much of the literature appearing throughout the 1990s centred on the competitive advantage to be gained by integrating the purchasing function into corporate strategy (e.g. Pearson and Gritzmacher, 1990; Freeman and Cavinato, 1990).

The purchasing function and strategic management

A useful starting point for examination of these recent perspectives is the survey by Ammer (1974) of top managements' perceptions of the purchasing function. Covering 750 companies, Ammer's study revealed a lack of importance attached to this area of business activity, leading him to remark that: 'There is a general, corporate-wide ignorance of what the purchasing process entails.' (1974: 36). His findings are particularly significant as the influence of the purchasing function within organizations is ultimately determined by top management. Although Ammer's data is drawn from US companies, the British experience in this respect tends to reflect that of the USA. The survey highlighted the following specific issues (Ammer, 1974: 37): management often encouraged 'passive' purchasing, i.e. purchasing simply as a reaction to the demands of departments within the organization; even in circumstances of 'enlightened' management, the role of purchasers was viewed as being limited to supplier selection and inventory management; management did not apply the same monitoring procedures to the purchasing function as they did to other areas of business activity; top management did not view purchasing as an area in which risks should be taken; there existed a discrepancy between senior managements' perceptions and those of purchasing managers as to the qualities required to be a successful purchasing manager; and management often regarded purchasing as a 'dead-end' job. Ammer's study, taken together with other academic evidence from this time concurs in suggesting that the purchasing function was poorly regarded and the concept of purchasing strategy in its infancy. Farmer's (1978) work supports Ammer's assertion about the perception of purchasing among top management. He argued that there was an acceptance by top management that the supply of products could affect profitability, but a realization that supply factors can also impact upon the long-term success of organizations was lacking.

As recently as 1994, in a review of key issues Baily, Farmer, Jessop and Jones (1994) identify a variety of reasons why the purchasing function continues to receive little attention from practitioners. The purchasing function is seen as involving little more than the administration of transactions, resulting in limited understanding of the potential benefits of operating efficiently in this area and the likely limitations of organizational success through inefficient purchasing. Often, corporate strategy is driven by the desire to increase sales. Certain departments, therefore, dominate company activity and purchasing is often overlooked. In addition, external influences contribute the continuing poor position of the purchasing function. If organizations experience no difficulties selling their products then they may pay insufficient attention to controlling input costs. However, this can cause problems as business environments become increasingly competitive. Baily, Farmer, Jessop and Jones (1994) also highlight problems of usability of the purchasing function stemming from the nature of the Institute of Purchasing and Supply, the professional body for those working in supply chain management. In the past there were relatively few members, little off-site training was provided and the organization lacked status. This has begun to change in the 1990s following the award of a Royal Charter.

From purchasing function to purchasing strategy

As previously detailed, academic literature identifies two levels of purchasing strategy. Earlier literature related primarily to strategies for improving the effectiveness of purchasing departments, rather than developing the role of the purchasing function in supporting corporate strategy. For example, Kotler and Levy (1973) identified strategies that can be adopted by industrial buyers to gain influence over the supply environment. Kiser (1976) notes that Kotler and Levy were the first to suggest that the scope of marketing should include buyer effectiveness, their work promoting an enhanced role for purchasing managers in stark contrast to that detailed in traditional operations management texts of the time.

Kiser (1976) developed this work by identifying 'key concepts' likely to have a bearing on the nature of strategies implemented by purchasing departments. This displays the increased complexity attached to the purchasing role as it moved from being merely 'transactional' to being proactive. These 'key concepts' can be summarized as follows.

- *Choosing which seller market to enter.* A vital consideration for industrial buyers is to source products that most precisely satisfy their organizations' requirements. Clearly, this is dependent upon the identification of, and effective communication with, appropriate suppliers. Kiser notes that the formation of relationships with appropriate suppliers carries with it a range of responsibilities, not least the mutual acceptance of legal contracts. It is also worth noting that failure to continually review the supplier market can lead to the extension of relationships between buyers and suppliers beyond their period of validity.

- *Choosing the most appropriate products from within the market.* After the seller market has been identified, purchasers source specific products that will most effectively satisfy organizational objectives. Kiser suggests that this is done by establishing restrictions and requirements that must be met. Choices are made by first applying the most inflexible requirements so as to confine the search to a limited number of suppliers. Such requirements would normally relate to product and price specifications.

- *Consideration of the 'product package'.* Purchasers are encouraged to envisage the 'product' which they buy as encompassing intangible aspects such as the '... functional utility of the goods, the service that the producer provides, technical assistance that may accompany it, assurance of delivery time, brand and reputation of the supplier, [and] the range of relationships that may develop between people in the buying and selling organizations' (Kiser, 1976: 5). The importance of such issues will be heightened in particular sectors of industry depending on the nature of the product and service that is on offer from the purchaser's organization. Kiser also notes that this area offers opportunities for suppliers to gain competitive advantage. This is increasingly the case as competitive pressures intensify within supplier markets.

- *Consideration of external influences on buyer decisions.* The suggestion here is that purchasers have to take into account the different perspectives of the purchasing function that will be held by others throughout the organization. Each department has a role to play in helping to fulfil organizational objectives, and key players within departments will often perceive purchasers as existing to assist them with that task. Potentially, this can cause difficulties for industrial buyers. It is likely that they will have to justify their decisions in ways that will be acceptable to those who are following different agendas.

Although these 'key concepts' of purchasing strategy may seem relatively comprehensive, they all relate simply to the supplier selection process. As Kiser (1976: 6) writes: 'The concept boils down to one basic question: what products or intangible services will the company buy from what groups of suppliers?'

Jain and Laric (1979: 3) suggest that the implementation of purchasing strategies can be influenced by the relative power of the parties involved. They provide a detailed model of influences on purchasing strategy that centres upon determining the relative strengths and weaknesses of buyers and sellers. Buyers' strengths are viewed as being dependent upon '. . . (a) size of organization (as compared to industry average) (b) purchasing volume in the past (c) size of future, expected orders (d) credit standing and (e) dependence upon seller'. The strength of sellers is determined by the quality of the product and service that they can provide. This model is useful, if only to highlight the extent to which purchasers need to use negotiation skills within markets where there is usually a degree of price flexibility.

Farmer (1978: 11) was one of the first commentators to articulate the importance of the purchasing function to the success of corporate strategy, stating that: 'Clearly, supply strategies do not stand on their own. The purpose of such strategies is to allow the buying firm competitive advantage in its own market. The company which ignores supply strategies of a creative rather than a defensive nature, is foregoing sources of such advantage.' He proposes that purchasers should not be involved solely with issues related to the supply environment, but should develop supplier relationships in ways that support corporate objectives, with similar attention paid to exploiting opportunities presented in the supply market as was tradition-ally paid to the sales market. Farmer presents alternative examples of purchasing strategies designed to secure long-term relationships with suppliers, reduce logistics costs attached to the supply of goods, and develop new sources of supply. Each of these examples is linked to the fulfilment of corporate strategy and in particular the maintenance of competitive advantage.

From purchasing strategy to corporate strategy

In the 1980s, academic literature relating to purchasing strategy began to stress more explicitly the benefits to be gained from closer integration of purchasing into corporate strategy. Spekman (1981) maintained that the purchasing function should be integrated into the strategic planning process. To do this, organizations would have to shed their traditional approach to purchasing, which involved managers becoming '... mired in day-to-day procurement decisions' (1981: 2). Rather, purchasing management should involve long-term planning relating to the supply environment. Interestingly, Spekman attempted to identify how procurement activities can influence organizations' competitive advantage. This is an issue on which there appeared to be growing consensus, but which lacked justification in the academic literature. He suggested that competitiveness in a sales market could be improved by gaining control over suppliers. This would lead to cost containment and the maintenance of high quality supplies. Spekman implied that the integration of the purchasing function into the strategic planning process was likely to be hindered by the lack of strategic orientation amongst existing purchasing managers. Central to his model for integration was environmental analysis by purchasing managers. This would include monitoring of suppliers, identification of likely future changes in the supply environment, analysis of the potential impact of such changes, and the formation of appropriate plans so as to manipulate the impact. The suggestion here was that adherence to this model would enable purchasing departments to influence the nature of corporate strategy, rather than simply reacting to it.

There followed a significant amount of published research debate detailing ways in which the evolution of purchasing can lead to its integration with corporate strategy. For example, Reck and Long (1988) identified a four-stage process (passive, independent, supportive and integrative) for the development of purchasing. In Stage 1, the *passive* purchasing department exists to react to the demands of other departments, uses unsophisticated supplier selection techniques and does not influence the supply environment. In the *independent* stage, the strategies adapted by the purchasing department are distinct from corporate strategy. The *supportive* purchasing department follows business activities that enhance the organization's competitive position. At the final stage, the *integrative* department has equal status with other business functions and contributes to the fulfilment of corporate strategic objectives. This model is based on Reck and Long's observations on a variety of organizations that sought to increase the contribution made by the purchasing function to business success. An important aspect of their study is that the purchasing function's role cannot be changed too rapidly. In order to make a worthwhile contribution to corporate objectives, purchasing staff must be experienced and understand the means by which integration can be achieved as well as the potential benefits of integration.

Pearson and Gritzmacher (1990) suggest that arguments focusing on the integration of purchasing into the strategic planning process actually fail to examine the role that can be played by purchasing in the strategic management decision-making process. However, their rationale for the inclusion of purchasing in strategic decision making is not entirely original. Its usefulness stems from the fact that it draws together a number of strands that previously appeared in literature, but not in a cohesive form. Their rationale is based on the following factors.

- *The supply environment.* Securing appropriate supplies is vital in establishing value added in the end products of organizations. In line with other commentators, Pearson and Gritzmacher establish the need for purchasing personnel to capitalize on opportunities in the supply environment by developing their negotiation skills. In addition, they note that purchasing departments can play a central role in identifying and analysing supply trends, which is crucial information for strategic decision making.

- *Intense competition.* As competition intensifies, often due to globalization, the role of the purchasing function should adapt. To be successful in an increasingly competitive environment firms must continually strive to update their product design and offer greater value for money. Pearson and Gritzmacher note that product design should not be the preserve of one department, but should involve purchasers who are responsible for sourcing the component parts.

- *The changing role of purchasing.* The case here is that the purchasing department should be viewed as a profit generating, rather than a cost cutting function. The authors maintain that this will help to improve the motivation and efficiency of employees engaged in purchasing and in turn lead to a widening of their remit. To be successful this would have to be accompanied by training for purchasing staff and improved communication with those in other departments.

Pearson and Gritzmacher go on to argue that the level of sophistication of the purchasing function determines the extent to which it can be integrated into strategic management decision making. They provide detailed analysis of the ways in which it is possible to identify the level of sophistication of the purchasing function. This claim supports that made by others such as Reck and Long (1988) and Freeman and Cavinato (1990) that the development of the purchasing function is necessary before its role within strategic issues can be established. Contemporary commentaries relating to the relationship between purchasing and strategic management are often more narrowly focused. Authors choose to analyse the contribution that can be made by the purchasing function to specific aspects of the strategic decision-making process (e.g. new product design, impact of supplier/buyer partnerships, the changing influence of purchasing managers, communication with other business functions). This seems like a rational and inevitable progression from debates that promoted the inclusion of purchasing in strategic management.

Having examined key developments in theoretical aspects of purchasing management it is possible to present a model relating to the business activities that would be involved in implementing purchasing strategy. This model (see Figure 5.1) encompasses the two levels of strategy that are identified in literature. Evidence would suggest that the business activities described within the lower-right quadrant of this model would raise the status of the purchasing function and subsequently facilitate its integration with strategic decision making at corporate level.

Strategy level	Business activity
Internal to purchasing department	Identification of supplier market (range of potential suppliers).
	Sourcing products in line with company objectives.
	Evaluation of 'product package'.
In support of corporate strategy	Monitoring of supply environment.
	Long-term planning relating to potential environmental changes.
	Communication with other business functions.
	Development of negotiation skills of purchasing personnel.
	Well-trained, professional purchasing personnel.
	Exploitation of relative power over suppliers.

Figure 5.1 Strategic purchasing business activities

Purchasing in the foodservice sector

It is not the purpose of this section to enter into a detailed discussion about the nature of food purchasing in the catering sector. The broad aim is to analyse the extent to which food purchasing is now integrated into strategic management decision making within foodservice organizations. There are three core observations worth highlighting before attempting to address this question. First, there is the scale and structure of the hospitality industry. This is well documented in various industry reports. For example, *British Hospitality – Trends and Statistics 1998* (British Hospitality Association, 1998) estimates that there were 300,505 catering units in the UK in 1996 (217,165 – 'profit' sector and 83,340 – 'cost' sector). Industry commentators estimate that approximately 70 per cent of units in the profit sector are small and privately owned, although the proportion in this category is declining. In 1996 the sector purchased food supplies to the value of £7676 billion in order to serve 8699 billion meals (British Hospitality Association, 1998). Providing focused commentary on the nature of purchasing in such a vast and heterogeneous industry is no easy task. Moore, Shaw and Sloan (1996) provide detailed analysis of food supply systems in the UK hotel, public house, and fast-food sectors, but little else has been written on these topics.

Second, the vast majority of academic literature on purchasing management draws on evidence from the manufacturing sector: most key purchasing management texts have a strong manufacturing bias (e.g. Baily, Farmer, Jessop and Jones, 1994). Given that the traditional focus of business management literature has been the manufacturing sector this is perhaps not surprising, although it is frustrating. It is also intriguing that this area still receives little attention from hospitality management academics. Given the proportion of total costs generated through food purchases and the changes that have occurred in this area of business activity, it is surprising that the topic does not appear to be of more interest to those specializing in operations management or marketing. As it is, most published sources on food purchasing in the catering sector tend to be found in the trade press and often relate to the experience of specific companies, rarely providing broader insights into the field.

Finally here, it is also still the case that literature relating to strategic management in the hospitality industry rarely makes mention of the role of purchasing management. This is interesting given the changes in industry practice that have been observed by those who have purchasing, rather than strategy, as their primary area of study. The focus of attention lies mainly within the areas of sales generation, product development and financial forecasting.

It is against this background that we examine the nature of purchasing management within the foodservice sector. The summary details relating to purchasing activity are derived primarily from research undertaken by the author and colleagues from the Strathclyde University Food Project, a food industry initiative, which undertook research and otherwise advised the UK food industry.

Food supply in the foodservice industry

It is worth noting the food supply routes that are available to foodservice operators. It is estimated that the sector obtains 79 per cent of its supplies from wholesale operators (Moore, Shaw and Sloan, 1996: 130). This includes national catering supply companies such as Booker Foodservice and Watson and Philip Foodservice for ambient (sometimes known as 'dry') products, and Brake Brothers for frozen products. Catering supply companies buy an extensive range of products before selling them on to caterers. They tend to offer a range of services such as sales and marketing support and menu development advice.

The wholesale market also includes regional specialists used for the supply of fresh fruit and vegetables, meat, poultry, fish and seafood, and bakery products. Specialist wholesalers are usually small companies that deal in single food groups. They often operate out of speciality wholesale markets (e.g. Billingsgate for fish and seafood, New Spitalfields for fruit and vegetables). Grocery wholesalers supply a range of food and household products to both retailers and foodservice companies. This category of wholesaler includes 'delivered trade' operators who charge an additional fee for product deliveries, and 'cash and carry' operators that trade from wholesale depots. In addition to food supply from wholesalers, a relatively small proportion of overall food supply (15 per cent) comes from retailers and direct from manufacturers (Moore, Shaw and Sloan, 1996: 105).

The extent to which foodservice companies implement purchasing strategies can be described employing the headings detailed in Figure 5.1. Available evidence would appear to suggest that the primary focus is still on strategies that are internal to purchasing departments, mainly in relation to product choice. Business activities would not seem to have developed to enable the optimum contribution of the purchasing function as a support to corporate strategy. Each is considered in turn as follows.

Identification of supplier markets

The identification of the range of potential suppliers available to foodservice companies is not an overly complex task. Within the ambient product market the range is normally limited to catering supply companies and grocery wholesalers, and for fresh products to specialist wholesalers. An additional limitation may result from the geographical location of foodservice units. However, in certain circumstances foodservice operators are guilty of failing to identify an appropriate range of potential suppliers. For example, large companies that operate centrally controlled purchasing systems tend to have small purchasing teams that may not have time to devote to this activity. Smaller operators often rely on their personal knowledge of the local supply market, which could result in them missing new supply opportunities.

Large operators often use 'nominated supplier' systems, which include a means of encouraging tenders from potential suppliers. This could be viewed as identification of supplier markets. In order to be categorized as a nominated supplier, and thereby have their products listed in purchasing manuals for all foodservice unit managers, supply companies have to show that they can meet a range of criteria. This is closely related to the product package consideration.

Sourcing products in line with company objectives and evaluation of product packages

There is a trend amongst larger foodservice companies towards greater centralization of the purchasing function and increased rationalization of the supplier base. This is partly so that purchasing activities can be coordinated in line with company objectives and is particularly notable in organizations that offer a standardized menu in their units. Centralized control contrasts with the traditional autonomous approach towards food purchasing which saw all responsibility resting with unit managers and individual head-chefs. Centralized control enables companies to use more sophisticated systems for sourcing products in line with company objectives. This could involve product reviews, menu analysis, requirement analysis, invitations to quote, cost comparisons, sampling, and trial periods (Moore, Shaw and Sloan, 1996: 164).

Clearly, the price of products is still the crucial factor when purchasers are attempting to source products in line with company objectives. Given the competitive environment in which foodservice units operate, the price at which they offer menu items to the public is of considerable importance.

Organizations must ensure that menu prices do not limit their ability to exploit target markets. It is therefore vital that they can source products at acceptable prices.

Monitoring of the supply environment

It appears that the ability of large companies to monitor continually the supply environment is limited by the size of their purchasing departments. It is often the case that the purchasing team consists of relatively few individuals, each of whom has responsibility for a particular product category. Business activities tend to be reactive, or even frantic, which is not conducive to undertaking supply environment monitoring. However, this should be offset against the fact that the supply environment for certain product categories (e.g. ambient products) contains few players. Monitoring the supply environment may not, therefore, be as complex a task as it can be in other industry sectors. In addition, these players tend to be proactive in providing purchasers with information about changes in product range, improvements in service and so on.

For the supply of fresh products, it is often the case that nominated supplier systems operated by foodservice companies actually assist with supply environment monitoring. By passing the onus to suppliers to meet a range of criteria before being granted approval, purchasers can restrict the level of environmental monitoring that they need to undertake. Where no nominated supplier systems are in place, foodservice companies tend to rely on the market knowledge held by unit managers and head chefs for informal monitoring of the supply environment.

Independent foodservice operators can join consortia that aim to provide some of the benefits of membership of larger groups. Most major consortia have purchasing departments, which hoteliers and restaurateurs can join, even if they do not wish to become fully incorporated into a consortium. The primary benefit to independent operators is that consortia can secure discounts from suppliers because of the levels of business that they generate. However, their scale also enables them to become involved in analysis of the entire supply market. It could be argued, therefore, that consortia undertake supply environment monitoring on behalf of independent foodservice operators.

Long-term planning relating to potential environmental changes

Long-term planning, which encompasses environmental analysis, is central to the concept of strategic management. Once again, the reactive nature of purchasing activity in large foodservice companies does not appear to complement long-term planning. In addition, even in those organizations that operate central purchasing systems it is common for day-to-day purchasing activities to be controlled by managers in individual foodservice units. This is not conducive to planning for environmental changes.

This approach is interesting given the broad strategic approach that is being adopted by a number of larger companies in this sector. For example, operators in the continually expanding branded food sector rely upon security and consistency of supply. Such companies change their menus infrequently, but when they do this has considerable implications for suppliers. It is inconceivable that purchasers should not be fully integrated into the long-term menu planning process, but this is often the case.

Communication with other business functions

Communication between purchasing departments and other business functions certainly occurs in foodservice organizations, but it still tends to represent an aspect of purchasing's supportive role, rather than being a sign of its integration. A key example of this comes from identifying typical communication between purchasing and marketing departments. Given that the nature of food on offer from foodservice operators often forms a central part of their marketing campaigns it would be natural to assume that two-way communication between marketers and purchasers would be commonplace. For example, a Scottish country house hotel, in either the chain or independent sector, may attempt to use its use of high quality Scottish products, from particular suppliers, as a marketing tool. In such a circumstance it would seem sensible to communicate with purchasers about their knowledge of the supply market, rather than simply outline the hotel's demands to them. The importance of such communication is heightened by the seasonality of many fresh food supplies.

Unfortunately, lack of two-way communication between purchasers and those in other departments characterizes the situation in many foodservice organizations. This may result from the apparent lack of status that is attached to the purchasing role, viewing it as being purely supportive.

Development of negotiation skills of purchasing personnel

As previously noted, there are relatively few players in the grocery wholesale market yet it is highly competitive. However, available evidence does not suggest that foodservice operators

Hospitality, Leisure & Tourism Series

develop the negotiation skills of purchasers so as to exploit the opportunities presented through buying in a competitive market place.

Well-trained, professional purchasing personnel

Large foodservice organizations usually have small teams of professional purchasing personnel. Individuals in these departments tend to take responsibility for contact with suppliers of particular product categories. They provide a single contact point for potential suppliers. In addition, purchasing departments oversee quality management in relation to food products from suppliers. The scale and complexity of the roles undertaken by those in central purchasing departments would indicate that they posses a high level of skill and professionalism.

However, it is usually the case that those who manage food purchasing on a day-to-day basis do not have purchasing as their primary role. Most large companies grant a high level of autonomy in purchasing matters to individual foodservice units where it is coordinated by head chefs or unit managers. It is worth contrasting this with the management of other business functions such as human resource management, for which individual units often have dedicated specialists.

Exploitation of relative power over suppliers

The mutually dependant relationship that exists between foodservice organizations and food suppliers limits the extent to which either side attempts to exploit their relative power over the other. However, there are examples of business activity that suggest that foodservice operators are making better use of their purchasing power to gain benefits from their supplier relationships. For example, chain hotels are moving away from the use of formal contracts with suppliers. This gives hotel purchasers more flexibility and potentially creates uncertainty in the supplier market, which can in turn shift power in supplier relationships in favour of purchasers. Small, independent foodservice operators can join consortia as a means of gaining benefits usually associated with large organizations. This collectivism is a means of gaining power in supplier relationships.

Conclusions

Do successful foodservice organizations, operating as they do in a competitive environment, therefore give due consideration to the role of the purchasing function? The evidence presented would suggest that the focus of activity within purchasing departments in foodservice organizations remains centred on product choice, rather than on supporting corporate strategy. This is despite the fact that many large organizations operate centrally controlled purchasing systems. Purchasing departments tend to contain relatively few members of staff, which helps to perpetuate the reactive nature of their work and limit their ability to become involved in long-term planning and analysis of the supply environment. This in turn contributes to the low status of careers in food purchasing and inhibits the development of the role. Commentators on purchasing strategy are in agreement that failure to integrate purchasing with other aspects of corporate strategy can seriously affect competitiveness. In the increasingly competitive foodservice sector this issue is therefore set to become of central importance.

References

Ammer, D. (1974) Is your purchasing department a good buy?, *Harvard Business Review*, March–April: 35–42.

Baily, P., Farmer, D., Jessop, D. and Jones, D. (1994) *Purchasing Principles and Management*, London: Pitman Publishing.

British Hospitality Association (BHA) (1998) *British Hospitality – Trade and Statistics 1998*, London: BHA.

Farmer, D. (1978) Developing purchasing strategies, *Journal of Purchasing and Materials Management*, Fall: 6–11.

Freeman, V. T. and Cavinato, J. L. (1990) Fitting purchasing to the strategic firm: frameworks, processes, and values, *Journal of Purchasing and Materials Management*, Winter: 6–10.

Jain, S. C. and Laric, M. V. (1979) A model for purchasing strategy, *Journal of Purchasing and Materials Management*, Fall: 2–7.

Kiser, G. E. (1976) Elements of purchasing strategy, *Journal of Purchasing and Materials Management*, Fall: 3–7.

Kotler, P. and Levy, S. (1973) Buying is marketing too!, *Journal of Marketing*, **37**: 55–56 (January).

Moore, E. J., Shaw, S. A. and Sloan D. (1996) *Supplier Opportunities in the Food Service Sector*, Letchmore Heath: IGD Business Publications.

Pearson, J. N. and Gritzmacher, K. J. (1990) Integrating purchasing into strategic management, *Long Range Planning*, **23**(3): 91–99.

Rajagopal, S. and Bernard, K. N. (1993) Cost containment strategies: challenges for strategic purchasing in the 1990s, *International Journal of Purchasing and Materials Management*, Winter: 17–23.

Reck, R. F. and Long, B. G. (1988) Purchasing: a competitive weapon, *Journal of Purchasing and Materials Management*, Fall: 2–8.

Spekman, R. (1981) A strategic approach to procurement planning, *Journal of Purchasing and Materials Management*, Winter: 2–8.

Watts, C. A., Kim, K. Y. and Hahn, C. K. (1995) Linking purchasing to corporate competitive strategy, *International Journal of Purchasing and Materials Management*, Spring: 3–8.

How does the media influence public taste for food and beverage? The role of the media in forming customer attitudes towards food and beverage provision

Sandie Randall

Introduction

In the United Kingdom today, the mass media is a characteristic feature of modern life. One noteworthy aspect of contemporary media production has been the growing prevalence of messages about food and beverages that testifies to their popularity. Some are news stories about the latest food poisoning scares or issues such as genetically modified foods. However, there is also a large and expanding range of texts that are presented as a media genre in their own right: good food and wine guides; food magazines; restaurant reviews; designated food and drink pages in newspapers and magazines; and television food programmes. In spite of this growth, the role of the food media has received scant attention within food and beverage management debates.

As we live in this mass-mediated world, Tolson (1996: ix) suggests that we should be asking 'what are the consequences of this way of living?' The purpose of this chapter, therefore, is to begin to explore the ways in which the media influences customer attitudes towards food and beverage provision. It begins by examining the historical relationship between the media and the construction of public taste in food and beverage provision and consumption. This is followed by an examination of some of the specific ways in which the media's communicative formats produce discourses about food and beverages that ensure audience consumption. Finally, the discussion seeks to identify the ways in which dominant meanings about food and beverage provision are currently presented within individual food texts. From this debate, insights may be gained about the nature of the media role that will inform food and beverage management strategies as they strive to understand and satisfy public attitudes and tastes.

Situated and mediated cultures

An important starting point for this discussion about the media's role is an examination of the ways by which societies construct sets of cultural values. In traditional societies, these cultural values and shared public tastes are situated in the interpersonal relations of the group in a specific place and time, to meet the conditions of their shared needs and experience (O'Sullivan, Dutton and Rayner, 1994). In contrast, modern societies, with access to technologies of media production, can communicate across the temporal and spatial boundaries of situated cultures. In this way, mediated messages have the potential to transform the values of other cultural groups.

In Europe, since the sixteenth century, new technology and increasing levels of literacy have led to a steady expansion of printed texts concerning food and beverages (Castiglione, 1528/1967; Erasmus, 1530; Della Casa, 1558/1958). Examples of the mid-twentieth century indicate that they echo the social role of their sixteenth century precursors: the role of food production and consumption is a source of elegance and gentility that offers 'the very dream of smartness' (Barthes: 1957/1993: 78) and allows the host to 'show off: impress your guests with your superior expertise; make them feel mildly inferior' (Mennell, 1996: 257).

However, in the late twentieth century, the pervasive influence of the mass media in modern societies creates important new implications. As a result of the expansion of global communications and the media industry during the last fifty years, the influence of the media has changed in terms of size, quality and scope. Today, with the ubiquitous influence of terrestrial broadcast television especially, all consumers, irrespective of literacy and economic status, have increasing access to a large volume of different mass mediated global cultures that offer potential experiences. As a result, Tolson (1996: x) suggests, the ways by which cultural values and practices are constructed has been profoundly changed. Today, 'we have increasingly learned to live not only in our situated culture but also in a culture of mediation' (O'Sullivan, Dutton and Rayner, 1994: 13). Moreover, and importantly, Tolson (1996: x) argues that 'the situated and mediated worlds gradually but inexorably, interpenetrate' to introduce a new dynamic quality to the construction of stable meanings. Thus, at a time when consumer tastes and behaviours are increasingly mediated and volatile, it is appropriate that food and beverage management should take a greater interest in the role of the media.

The production/consumption context

The implications of these developments in mass communications can be better understood by an examination of the changes in the nature of production that occurred during the same period. In the United Kingdom, the momentum of capitalist expansion has led to the construction of new types of products and markets: those for cultural consumption (Bourdieu, 1984; Featherstone, 1991; Freeman, 1989: 179; Finkelstein, 1989). As Featherstone (1991: 19) suggests: 'in this context, knowledge becomes important: knowledge of new goods, their social and cultural value, and how to use them appropriately. This is particularly the case with the aspiring group who adopt a learning mode towards consumption and the cultivation of a lifestyle.'

Dissemination of this type of information has been assumed by the media, who in addition, sought to increase the currency of those cultural goods such as foods and beverages, with additional values concerned with social status (Bourdieu, 1984: 359; Featherstone, 1991: 19). It is these secondary meanings that now control their market value (Farb and Armelagos, 1980: 266). In an era of mass production, as Fischler (1993: 390) suggests, consumers turn increasingly to the media for guidance, to allay their anxieties about contemporary cultural life when faced with so much choice.

Significantly, the media role has extended beyond solely that of the promotion of goods. The media industry now produces cultural products and services in its own right: newspapers; books; journals; films; videos; websites; and television programmes. In so doing, it has produced a new social class, the cultural intermediaries, who associate with the experts, but subvert the experts' class interests by disseminating their esoteric expertise to the lower classes. In this way, the media contribute further competitiveness to the class positioning system, as the higher classes look for new ways to distinguish themselves (Bourdieu, 1984; Featherstone, 1991: 18). In addition, the media industry is now obliged to innovate and promote its own products in order to perpetuate its own interests. However, the rhetorics adopted may not necessarily be directly allied to the entrepreneurs' or the consumers' perceived traditional values and interests (Bourdieu, 1984: 359; Finkelstein, 1989; Featherstone, 1991: 19).

In modern post-industrial societies such as the United Kingdom, therefore, dominant contemporary cultural meanings about food, drink and dining out will be produced and circulated within this mediated cultural experience. If the hospitality industry is to proactively manage the provision of food and beverage services to meet consumer needs, it seems clear that the ways in which the media constructs messages about hospitality and its constituent parts must be better accessed, identified and understood.

Interpreting media texts – semiotic theory

The ways in which cultural messages are produced and circulated via the media are complex and subtle. Today, media messages must be designed to appeal to a mass audience, sharing a range of mediated as well as situated values and experiences. The lack of previous concern with the media influence in food and beverage management can be partially explained by the problem of finding a methodology that will allow the systematic interrogation of texts for meaning (Tolson, 1996: 4; Randall, 1999: 42). Such an investigation must identify a number of different issues: the role of media technology and the character of the consumption experience; the way that the text speaks to the reader; the self-referential nature of mass mediated texts; the ways by which dominant or preferred meanings are constructed; and their openness to reader interpretation.

Although there is no such research tradition within the field of food and beverage management, the theory of semiotics is a well-established approach within cultural and media studies (Barthes, 1957/1993; 1977; Coward, 1984: 110; Randall, 1999). Semiotic theory is the science of signs. It not only allows access to meanings presented in media texts, but also allows us to identify the specific ways in which the media presents its messages to foster mass audience consumption and adoption (Barthes, 1957/1993; 1977). As Tolson (1996: xv) confirms, it is through an examination of these methods of production, or discourses, of the message that it is possible to identify how the text invites 'participation in organised (and institutionalised) cultural practices'. Semiotic analysis, therefore, offers a tool by which one can interrogate the seeming transparency of media food texts, to identify how they invite participation in contemporary cultural practices associated with the provision of food and drink (Barthes, 1977: 89–91; Strange, 1998: 301).

Television food programmes

Undoubtedly, one of the most important and far reaching developments in mass media has been that of television. In the United Kingdom, not only does broadcast terrestrial television reach a potential audience of 99 per cent of British homes (O'Sullivan, Dutton and Rayner, 1994), but significantly, it requires no level of literacy for satisfactory consumption. An increasingly noticeable element in broadcast television output is the 'food' programme. From the occasional half hour series of the 1950s, an average week of television programmes offers the viewer up to twelve hours of designated food programmes, as well as a range of shorter programmes and food slots (Randall, 1999: 42). It is therefore surprising that the effects of the proliferation of the most significant example of mass mediated food texts, television food programmes, have largely been ignored (Strange, 1998; Randall, 1996; 1999). As Strange (1998: 301) argues: 'this neglect suggests the assumption that cookery programmes . . . are transparent: that they are merely about food and the instruction of cookery methods and as such, do not merit closer examination'.

In this chapter, television food programmes provide a conceptual focal lens to identify and illuminate the issues relevant to the examination of the media role. Broadcast television food programmes offer the discussion an example of contemporary mass mediated food texts par excellence. Food programmes regularly attract audiences of several millions, and achieve high ratings within the top ten BBC 2 programmes (BARB/RSMB,

1998). For this reason, a good deal of the discussion will be centred in this area. However, in sorting out the complexities and subtleties of television for meanings about food and drink, it is noteworthy that we will, in any case, be obliged to take into account the role of other types of food media (see also Chapter 10, where some of those themes are developed in the more specific context of 'television' cooks and chefs).

Media formats and discourses

As Barthes (1957/1993: 109) has indicated, one of the important features of the relationship between the media and cultural meanings is the centrality of the role of the discourse. Thus, it is with an examination of this aspect of the media role that the discussion begins. At first sight, as with so many aspects of the media, the role of technology and communicative formats is unobtrusive and largely taken for granted. However, the ways in which messages are presented are very specific and selective (Tolson, 1996; Randall, 1999: 43).

Media food genres

One established and taken for granted way by which the media organizes the presentation of its meanings to influence the consumer is through the creation of different genres. The increasingly large and heterogeneous range of television food programmes have been organized in specific ways to be recognized as distinctive programme types, with some clear subgroups (Randall, 1996: 5). These food programmes are more readily understood by the viewers as they share many characteristics with established television genres: the competition/game food show (*Ready Steady Cook*); the documentary/magazine show (*Food and Drink*); the travel show (*Rick Stein's Seafood Odyssey*); and the personality programme (*The Naked Chef*).

We should consider the motivations of the media industry when it chooses to differentiate food texts into distinctive genres. One result is that the distinction can be used to market its own products more effectively (Bennett and Woollacott, 1987). The *Radio Times*, for example, lists all the food items/programmes on television and radio for the week, together with copy on food topics, within its designated 'Food' pages (Randall, 1996; 1999). Through these genre relationships, 'readers' views and expectations feed back into the production process which ... will serve to reinforce a "game" which is well understood by all concerned' (Tolson, 1996: 86).

Secondary texts and inter-textuality

These genres do not exist in isolation from each other. The food media operate in relationships that are deliberately incestuously inter-textual, so that the influence of any individual food text is amplified and legitimized through the production of complementary and supplementary texts in other media formats: Ainsley Harriott in *The Times* feature on barbecues (Heiney, 1999: 1); the guest appearance of Jamie Oliver, the 'Naked Chef', in *Veg Talk* on Radio 4 (BBC, 1999a).

In addition, producers of food media texts deliberately and systematically seek to generate additional complementary material in the 'official' secondary texts that spin off from television food programmes: television scheduling journals such as the *Radio Times*; specialist food journals such as *BBC Good Food*; and most importantly, the recipe books to accompany the series (Stein, 1995; Oliver, 1999a). In particular, the recipe books achieve enormous sales (Randall, 1996: 115): for example, the recipe book accompanying the *Naked Chef* television series sold 5357 copies in the week ending Saturday 26 June 1999, and was the second highest selling hardback book that week (Waterstones, 1999).

In these ways, secondary media texts construct the viewers'/readers' reading formation. It is inevitable that both producers and consumers of new food and beverage texts will adopt a position that has been predetermined, to some extent, by familiarity with the discourse and meanings circulating in other media products (Bennet and Woollacott, 1987). These secondary texts reproduce and potentially extend the messages about food and beverage found in the programmes. For example, the text anchoring the recipe page in the men's *GQ* magazine confirms the discourse of increasing cultural diversity found in the recent *Naked Chef* programme: 'Resident chef Jamie Oliver delivers a dish even his dumbest mates have mastered' (Oliver, 1999b: 75). Furthermore, it is of interest to note that the recipe book accompanying Martha Stewart's television food programme in the USA echoes the reading formation of those found in the United Kingdom (Stewart, 1994; Stein, 1995). These examples highlight the global currency of mediated food meanings.

Moreover, the role of the recipe book also alerts us to potential new purposes of the television food programmes. These programmes do not seek to show the viewer exactly how to create the dishes at home as their chief purpose, as they once did historically (Randall, 1996, 1999; Strange, 1998). They now offer scope for additional projects which may be of direct concern to the food and beverage industry. This self-referential inter-textuality of media products benefits all the media interests involved, as well as that of the food and beverage industries in general. Even though these products may occasionally be bad publicity, the media interest still further promotes and legitimizes the consumption of food and drink, and its media discourses, as an important and desirable cultural activity, to stimulate demand (Atkinson, 1999: 24; Ferguson, 1999: 18, Fletcher, 1999: 24; Marshall, 1999: 24; Winner, 1999: 24).

Personality, intimacy and trust

Another important function of secondary texts is found in the contribution they make to the construction of the food presenter/ writer as celebrity personality. The discourse of the food personality is not solely the product of media vanity, it has an important role in producing convincing and authoritative messages for the audience.

One way by which this is achieved is through the simulation of a para-social interaction between the presenter/writer and individual members of the audience (Horton and Wohl, 1956: 215). Strategies are adopted to develop a 'communicative ethos' of intimacy, immediacy and co-presence with the presenter (Scannell, 1989: 152). In television food programmes, for example, the life-size close-up face work of the camera, the simulated eye contact of everyday conversation, the everyday locations of work and leisure, the adoption of informal styles of address and language, the inclusion of local accents and slang, and the elision of time, create what Langer (1981: 362) calls a 'sustained impression of intimacy', to change the viewer from detached onlooker to engaged collaborator. Within this context, the constant alignment of 'you' the viewer, with 'I' the presenter, reinforces this relationship between insiders, 'we', against outsiders, 'them' (Moores, 1995; Randall, 1999: 45). As Moores argues, these modes of address foster trust and reduce risk, to invite the audience into a complicity with the presenter that acknowledges and accepts unspecified shared values and norms (Langer, 1981: 361; Giddens, 1990; Moores, 1995). In these ways, audiences are seduced into consuming the shared rhetoric of the programme, even though it may be directly criticizing a lifestyle or taste that is in reality the viewers' own (Randall, 1999: 45).

This intimacy and trust also derives from the construction of the presenters of food media texts as authentic and authoritative personalities. During the television programmes, the audience is invited to enter the personal lives of these presenters: for example, to get to know their staff, family, home, friends and even pets. This personality status is developed further via other media sources as the food presenters/writers become newsworthy: for example, a feature article on the food critic, A. A. Gill (Smith, 1999: 10). The nation is regularly made aware of the daily lives and personal problems of food media personalities, through articles in newspapers and magazines (Fracassini, 1998a: 5; 1998b: 5; Gibson, 1998: 13; Urquhart, 1998: 20). Moreover, the concept of food 'personality' is circulated to a widening non-food media audience through references in other top rated television shows of other genres: a situation comedy about a personality chef; satirical entertainment with impressions of food personalities; guest personality appearances in game shows and chat shows; choices of music for Radio Three programmes and the 'BBC Proms' promotional material; articles about holidays for travel sections of newspapers; subjects for University Challenge questions (Randall, 1996: 110; Randall, forthcoming). These personal details fuel the spiral of demand for knowledge about the presenters' qualities and shortcomings that Langer claims is the hallmark of the personality (Langer, 1981; Randall, 1996: 114).

Polysemy and dominant meanings

Even with these communicative discourses, every media text has the potential to present multiple meanings. As Barthes (1957/1993) suggests, the polysemy of these food texts is reduced through the particular depictions of the individual signs and their association together, to produce preferred, dominant chains of meanings. In addition, the potential range of meanings is made more specific by the anchorage of the verbal text. In these contemporary texts, preferred meanings for mass audiences are also produced through the use of references to conventional cultural meanings and values derived from other mass mediated genres. In television food programmes, inter-textual references such as the BBC shipping forecast, well-known novels, TV serials, popular films, music or widely recognized iconic images are all incorporated, to connote meanings that have common currency with contemporary society (Randall, 1996; 1999). In this way the situated and mediated can be satisfactorily integrated to overcome the potential breakdown of communication to a mass audience with different experiences (Barthes, 1977: 89–91; Tolson, 1996: 7).

Once common and significant feature of food texts is the limited amount of time actually devoted to the cookery/food elements. We should question the purpose of these non-food segments to the overall project of the text. It is noteworthy that it is with these segments that the texts produce chains of meaning that are designed to reduce the diversity of reality into a number of taken for granted, cultural norms, as Barthes predicted. Food texts, such as television food programmes, produce a limited number of overarching cultural myths about traditional communities; nature; traditional forms of work; communities and belonging; traditional celebrations and feasts; and distinctive local produce (Randall, 1996: 18; 1999: 45; Strange, 1998). These cultural norms resonate powerfully with audiences who 'understand' these idealized conventional values, even though they do not represent the lived realities of their own lives or are necessarily in their best interests. These myths appear to be naturalized and common sense views, but as Barthes (1957/1993: 129) argues, in fact they seek to 'transform(s) history into nature' and disguise their origins as products of the powerful classes in history to become ideologies.

In reproducing these myths, meanings about food and beverages are produced within nostalgic symbolic fictions of imagined communities (Anderson, 1983; Hobsbawm and Ranger, 1983): the hen night; Mayday celebrations; the cricket club; the island community; the lifeboat men. Moores (1995) argues that these strategies are additionally successful because they re-embed the fragmented social relations of the modern, mass mediated world (cf. Giddens, 1990). In addition, they recirculate meanings about food and beverages that are regularly found in the fictional constructions of community of the soap opera, that are regularly defined by sites for the consumption of food (Bell and Valentine, 1997).

Simultaneously, these food texts produce other sets of meanings, that are often seemingly contradictory, within these chains of conventional values. The function of the overarching myths provides the reassuring and legitimizing context for the juxtaposition of this second set of dominant meanings. Combined with the overarching discourses of the programme format, the viewers/readers are seduced into a voluntary and unwitting adoption of the new and potentially contentious meanings that are not necessarily in their best interests. These new and contradictory meanings are added to the established norms in an evolutionary process, so that the media produces dominant meanings that can transform the audience's cultural values (Fiske, 1990: 90).

Innovation and sophistication

An analysis of these other sets of meanings highlights the additional ways in which the food media seek to influence consumer values about food and beverages. The promotion of innovation and change in food and beverage practices is constructed, paradoxically, contrary to the overarching context of tradition, with a palpable sense of excitement that uses discovery and adventure, and the sense of the idealized exotic that is derived from the 'foreign' (Said, 1985; Kabbani, 1986; Randall, 1999). For example, on the one hand 'you can't beat old fashioned simplicity', on the other 'this guy's [the chef] got a spirit of adventure' (BBC, 1999d).

An additional and significant way in which innovation is promoted is by the sophistication and artistic talent of the food presenter. Food texts seek to promote the quality of raw ingredients in terms of their naturalness and simplicity. This strategy embeds food and beverage products 'within a contemporary discourse of ecological correctness at a time when fear and anxiety about the purity of food and trustworthiness of production practices is high' (Randall, forthcoming). However, the main project of these texts is to use this naturalness to point up the sophistication of the transformatory artistic role of the presenter, to link the gastronomic and artistic concepts of taste (Gronow, 1997; Randall, 1999).

Food and class

The sophisticated taste of the presenter/writer is reinforced in other significant class constructed ways. Although this takes different forms, concepts of food quality articulate with expense and luxury to demonstrate the social prestige of economic capital. At the same time, class positioning is displayed through the cultural capital associated with the acquisition of esoteric knowledge, cultured disposition and the transformatory practices of the art of cooking (Randall 1996, 1999).

In the printed media, different types of product target different market segments: for example, the food pages of *Vogue* are different in format and tone to those of *Woman's Own*. In the mass mediation of television, these sub-cultural differences are accounted for, to some extent, by the nature of the sub-genre of food programme, and their time scheduling: for example, competition game shows are shown to daytime audiences (retired, unemployed, housewives, mothers, children), whilst the personality programmes are shown at peak night-time viewing (working adults with higher disposable incomes). However, the promotional objectives of the discourse of class are highlighted by recent developments in television personality and travel food programmes, which seek to increase the cultural diversity of the discourse, to widen the potential audience range by, for example, the introduction of non-white presenters in programmes that are not exotically foreign, as with *Ainsley's Big Cook Out* (BBC, 1999b);

the introduction of young, male and seemingly working-class personalities, speaking in estuary English such as *The Naked Chef* (BBC, 1999c); or the introduction of a hip young male chef who is a reformed drug addict, and a young, black Caribbean male designer, in Stein's *Fresh Food* (BBC, 1999d). Other media examples support this move to access new non-standard audiences: for example, separate children's newspaper cookery columns (Preston, 1999). For a genre whose audience has been essentially female, middle aged and middle class, these developments open up the mediated food and beverage discourses to include much wider sociocultural groups in terms of ethnicity, age, gender and class.

Self indulgence and pleasure

Another way in which the media influences consumer tastes is by creating tantalizing fictions of self-indulgence and pleasure derived from the Epicurean. This occurs in many different ways. One way is through the production of excitement. This excitement is constructed with iconic concepts and is anchored by the verbal text. A sense of romance and magic are similarly reproduced with dramatic sunsets, seascapes, moonlit scenes, fun parties and sophisticated dinners (Randall, 1996, 1999).

Excitement, entertainment and theatrical performance have been significant aspects of television food programmes from the early days of Fanny Cradock. One development has been the fusion of cookery elements with comedy, entertainment and competition as with, for example, *Ready Steady Cook*. Another has been the increasingly exciting cooking locations and challenges for the presenters (Randall, 1999: 49). This sense of Epicurean pleasure has been expanded by the media through the aestheticization of food and beverage provision that presents them as cultural artefacts to be consumed as works of art (Randall, 1999: 47; Randall, forthcoming). This media emphasis upon the artistic role of the chef promotes the *embourgeoisement* of the traditional working-class chef *métier* (Chivers, 1973) which may lead to the improved social status of the food and beverage industry as a whole (Randall, 1999).

Another crucial component of this sense of pleasure is the sensuality and self-indulgence derived from food and beverage consumption. The viewer is offered palpable sensations of touch, smell, sight, sound and taste (Randall, 1996, 1999). Presenters handle food in very tactile ways, almost caressing the raw materials, or eat with their hands, or use a range of language and gestures that transforms the most ordinary food and beverages into a sensuous exotic pleasure: for example, Ainsley Harriott

(BBC, 1999b); Rick Stein (1995; BBC, 1999d); and Jennifer Paterson (BBC, 1999e). The accompanying verbal text anchors these meanings more precisely, whether in the modern vernacular of *The Naked Chef*, 'wicked' (BBC, 1999c), or with the more sophisticated language of Stein 'It's so rich and warm. . . . It's so inviting' (BBC, 1995), or unambiguously anchoring an image of a Pavlova on a Sunday supplement's front page, 'Pure indulgence!' (Lawson, 1999: 1). Strange confirms Coward's view that in these ways the media has eroticized the provision of food and beverages (Coward, 1984; Strange, 1998).

Conclusions

This chapter has sought to explore the ways in which the media influence the formation of customer attitudes to food and beverage provision. Although the strategies adopted by the food media have not been left to chance, they can be seen to be varied and subtle. The discourses adopted are designed to make food texts as attractive as possible to a wide and diversified mass audience. These derive in part from the communicative formats and techniques of the media genre itself; the organization of genres; the use of inter-textuality and secondary texts; and the manipulation of the communicative format to produce an ethos of intimacy, trust and celebrity personality. Other powerful influences derive from the way that the texts themselves seek to close down alternative interpretations, to produce a dominant meaning. This is achieved through the connotations evoked by the choice and depiction of signs, and their association together, to form particular chains of meaning; and the reliance upon the reproduction of a limited number of conventional ideologies.

Thus, the media construct convincing meanings about food and beverages that resonate with audiences' existing cultural values. Food and beverages are articulated by the media with universal concepts of tradition, community, and belonging. However, subsumed within these conventional norms are other sets of values which promote more precise meanings about food and beverages. Food and beverages are promoted as exotic and exciting commodities that are a source of fascination, narcissistic desire and hedonic satisfaction (Featherstone, 1991: 22–23; Randall, forthcoming). In addition, and importantly, consumption of these commodities is perceived to bring social and emotional benefits that are associated with the display of taste, class status, self-esteem and self-aggrandizement. Acceptance of this role for food and beverages invites media audiences to become willing consumers in an inflationary and diversifying consumption process that benefits the media itself, as well as the food and beverage industry. Potential customers are introduced to new concepts and values that allow them to widen their culinary experiences, both in the home, and more importantly, in commercial hospitality establishments.

In an increasingly competitive and mass mediated world, knowledge of these contemporary tastes, as well as the ways in which the media communicates to the consumer, can assist the design and management of food and beverage establishments and their products.

References

Anderson, B. (1983) *Imagined Communities: Reflections on the Origins and Spread of Nationalism*, London: Verso.

Atkinson, D. (1999) Letters, *The Sunday Times (Style)*, 27 June: 24.

BARB/RSMB (1998) What the Nation Watched, *Radio Times*, 21–27 November: 160.

Barthes, R. (1957/1993) *Mythologies*, London: Vintage.

Barthes, R. (1977) *Image – Music – Text*, London: Fontana.

BBC (1995) *Rick Stein's Taste of the Sea*, BBC 2, 26 September, 8.30pm.

BBC (1999a) *Veg Talk*, Radio 4, 2 July, 3.00pm.

BBC (1999b) *Ainsley's Big Cook Out*, BBC 2, 6 July, 8.30pm.

BBC (1999c) *The Naked Chef*, BBC 2, 16 June, 8.00pm.

BBC (1999d) *Fresh Food*, BBC 2, 1 July, 8.30pm.

BBC (1999e) *Two Fat Ladies*, BBC2, 28 September, 8.30pm.

Bell, D. and Valentine, G. (1997) *Consuming Geographies*, London: Routledge.

Bennett, T. and Woollacott, J. (1987) *Bond and Beyond: The Political Career of a Popular Hero*, London: Macmillan.

Bourdieu, P. (1984) *Distinction: A Social Critique of the Judgement of Taste*, London: Routledge and Kegan Paul.

Castiglione, B. (1528/1967) *The Courtier*, Harmondsworth: Penguin Books.

Chivers, T. (1973) The proletarianisation of a service worker, *Sociological Review*, **21**: 633–56.

Coward, R. (1984), *Female Desire*, London: Paladin.

Della Casa, G. (1558/1958) *Galateo*, Harmondsworth: Penguin Books Ltd.

Erasmus, D. (1530) De civilitate morum puerilum (Cologne edn), cited in N. Elias (1994) *The Civilising Process: The History of Manners and State Formation and Civilisation*, Oxford: Basil Blackwell.

Farb, P. and Armelagos, G. (1980) *Consuming Passions: The Anthropology of Eating*, Boston, Mass: Houghton Mifflin.

Featherstone, M. (1991) *Consumer Culture and Postmodernism*, London: Sage.

Ferguson, G. (1999) Laying off the barbecue sauce, *The Scotsman*, 7 July: 18.

Finkelstein, J. (1989) *Dining Out: A Sociology of Modern Manners*, Cambridge: Polity Press.

Fischler, C. (1993) 'L'(h)omnivore: le gout, la cuisine et la corps', n.p.: Editions Odile Jabob, cited in A Warde (1997) *Consumption Food and Taste*, London: Sage.

Fiske, J. (1990) (2nd edition), *Introduction to Communication Studies*, London: Routledge.

Fletcher, M. (1999) Letters, *The Sunday Times (Style)*, 27 June: 24.

Fracassini, C. (1998a) Delia cracks the secret of success in shops' sales, *The Scotsman*, 19 November: 5.

Fracassini, C. (1998b) Fat lady turns up heat on rector bid, *The Scotsman*, 19 November: 5.

Freeman, S. (1989) Mutton and Oysters: The Victorians and Their Food, London: Victor Gollancz cited in A. Beardsworth and T. Keil (1997) *Sociology on the Menu*, London: Routledge.

Gibson, J. (1998) Delia's basic recipe for book success, *The Guardian*, 17 October: 13.

Giddens, A. (1990) *The Consequences of Modernity*, Cambridge: Polity Press.

Gronow, J. (1997) *The Sociology of Taste*, London: Routledge.

Heiney, P. (1999) Burning question: why do men BBQ? *The Times (Weekend)*, 3 July: 1.

Hobsbawn, E. and Ranger, T. (1983) *The Invention of Tradition*, Cambridge: Cambridge University Press.

Horton, D. and Wohl, R. (1956) Mass communication and para-social interaction: observations on intimacy at a distance, *Psychiatry*, **19**(3): 215–219.

Kabbani, R. (1986) *Europe's Myths of the Orient*, Basingstoke: Macmillan.

Langer, J. (1981) Television's 'personality system', *Media, Culture and Society*, **3**(4): 351–365.

Lawson, N. (1999) Pure Indulgence! *The Observer (Life)*, 27 June: 1.

Marshall, M. (1999) Letters, *The Sunday Times (Style)*, 27 June: 24.

Mennell, S. (1996) *All Manners of Food: Eating and Taste in England and France from the Middle Ages to the Present*, Urbana, USA: University of Illinois Press, 2nd edition.

Moores, S. (1995) TV discourse and 'time space distanciation': on mediated interaction in modern society, *Time and Society*, **4**(3): 329–344.

Oliver, J. (1999a) *Jamie Oliver: The Naked Chef*, London: Michael Joseph.

Oliver, J. (1999b) Seared Salmon steak, *GQ*, July: 75.

O'Sullivan, T., Dutton, B. and Rayner, P. (1994) *Studying the Media: An Introduction*, London: Edward Arnold.

Preston, J. (1999) Juliet Preston's Shortbread, *The Guardian (Weekend)*, 10 July: 53.

Randall, S. (1996) *Television Representations of Food: a Case Study of Rick Stein's Taste of the Sea*, unpublished MSc dissertation, Edinburgh Queen Margaret University College.

Randall, S. (1999) Television representations of food: a case study of 'Rick Stein's Taste of the Sea', *International Tourism and Hospitality Research Journal: The Surrey Quarterly Review*, **1**(1): 41–54.

Randall, S. (forthcoming) 'Mediated meanings of hospitality: television personality food programmes', in C. Lashley and A. Morrison (Eds) *In Search of Hospitality: Theoretical Perspectives and Debates*, Oxford: Butterworth-Heinemann.

Said, E. (1985) *Orientalism*, London: Penguin.

Scannell, P. (1989) Public Service Broadcasting and Modern Public Life, *Media Culture and Society*, **11**(2): 135–166.

Smith, A. (1999) A perfect swine of a critic, *The Scotsman*, 7 July: 10.

Stein, R. (1995) *Rick Stein's Taste of the Sea*, London: BBC Books.

Stewart, M. (1994) *Martha Stewart's Menus for Entertaining*, New York: Clarkson Potter Inc.

Strange, N. (1998) Perform, Educate, Entertain: Ingredients of the Cookery Programme Genre in C. Geraghty and D. Lusted *The Television Studies Book*, London: Edward Arnold, 301–312.

Tolson, A. (1996) *Mediations*, London: Edward Arnold.

Urquhart, C. (1998), Knives are always out among TV chefs, *The Scotsman*, 27 October: 20.

Waterstones (1999) Best sellers, *The Independent on Sunday (Culture)*, 27 June: 13.

Winner, M. (1999) Winner's Dinners: Frederick the Great, *The Sunday Times (Style)*, 27 June: 24.

CHAPTER 7

Do restaurant reviews really affect an establishment's reputation and performance? The role of food journalism in restaurant success and failure

Joseph E. Fattorini

Introduction

Loved and loathed, usually at the same time, restaurant critics have become an indispensable part of newspaper feature pages and style magazines. This chapter examines the forms restaurant criticism takes, considers what purpose it serves and how influential it is in the success and failure of restaurants.

Without delving into the history of restaurant reviews, it is clear why they emerged and what purpose ostensibly they serve. Outside the realm of theme restaurants and chains, lunch and evening dining is an extremely diverse product. This diversity comes on many different levels too. There is diversity of price, market, style, size, ambience, service level and quality, location and consistency. Yet meals out are not trivial purchases. Consumers are wary of spending between £30.00 and £100.00 plus on a product about which they know little or nothing and without taking some reasonably objective advice. Furthermore, unlike clothing or many other products that cost about the same amount of money, they cannot test the meal beforehand or take it back later if they are dissatisfied. It is not only money that is at stake when dining out either. Restaurant dining is a matter of fashion, style and taste in the more general sense of these terms, as well as taste in the gustatory sense. Research highlighted later in this chapter indicates that those who are most likely to read reviews are also most likely to eat out and have a more general interest in food. In the parlance of informal social groups in the UK, they are what might be termed 'Foodies'. MacClancy (1992: 210) disparagingly notes of foodies:

> Foodies see themselves as individualists though they are, of course, members of a collective social movement, one of their own making . . . [.] They do not go to an expensive foodie restaurant because of the chef, but because the place is in vogue. They go to see and be seen, and to be able to boast about the experience later. They are sheep, led by the nose, and often paying through it as well.

Or as Warde (1997, 185–186) suggests rather more coolly, 'exposure given to different styles of restaurants rises and falls, as if in a fashion cycle'. In other words, consumers need to feel reasonably convinced that a meal will be good (both for their palate and their social standing) before they go. For that they turn to several sources of advice, including restaurant critics.

Restaurant critics also serve another purpose explored in this chapter, one associated with the sentiments expressed by MacClancy. Food and restaurants capture the public imagination. Dining out is glamorous and desirable. As Bell and Valentine (1997: 5–6) suggest: 'Professional and amateur chefs are household names . . . their restaurants given the status of temples of consumption in countless guides and features; food writers . . . show us not only how to cook, but tell us what, when, where, how – and even why – to eat and drink.' But it is also reasonably costly, with limited opportunities (only a maximum of seven, evening, meals a week) and in many cases needs prior planning in the forms of booking, babysitters and in economic terms, the opportunity cost of not slouching in front of the television. Restaurant critics allow their readers to dine out by proxy. It is possible to be reasonably well informed about a city's restaurant scene without ever ordering a martini. Some restaurant critics see their main purpose as entertainers, not assessors, and it is the dual nature of restaurant critics that often makes them such controversial figures. This chapter considers how the sometimes explosive relationship between critic and restaurant can be managed or indeed whether changing it would be desirable.

Why are restaurant reviews taken so seriously?

Some may approach the question above by replying 'are restaurant reviews taken seriously?' The answer seems to be an emphatic 'yes'. During the writing of this chapter the restaurant manager of a newly opened restaurant in Glasgow contacted one of the city's newspapers to demand why the restaurant had been given such a poor review over the weekend. The manager pointed out that the restaurant had been reviewed favourably by most major national and regional papers, and had in fact received a favourable review from the paper in question only a few weeks earlier. The Features Editor replied that she was confused. Yes, she remembered the earlier, favourable review, but was not aware of any further coverage. It then transpired that the irate manager had not actually seen this supposed poor review, she thought she had heard someone discussing it in the restaurant. Rather shame-faced, the manager apologized and put down the phone. Yet this is only the mildest form of rebuke newspaper editors and their restaurant reviewers receive for their work. Dornenburg and Page (1998) in their excellent book on US restaurant criticism, describe how critics have received veiled threats from mobsters and even explicit death threats from irate chefs after poor reviews.

So why do restaurant reviews, whether real or imagined, generate such passions? The answer would appear to be threefold. First, the restaurant is someone's livelihood. All the more so in the case of the chef-proprietor who may well have invested everything and taken out a very substantial loan in order to set the restaurant up. Even employees though are aware that if a restaurant fails to work, they will be out of a job. And so clearly, if owners and staff feel that reviews have the potential to ruin their livelihoods they will be passionate about them.

A second reason that perhaps explains why restaurant reviews in particular are capable of arousing fiery moods and passions concerns the fact that the hospitality industry is a service industry and good service is personalized. In good restaurants, the chef is, in his or her own mind, and sometimes that of their customers, an artist, putting their own personality on the plate. The ambience of the restaurant too, its fixtures and fittings and overall style of service, is a reflection of the personality of the owner and designer. As Marco-Pierre White (1990: 28), a chef renowned for his fiery temper points out, 'If I came to your house for dinner an hour late, then criticized all your furniture and your wife's haircut and said all your opinions were stupid, how would you feel?'.

The third reason is one often associated with feelings of anger and rage, that of helplessness. The classic model of ownership in many restaurants is that of the chef-proprietor. For this owner the food is all-important and quite rightly they concentrate their efforts behind the stove. Yet this means that the people who have contact with customers, including restaurant critics, are waiting staff, who may well be poorly paid, poorly motivated and more likely to give a poor impression of the restaurant. Thus the person with the most to lose from a poor review is the one least likely to interact with the customer. One further issue may exacerbate this. As noted elsewhere (Fattorini, 1994: 26) 'front-line' workers in hospitality are among the least likely to be targeted by the style magazines and broadsheet newspapers that carry restaurant reviews. They are 'those on the very lowest pay levels within the industry who thus also usually have a minimal level of disposable income and therefore fall well outside the target market of consumer based magazines'. As a consequence, it may be the case that they are the least likely to appreciate the importance of reviews or the qualities in staff that make for good reviews. However this is supposition, and further research on this topic is needed to develop the issue.

Forms of restaurant criticism

Up to now this chapter has used the terms 'restaurant review' and 'restaurant criticism' without considering what these terms encompass. Not all restaurant reviews are the same and restaurant critics themselves come in a number of different forms. Yet research on the topic has often done little to distinguish between the various types.

The first distinction to make is between what we will term 'graders' and 'writers'. Those that would be included within the first category would be the guides of the motoring organizations, the AA and RAC, Michelin, Egon Ronay, Which?, Johansens and the Good Hotel/Pub/Food Guides. On the whole this chapter is not concerned with these. There are several reasons for this. First, whilst several of these may have a narrative attached, they are not primarily 'journalism'. Second, they are a subject worthy of a chapter themselves. Among the full list of guidebooks are those that can claim to be entirely independent with paid inspectors, to those that are little more than a collection of paid-for advertisements, with entries based upon the proprietors' own comments about the restaurants. Where comments are independent, some guides use inspectors with long experience of the industry, often chefs or restaurant owners themselves, whilst others rely on submissions from readers to provide comments. Furthermore, in recent years considerable controversy has surrounded several guides with parties going to court over allegations of poor review quality and falling standards within the Egon Ronay Guide.

'Writers', the second group, is the main focus of interest in this chapter. These are writers who review restaurants for newspapers and magazines, usually as part of a series. It is this group that seemingly causes the most controversy, and anguish for chefs and restaurant proprietors. In some cases particular reviewers are vilified, in others the whole notion of restaurant reviews called into question. The rest of this chapter explores a range of issues that confront this group of writers, not least how much influence they have over the places they review. The first issue is 'who is qualified to be a restaurant critic?'.

Who is qualified to be a restaurant critic?

The brief answer to the question would appear to be almost anyone. Laurence (1994: 4) writes in a guide to food and cookery writing:

> Don't be daunted by not having a cookery diploma or a home economics degree. There are editors who believe that a formal training hampers creativity . . . [.] Take a look at this list and consider whether:
>
> • You produce food people like to eat;
> • You love cooking;
> • You have a deep interest in a particular aspect of food;
> • You love to eat;
> • You have an enquiring mind.
>
> If you can answer yes to one or more of the above, you could be qualified to write about food or cookery.

Even so, in one area of food writing experience is vital. The brief discussion of restaurant guides above noted that several (invariably the most reputable) used experienced industry professionals to assess and grade restaurants for their guides. The same is not necessarily true of restaurant reviewers in journalism. There are essentially three groups: 'serious' food journalists; feature writers; and readers who have submitted reviews.

Dealing with the three in reverse order, reviews from readers are most common in local newspapers. Readers may be invited to submit copy or alternatively a group of regular readers may take it in turns to produce reviews. Clearly the advantage to the paper is that this is cheap. Laurence (1994) suggests that in some cases reviewers may expect to have part of the cost of their meal repaid by the paper, in others the reviewers are just happy to see their name and/or work in print. A disadvantage of this approach lies in the quality of the reviews. Informal analysis of one local English paper over a period of months revealed that the review was almost always of public houses, often serving identical menus as they belonged to the same parent firm. The reviewers apparently did not notice this. One reviewer always chose steak wherever they were, whilst generally the reviewers were unadventurous in their choice of food. The quality of writing was also unadventurous. All reviewers 'plumped' for their various courses and assessment of the food was limited largely to 'nice' or 'bland'. For one reviewer vast helpings became the main criterion of quality, and the final verdict was decided by how 'stuffed' they felt at the end of their meal. Yet, whilst it may be easy to criticize these reviews, many restaurants in the local area proudly displayed their latest write-up. This must indicate that even this most lowly form of restaurant criticism is regarded as carrying some weight by restaurateurs.

The next group of reviewers is newspaper feature writers. These may well be writers who have a considerable interest in food but have not specialized in food writing in their career. They are often chosen for their entertaining copy as much as their skills in reviewing meals and restaurants. Despite their non-expert status these writers can often wield considerable influence, all the more controversially because they are not perceived by chefs as having the 'inside' knowledge necessary properly to assess the food and service they have received. The most notorious of this group is arguably Michael Winner, a film director, who writes for *The Sunday Times*. Acerbic in his criticism and of forthright opinions, Winner has been banned from a number of restaurants and is seen as a highly influential presence on the London restaurant scene in particular. Yet his entry to restaurant journalism came after he wrote a one-off piece in 1992 on the appalling service he felt he had received from Conran's Pont de la Tour restaurant. Soon after, the then editor of *The Sunday Times* invited Winner to write a regular column for the paper. But despite his influence Winner claims no particular expertise or special ability in reviewing restaurants, instead he simply applies himself with a precise and methodical approach to assessing how well he was cared for and fed.

Finally there are those restaurant reviewers that are to a greater or lesser degree experts in food, cooking or restaurants. Food writing has not always been considered the highest journalistic calling. Dornenburg and Page (1998: 36) note that in the USA in the past 'cooking was seen as a blue-collar profession, and food writing as something that "anyone" could do' and they cite Alison Cook, a restaurant critic who says:

> . . . there is still a sense in which food writing is devalued . . . I once wrote an article on the ten best and worst legislators for *Texas Monthly*, and one of the ten worst dismissed it, saying, 'Oh, she's just a food writer, anyway'.

This view of food as a field that all are experts in is reflected to a degree by the use of readers as a ready source of restaurant critics in the UK regional press. Fattorini (1994) notes that romanticized images of hospitality work in various parts of the media, not least fictional portrayals of work in the hospitality industry in television drama, have lent support that food is a field in which all are expert.

Yet many in the field of catering as well as, interestingly enough, in the media, feel some experience in the hospitality industry is vital. Dornenburg and Page (1998: 187) note that several of the most highly regarded restaurant critics in the USA have spent at least some time working in restaurants. They asked a small sample of highly regarded critics from other fields what qualities make a good restaurant critic. David Shaw, a media critic from the *Los Angeles Times* replied that:

> they should probably have some cooking training, either professional training or experience working in a restaurant, so that they know something about food preparation and service. I find that restaurant critics who cook have more acute palates, and are better able to discern what the ingredients are in a dish or why something didn't work.

Despite this Dornenburg and Page (1998: 28) note:

> Most restaurant critics were simply journalists who eventually combined their loves of writing and food . . . [.] The other most popular, albeit circuitous 'routes' into restaurant criticism include earlier pursuits related to music, sociology, travel, and even restaurant work.

Interestingly, readers of restaurant reviews are not ambivalent on the issue of restaurant critics' qualifications. In their study into the influence of restaurant critics Barrows, Lattuca and Busselman (1989: 91) found that some respondents to their questionnaire:

> mentioned that reviewers could more often show a greater sense of professionalism, citing degrading reviews as examples. It was also mentioned that reviewers could be required to have some common background which might include knowledge of food, restaurant experience, journalism experience, and a greater sense of objectivity and integrity.

The purpose of restaurant criticism

A subject intimately linked to the qualifications of a restaurant critic is their purpose or motivation. An expertise on food and cooking techniques is useless if the purpose of the column is solely to entertain.

There would appear to be a continuum along which most, if not all, restaurant criticism can be placed when it comes to assessing its purpose. In the middle is an almost Reithian ideal, an article that educates, entertains and informs. Then at one extreme are reviews that are purely informative, that attempt to look as coldly and objectively as possible at the restaurant, and particularly its food. The form of review and grading systems used in guidebooks typifies these. Certainly few people would read restaurant guides purely for entertainment. This approach is described by Simon Wright, an AA inspector who was shadowed at work for the _Caterer and Hotelkeeper_ trade magazine (Wood, 1998: 66). He comments, 'in your mind you go through how each dish works, how its components interact – but without destroying the process by being overanalytical'. When the reviews of these inspectors are published, they may contain descriptions of the food, but assessment is most usually kept to the form of a grading system.

The other extreme is where the purpose of the review is primarily entertainment. This is what Michael Winner claims his articles have to do, to be both entertaining and funny. Clearly where this is the case, the qualifications of the 'good' restaurant critic are far more likely to be those of a good writer than an experienced cook. But this does raise the question of whether this is really restaurant criticism and whether it can be morally or ethically acceptable for newspapers to carry columns that criticize restaurants purely for entertainment value, as Webster (1999: 28) suggests in an interview with Winner:

> Entertainment may be all very well for the reader. But what about the owners? Is their hard work being ridiculed for the sake of entertainment? Winner becomes more serious. 'I have no doubt that Andrew Neil [former editor of *The Sunday Times*] would have liked me to go out every week and murder a restaurant. But of course you can't do that. Because first of all it wouldn't be true. Most restaurants are really rather good, there's no question of that!

There is also a third aspect to the work of the restaurant critic, to educate. Fine (1996: 155) notes, 'critics, like cooks, see their task to educate the public' and cites several examples (*nouvelle cuisine*, spicy Szechwan food) where the efforts of several critics popularized novel foods. Indeed, Fine even goes so far as to suggest that areas with a reputation for adventurous cooking owe that reputation in large part to the educative and innovative influence of their critics. Citing the examples of Minneapolis and St Paul (the 'Twin Cities'):

> Minneapolis's restaurant scene expanded during the 1980's from its sleepy senescence of the decade before. In contrast, without adventurous or sophisticated critics – without any regular critic for much of the decade – St. Paul never did develop a viable restaurant market. While other explanations might be given, the fact that Minneapolis critics were more likely to review and praise Minneapolis restaurants, and the reality that most of their readers resided in that Twin City, influenced the two restaurant communities by affecting audience knowledge.

Thus we can see the potential for conflict between various parties building up already. Not only are there several types of review, reviews are also carried out by several very different groups of people often with wildly differing levels of expertise. Add to that the editor keen for amusing copy on one side, and the restaurateur keen to keep their reputation on the other, and the mix looks explosive. Finally, the precise definition of what is to be reviewed is not universally agreed upon.

What should restaurant critics review?

Undoubtedly one of the most influential pieces of work in food and beverage management in the post-war period has been Campbell-Smith's (1967) *The Marketing of the Meal Experience* (see Chapter 3). This set out the now implicit concept that customers to restaurants bought not simply the food and drink they consumed, but also the service and atmosphere of the restaurant – in other words a 'meal experience'. However, the role of food remains for many predominant. Again the contrast between food guides and journalistic commentaries is illuminating. Wood (1998: 66) comments:

> Wright is impressed by the standard of staff service in Kings [a restaurant he is reviewing] but as far as the restaurant award scheme is concerned this, like ambience and décor, is irrelevant: AA rosettes are awarded only on a restaurant's standard of food.

A similar view is reflected in the highly influential French guide *Gault et Millau* (cited in Dornenburg and Page, 1998: 72):

> Rankings reflect only our opinion of the food. Other important considerations – the décor, service, wine list, and atmosphere – are commented upon in each review. What is on the plate is by far the most important factor.

On the other hand Webster (1999: 28) notes of Michael Winner:

> What Winner looks for is not just good food, but an overall experience, starting from the moment he enters the restaurant. 'I have great respect and sympathy for the chefs – they all try very hard. But again and again they are let down at the front line. They are so busy poncing about getting the carrots to look neat that they're not concentrating on the people the customer meets. Before the customer meets the food, he's meeting the staff.'

As might be expected, the second, inclusive approach is by far the more common in newspaper and magazine restaurant criticism.

Remember the comments of MacClancy (1992: 210), '[foodies] do not go to an expensive foodie restaurant because of the chef, but because the place is in vogue'. This is undoubtedly the appeal of these columns for editors. Aspiring journalists are encouraged to include human interest in their stories. The latest places to see celebrities and be seen yourself conflict with haughty head-waiters, slovenly waiting staff and similar characters: all these make for very strong copy.

Dornenburg and Page also note the importance of other factors in restaurant reviews, although food is undoubtedly the dominant factor. Some of the critics interviewed suggested that they allocated a particular weighting to food and other factors in their assessment, with weightings varying from less that 50 per cent to over 85 per cent. Other reviewers suggested that food remained all-important but that, if particularly bad, other factors could drag down a restaurant's review.

How influential is restaurant criticism?

Irrespective of who carries out a review, based on whatever criteria and with whatever prejudices in mind, for the restaurateur one question remains: how influential are they? At the beginning of the chapter, it was noted that restaurant reviews, particularly bad reviews, could arouse great passions in restaurateurs, even to the extent of threats and aggressive behaviour. But does this necessarily mean that the reviews are influential? This chapter has already noted that the personalized nature of comments in reviews, whether intentional or not, can themselves be extremely hurtful and upsetting.

Some empirical research into the influence of restaurant reviews has been carried out. Jolson and Bushman (1978) and Barrows, Lattuca and Busselman (1989) are responsible for two well-known articles that addressed the influence of restaurant critics. Jolson and Bushman found that there was widespread use of restaurant reviews. However their use was usually as a third-party source of information, after the diner had found out more from family and friends. They found that restaurant reviews were perceived as being particularly useful when diners ate out in restaurants for the first time or where the restaurant they intended to dine at was more expensive.

Barrows, Lattuca and Busselman (1989: 84–85) surveyed 420 college faculty and staff members and asked them various questions about their dining habits and the influences that acted upon them in choosing a good restaurant. They began by highlighting three issues that were generally agreed upon by both reviewers and restaurateurs from a survey carried out earlier:

- 'Restaurant critics are too often uninformed and simply do not have the necessary knowledge of the food that they are eating of the restaurant business.

- Critics can often have more influence upon the restaurant in terms of operational changes than they may have upon its readers.

- A review may not make or break a restaurant, but it can help to facilitate a restaurant's ultimate fate.'

The researchers then sent a questionnaire to various staff members within their college. The findings are in part hard to translate directly into a UK context because of the very different nature of newspaper readership in the USA, where local rather than national newspapers tend to be most commonly read, but their findings are interesting nonetheless. They found that on the whole almost two-thirds of respondents (65 per cent) read restaurant reviews occasionally (at least once a month) with most of them reading reviews in their local or regional newspapers. Where respondents liked a review, the review would not usually cause them to visit a restaurant immediately, with most saying that they would wait until an opportunity arose to go out before visiting.

The researchers then tried to assess the extent to which reviews influenced restaurant diners. These findings were among the most interesting. While 38.2 per cent said that a favourable review would make them very likely to visit the restaurant, 70 per cent said that a negative review would make them not likely to visit at all. Thus, reviews seem to have a much greater power to turn customers off a restaurant than to make them visit. This was particularly important in light of the (hardly surprising) finding that review readers were more likely to eat out than those who never read reviews at all and spent more on their meals when they did so.

Several other interesting findings regarded the critics themselves. Dornenburg and Page's (1998) study was very much one of the cult of critics' personalities rather than the process of restaurant criticism, yet Barrows, Lattuca and Busselman discovered that for the respondents in their study, *where* the review appeared was more important than *who* wrote it. Barrows, Lattuca and Busselman found that recommendations from friends were the most valued factor when deciding where to eat out in restaurants. This was followed by the general reputation of the restaurant (although the authors do not specify what is meant by this term), the menu, price, discounts and advertising – with reviews of only minor importance in decisions to select a restaurant.

This once again begs the question why reviews arouse such passions if, as this research suggests, they are of only minor importance in helping consumers decide where to eat. One factor is contained in the study. Reviews have a far greater power to deter than to encourage custom. They can, therefore, be seen as potentially highly dangerous, but of little or no benefit if they are good. Second they are very public. Many thousands of customers could relate tales of poor meals to their friends, and the restaurateur might never hear of it. But even mildly negative comment is very clearly and directly communicated in a review.

Do restaurant reviews really affect an establishment's reputation and performance?

The short answer to this is 'yes'. The evidence appears to indicate that both good and bad reviews can affect a restaurant's reputation. Barrows, Lattuca and Busselman (1989: 91) claim, 'when a restaurant receives a positive review in a source with a high profile, it is likely that the review will have an almost immediate effect upon sales. The same could also be true of a restaurant which receives a negative review, only the resulting change in sales might be more drastic and abrupt.' Restaurant reviews also appear to have an influence on restaurant performance. This happens in two ways. As noted earlier, Fine (1996) suggests that knowledgeable and active restaurant reviewers in a particular location can actually have the effect of improving a city's restaurants. Indeed he goes so far as to suggest that cities with pedestrian and lacklustre restaurants may well lack dynamism because they lack good or active reviewers. This remains a hypothesis though and research needs to be undertaken to establish the accuracy of such a view. Fine also notes that reviews can affect restaurant performance in another, more direct manner. He claims (1996: 155–156):

> The mass media is integral to the organizational environment in which restaurants compete and, by affecting the success of a restaurant, has an effect of the lives and positions of kitchen workers. Positive notice creates a buoyant kitchen, whereas criticism affects not only the bottom line but also the relations within the kitchen as blame must be assigned and changes must be plotted.

Conclusions

Finally, how can these various findings be placed in the context of the restaurant industry's media relations and modern food and beverage management? A conclusion of many of these cited earlier was that there was a need for greater understanding and dialogue between chef/restaurateur and reviewer. Mandatory qualifications for reviewers were generally seen as prohibitive to enforce and overly restrictive. Instead, where reviewers were unreasonably harsh simply for the sake of good copy, the responsibility they bore (indeed quite possibly the responsibility for the restaurateur's livelihood) should be impressed upon them. Beyond this little could be done to assist the relationship. Where reviewers have given restaurateurs the opportunity to answer back, perhaps a week after the review, the response was seen as having little impact and generally treated by readers as 'well he would say that wouldn't he'.

More generally, little is known of the precise impact of restaurant reviews and further research could illuminate this. Also, studies into the influence of reviews have addressed only the most general questions, whilst being limited in focus to the USA. More work could provide greater detail into the influence of reviews, particularly in the UK. Finally, those who work in restaurants appear to treat reviews with more passion than they really deserve. Were food and beverage managers better informed about the precise nature and influence of reviews, and how they could usefully be integrated into the quality management systems of a restaurant, more hysterical reactions to negative reviews might be avoided.

References

Barrows, C. W., Lattuca, F. P. and Busselman, R. H. (1989) Influence of Restaurant Reviews Upon Consumers, *FIU Hospitality Review*, **7**(2): 84–92.

Bell, D. and Valentine, G. (1997) *Consuming Geographies: We Are Where We Eat*, London: Routledge.

Campbell-Smith, G. (1967) *The Marketing of the Meal Experience*, London: University of Surrey Press.

Dornenburg, A. and Page, K. (1998) *Dining Out: Secrets from America's Leading Critics, Chefs, and Restaurateurs*, New York: John Wiley & Sons, Inc.

Fattorini, J. E. (1994) Food Journalism: A Medium for Conflict?, *British Food Journal*, **96**(10): 24–28.

Fine, G. A. (1996) *Kitchens: The Culture of Restaurant Work*, Berkeley and Los Angeles: University of California Press.

Jolson, M. A. and Bushman, F. A. (1978) Third-Party Consumer Information Systems: The Case of the Food Critic, *Journal of Retailing*, **54**(4): 63–79.

Laurence, J. (1994) *The Craft of Food and Cookery Writing*, London: Allison and Busby.

MacClancy, J. (1992) *Consuming Culture*, London: Chapmans.

Warde, A. (1997) *Consumption, Food and Taste: Culinary Antinomies and Commodity Culture*, London: Sage.

Webster, J. (1999) Taking the Michael, *Caterer and Hotelkeeper*, 4 February: 27–29.

White, M.-P. (1990) *White Heat*, London: Pyramid Books.

Wood, J. (1998) Days of Wine and Rosettes, *Caterer and Hotelkeeper*, 1 October: 64–66.

Can hotel restaurants ever be profitable? Short- and long-run perspectives

Michael J. Riley

Introduction

In a 1990s cinema remake of 'Robin Hood', the Sheriff of Nottingham, out of pique, orders Christmas to be cancelled. Hoteliers could be forgiven for being similarly tempted to do the same to lunch-time. It is problematic. Worst than that, the problem of hotel restaurants at lunch-time is one of those problems where the causes are obvious but the solutions are not. What makes it even worse, however, is that the problem of lunch is only a particular issue of the more general problem of restaurants in hotels – one that can affect dinner-time too. Restaurants are part of the image of the hotel yet it is hard to make them profitable because of a lack of demand. What is more, the issue of profitability is exaggerated by comparisons with the profitability of rooms. Indeed it is the comparison with rooms that has led to two current trends in hospitality management, namely, that of out-sourcing restaurants in hotels, and that of talk of a schism in the skill requirement of hotel managers which suggests that hoteliers should concentrate on the so called 'core skills' of room management and leave restaurants to the food and beverage specialists. Both views are perfectly legitimate. It is undoubtedly true that technology is changing occupancy management and making it more complicated.

It is also true that the restaurant industry is becoming more specialist but, to a degree, both these ideas represent an imposition of large-scale corporate management thinking on to an industry which encompasses more than just corporatism. How widespread these ideas are or how permanent they are is as yet unknown. Recent evidence from career studies indicates that hotel management has taken on board corporate management thinking whilst building careers based on food and beverage knowledge (Ladkin and Riley, 1996). In constructing a career hotel managers sought both rooms and food and beverage experience and saw their role in terms of what might be described as a 'traditional' one with modern techniques grafted on. In a way, the schism may be the equivalent of asking the above mentioned Mr Hood to stick to archery and let someone else swashbuckle with the sword. Time will tell if the schism becomes more than just talk plus the behaviour of the corporate 'big boys'.

That might sound a little glib but it is not intended to demean the importance of what happens in terms of pro-gressive trends in corporate hospitality management, but merely to highlight that 'chain operations' are not coterminous with the concept of the industry. But, having said this, the relationship between corporate hospitality and small-scale entrepreneurship is important because it sits at the centre of evolutionary development in what is a very fragmented indus-trial structure. For one thing it controls the passage of ideas and good practice around the industry but more importantly, the competition between independent operators and chain operators is direct and local. A thumbnail sketch of compar-ative advantage might suggest that the former have advantage on differentiation and flexibility whilst the latter have it on marketing and purchasing economies of scale. The big issue in the case of hotel restaurants, however, is that of local versus global – the size and needs of the local market versus that of the global, or, if not exactly global, the larger market repre-sented by hotel room guests. The point here is that hotel restaurants need to capture their local market as well as their guest market to achieve and sustain profitability.

Stating the problem

Riley and Davis (1992), as part of a general defence of the importance of food and beverage, make three important points which are, first, that it is easy to underestimate the profitability of food and beverage operations in hotels both through variable overhead allocation systems and by direct comparisons with room revenue. Second, it is easy to exaggerate the problem of demand at lunch-time and point out that whilst there is still a problem, the surrogate – 'bar snacks' – has shown remarkable growth. Third, they argue that food and beverage's contribution to cash flow, particularly in times of recession, is a crucial factor in a hotel's overall performance.

Accepting these points it would be useful to outline the problems of restaurants in hotels. A shorthand sketch would go something like this: guests do not want to eat all their meals in the place where they are staying therefore there is a lack of demand especially at lunch and dinner. Another way to put the same problem is that restaurant cannot compete effectively with local independent restaurants. In psychological terms it is represented by the desire to 'get out', for something different and the need to explore. In sum, pull and push factors both work against the hotel restaurant. Yet restaurant space is deemed necessary because breakfast is necessary and what is more, any competent banqueting department should make profits. Add to this the financial perspective about overheads and expensive physical space and the problems mount. Furthermore, there are a couple of 'own goals' to take into account. In many hotels there is still a problem of direct access from the street. The absence of this is seen as a deterrent to non-resident customers because entrance through the hotel makes the restaurant invisible but, even if it is visible, passage through the hotel carries overtones of social thresholds which may add to the deterrent effect (Riley, 1984).

If , for a moment, the economic arguments are set aside and the overall problem is confined to one of demand then three consumer psychology problems can be identified which are, for residents, that of needing to 'get out' and that of wanting to explore, and for non-residents, perception of the hotel image and the thresholds it entails. These are largely the province of antecedent attitudes and are therefore the stuff of marketing. However, the response of the corporate sector of the industry is to combine marketing solutions with economics.

Modern solutions and their implications

The response of some in the hotel industry to lack of restaurant profitability is to go for some form of out-sourcing such as buying-in an established concept or contracting out management: in other words, the problem is passed on to someone else (Mitchell, 1997; Perrin, 1997). Rationales for this strategy include: to gain access to special expertise, to buy into an established image in a co-branding operation and to have access to greater purchasing muscle (Hemmington and King, 1998). The issues with out-sourcing are essentially marketing and expertise. In one sense it is just a matter of size but in another it raises a question mark over the training of hoteliers. If an established restaurant concept is brought within a hotel then the efficiency of 'practice' accrues to the hotel operation as does market identity. At a simple level it saves the guest the need to go and find it on the high street. By doing this the hotel may be capturing antecedent consumer preference and have marketing expenses carried by the image of the brand. The economies of scale are in terms of both productivity and marketing costs.

Contracting out the management of a food and beverage operation goes to the heart of the issue of expertise. In a sense, the schism referred to earlier is an affront to the traditional education and training of hotel managers. They are supposed to know about food and beverage. However, this may be a case of education and training being out of step with market demands. Food and beverage operations in hotel are built on the product knowledge of the management and the relationship between managers and chefs. In other words the paradigm is skill, product knowledge, the ability of quality to sell itself and organizational role relationships. In contrast, consumer demand is looking for innovation and appears to be susceptible to being sold novelty. It is possible to suggest that there is a 'new think' 'old think' dichotomy at the base of the supposed schism. 'New think' is about product development, marketing and retailing rather than about skill and production. The most significant point about this dichotomy is that the real point of diversity is also residually what they have in common. The old school have the idea that quality sells itself, the new school knows it doesn't but both know that consistent quality is the bedrock of attraction. There are bridges to be built here; food and beverage is not simply concept and marketing – someone has to produce the stuff! It is a challenge for vocational education (Cattet, Baker and Riley, 1995). Another key difference with the new paradigm is that it is not just marketing based but also design centred. Décor and food and linked in a conceptual design and the detail involved in this incorporates productivity into restaurant concepts. In the 'new think' marketing and economics come as a single item.

However, given a trend towards out-sourcing it is worth asking whether expertise takes away the problems? It is unlikely to do so but it does draw attention to the need for marketing even for independent operators. The arguments of Cooper (1967) about the inappropriateness of marketing to the restaurant business can now be seen as dated. The clear and simple techniques advocated by Lawson and Stevenson (1992) make the appropriateness argument redundant. The argument that the food and ambience of a restaurant sell the restaurant is not negated by the suggestion that a spot of marketing might help!

Perhaps the strongest argument for out-sourcing to professional restaurateurs is that it is the restaurant sector that has been the most innovative. Riley (1994) argues that it is because eating out is not embedded in British cultural life that novelty and innovation are so effective in encouraging the population to eat out. The growth of fast-food outlets, themed restaurants and new forms of higher cuisine is testament to this. However there is an argument to suggest that these innovations have a perishable life cycle. The problem with innovation within hotel food and beverage departments is that it goes unnoticed in the outside world. The real point is that innovation is necessary in food and beverage in any circumstances. If the schism between rooms and food and beverage has any meaning it is not about different skills but about the need for creativity in food and beverage and for other dispositional attributes in rooms.

Encouragement from the long view

If there is to be just one beneficiary of the postmodernism that has taken hold then a good bet, apart from sociologists who write about it, might be lunch-time. Already flexible, vague and given modern time-zone travel, open to wide interpretation, it is a ready-made postmodern entity. What this might mean is that lunch-time may become a moveable feast (no pun intended) with lunch itself becoming unhinged from some designated period called lunch-time. Longer and flexible working hours in the general population may mean that restaurants have to open longer hours. This is an argument for the ubiquitous 'coffee shop' and for buffet service. The blurring of boundaries between designated eating periods and elongated opening hours may be the appropriate response of hotel restaurants

If the trend towards living alone continues then its consequences have important implication for restaurants. One line of argument goes that such atomized lifestyles encourage materialism (Goldthorpe, Lockwood, Bechhofer and Platt, 1968) but the question this raises is what happens to surplus income once home based needs are satisfied? The answer appears to be consumption of leisure activities which include eating out. This brings eating out directly into competition with cinema, television, theatre, video hire, sport, fitness and other pursuits. One strategy in response to such competition is to ride along with the others to get a part of the general expansion. For example, pubs have gone some way to incorporating restaurants and television. Similarly, hotels have become sports venues. However, what distinguishes eating out is that its context and purpose are purely social. If isolation is a way of life, then the argument is that it creates not just materialism but a need for 'relational goods' which is, in a way, a fancy term for the need for a social life. Relational goods are needs that can only be satisfied by contact with others (Uhlaner, 1989). Purposeful social interaction requires a venue where sociability and hospitality enable such needs to be met (Telfer, 1996). Food and beverage outlets are an obvious source.

A central argument advanced by Riley and Davis (1992) is that irrespective of visitors from outside the locale staying in the hotel's rooms, food and beverage has to service a local market as well and in so doing buttress the business against recession in the rooms department. There is a need for the hotel to be part of the community serving the local market. In the same way as a pub is referred to as a 'local' by locals a hotel needs that kind of identity. It could be suggested that this idea applies only to small hotels in urban or rural areas but the arguments apply irrespective of size or location. There are problems attached to this notion. Threshold conventions have dogged hotels for a long time. On top of this are the numerous connotations of social difference between visitors and local people. Policies and practices which develop bridges between local social activity must have beneficial effects on food and beverage performance. Not least of these would be access to the restaurant from the street. At present conference and banqueting are seen as venue providers and this may not in the future be enough. The extension of hotel management may well include activity organizing, and activity and club management. In other words, the hotel becomes a purveyor of management as well as facilities and services. The use of the word community used in the same sense as 'community college' would not be misplaced in this set of arguments.

References

Cattet, A., Baker, M., and Riley, M. (1995) Practical food and beverage training in the UK: a study of facilities and a debate on its relevance, *International Journal of Contemporary Hospitality Management*, **7**(5): 21–24.

Cooper, D. (1967) *The Bad Food Guide*, London: Routledge and Kegan Paul.

Goldthorpe, J. H., Lockwood, D., Bechhofer, F., and Platt, J. (1968). *The Affluent Worker: Industrial Attitudes and Behaviour*, Cambridge: Cambridge University Press.

Hemmington, N. and King, C. (1998) Hotel Restaurants: key dimensions of co-branding, in J. Edwards and D. Lee Ross, (Eds) *Culinary Arts and Sciences II: Global and National Perspectives*, Bournemouth University, 5–14.

Ladkin, A. and Riley, M. (1996) Mobility and structure in the career paths of UK hotel managers; a labour market hybrid of the bureaucratic model?, *Tourism Management*, **17**(6): 443–452.

Lawson, S. and Stevenson, A. (1992), Sales and Marketing, *Caterer and Hotelkeeper*, 27 February, 38–45; 5 March, 50–54; 12 March, 44–48; 19 March, 42–44; 26 March, 38–42; 2 April, 52–56.

Mitchell, J. (1997) Passing it on, *Caterer and Hotelkeeper*, 13 November: 66–68

Perrin, J. (1997) Hotel Restaurants: do the sums really add up? *Hospitality*, June: 27–28.

Riley, M. (1984) Hotels and Group Identity, *Tourism Management*, **5**(2): 102–109.

Riley, M. (1994) Marketing eating out: the influence of social culture and innovation, *British Food Journal*, **96**(10): 15–19.

Riley, M. and Davis, E. (1992) Development and innovation; the case of food and beverage management in hotels, in C. Cooper, (Ed) *Progress in Tourism, Recreation and Hospitality Management, Vol 4*, London, Belhaven Press, 201–208.

Telfer, E. (1996) *Food for Thought*, London: Routledge.

Uhlaner, C. J. (1989) 'Relational goods' and participation: incorporating sociability into a theory of rational action, *Public Choice*, **62**: 253–285.

CHAPTER 9

How can we better understand operational productivity in food and beverage? A resource substitution framework

Michael J. Riley

Introduction

The purpose of this chapter is to draw attention to the fundamentals of productivity and present a simple descriptive framework which displays the factors which contribute to productivity in restaurants and bars. An additional aim is to show what a strategy for productivity might look like. The concern throughout is with productivity, not with *relative* productivity and the measures used to make comparisons. At the outset it is important to note that ownership is irrelevant to the arguments and therefore considerations of such modern trends as out-sourcing food and beverage operations are not discussed (see Chapter 8).

The literature on productivity in the hospitality industry contains two broad themes. The first which exposes the inherently problematic nature of the topic is its ability to distract the focus. Whilst most writers agree that productivity is about inputs and outputs, thereafter there is a tendency to jump too soon from what productivity 'is' to either how it is to be achieved, or considerations of quality, or, how it is part of a holistic system or process (Jones and Lockwood, 1989; Jones, 1990; Heap, 1996). The effect of this is that examination of what productivity is remains rather cursory (readers interested in pursuing this claim could do worse than read Pickworth, 1987, who pauses long enough to consider the nature of productivity, to give an integrated picture of its relationship to quality and how it might be accomplished, and Gronroos, 1984, whose model offers a less positive view on the relationship with quality, and one which highlights the dangers which productivity brings to quality). The second theme in the literature is largely a consequence of the first and points up the poor joinery between notions of what productivity is and how it might be measured. In measurement terms comparisons rule. The problem is that productivity expresses the relationship between outputs and inputs but does so without regard for the value it creates for the organization, and this despite 'value added' being a common estimate of output in productivity measurement. Productivity is about optimally deploying resources and, although it can be indicated by measures, the outcomes of any level of productivity work their way through in normal business measures such as profitability. In the same way as intelligence tests provide indicators of intelligence but do not measure it, productivity measures only capture indicators.

These issues notwithstanding, it is when confronted with the problems of measurement in the hospitality context that the real value of looking at the nature of productivity becomes clear (Baker and Riley, 1994). The problem is the nature of demand itself and it is possible to suggest that in 'jumping too soon' the full significance of this has not been appreciated in the literature. The assertion that the nature of demand is the crucial factor in understanding productivity in hospitality, together with the fact that productivity carries an irresistible affirmative logic around with it, which, crudely stated, means it is always in the interests of a business of any size to be increasingly productive, are the guiding assumptions of the analysis which follows. Furthermore, it is suggested that the nature of productivity in action is directly connected to strategies to improve it through the fundamental process of deploying proportions of capital and labour. This process, it will be suggested, is not a dry economic theory but an ever-present framework of options for decisions.

Productivity and strategy

It is possible to suggest that within the realms of strategic thinking productivity is always the bridesmaid and never the bride. We are accustomed to global positioning strategies, entry strategies, marketing strategies, financial strategies, risk management, operating strategies and quality procedures all coming with sub-strategies and variations but rarely do we see a stand-alone productivity strategy, Yet it is always there and always implicit. There are good reasons for its absence. For one thing, it could be argued that strategies for profitability demand efficiency and that therefore a productivity strategy is unnecessary. For another, the fragmented structure of the industry separates corporate management from operating units and consequently a broad operating strategy is deemed sufficient with local management dealing with the contingency. Furthermore, given the character of the industry which is dominated by many small businesses, it is doubtful whether, at least for some, productivity takes precedence over the 'way of life' motivation that many have for entering the sector. None of this demeans the importance of thinking about productivity but it does reduce its status to that of a 'hidden hand'. The rationale for what follows is that, because it is implied in other realms of thought and areas of goal construction, it is possible for productivity to be invisible and for its significance and its fundamentals to be overlooked.

To put this problem in a more pragmatic way, one business question that is rarely asked is: 'On what does any level of profitability depend?' The obvious answer is sales volume, prices and costs but whilst this is true, it is not the complete story. All three factors, but particularly costs, are dependent on the productivity of the operation, its efficiency. The gap between costs and revenue has to be achieved by operating efficiency. Never mind the strategic level, it is perfectly understandable at the operational level that the focus will be on such tangible functions as sales and marketing and finance and control because attention to them is essential to success. The hidden hand only tends to come to the fore at the design stage of a food and beverage operation or when the profit trend line is going south. In fact productivity is a daily issue but one which is difficult to keep in focus. This is especially true with the general pace of life in restaurants and bars.

Productivity and the nature of demand

At the outset it is worth pausing to take on board the major assumption of this analysis, which is that in terms of an input-output model, food and beverage operations, like other tourism activities, exhibits the reverse of the normal engineering assumption that inputs determine output. Here it is being suggested that output drives input. Mechanical engineers with power-weight ratios such as brake horsepower engraved on their hearts, or economists with production functions tattooed wherever economists have things tattooed, would shudder at the thought. This is not a criticism of macro input-output models merely a statement that at the operational level the location of the drive is with output. The two positions are not inconsistent, they exist at different levels and with different spans of explanation (Riley, 1999). The initial feasibility of most tourism and hospitality operations is built around estimated throughput, but when up and running its importance does not diminish. It is often said that the customer is king but, in the sphere of productivity, the throughput of customers is always king.

The productivity dilemma

Hotels and food service operations are part of a class of units which share characteristics of having perishable products, a within-unit product range, and demand which is stochastic in the very short run. These characteristic bequeath to the task of achieving and measuring productivity two intractable problems which are:

- that of having to account for very short-term changes in demand;
- because there is a range of mainly perishable products and services, having to account for the discrepancy between those consumed and those provided.

These problems can be most usefully seen as two sources of uncertainty: never being sure how many customers will arrive, and not knowing what they will consume from what is on offer. The principal dilemma of food and beverage comes from the fact that to entice customers into the restaurant you may have to offer a wide range of dishes but once inside the customers may choose narrowly. Alternatively, you may choose to offer a narrow range of dishes and the customer wants something outside your range and dines elsewhere. What is good for marketing may not be good for productivity and vice versa.

Reconciling this conundrum is at the heart of productivity and successful food and beverage management.

What would a productivity strategy look like?

As with any strategy, a food and beverage strategy has to have direction and completeness. In other words, it must 'embrace' the operation and have clear aims attached. This means that productivity itself should be expressed as a set of aims and that these aims should start their life as part of the design process.

The aims of productivity strategy

In all circumstances, a productivity strategy would have three clear aims, namely:

1 To lower and control costs (both operating and capital costs).
2 To increase the efficiency and quality of the product or service.
3 As consumer demand is stochastic in the very short term, a further aim needs to be added, which is to increase the capacity of the operation to adjust resources in response to variable demand.

This last aim is not coterminous with lowering costs and increasing efficiency. It may achieve both but it should be considered as an aim and objective in its own right. You can lower material purchasing prices and reorganize the kitchen to produce better food but neither will help to cope directly with fluctuations in demand. They may lower the cost of ensuing wastage but that is all. Responsiveness should be seen as a separate aim.

Productivity design and process

At its most fundamental level productivity comes down to decisions on how much capital and how much labour to deploy and in what proportions. In all businesses capital and labour are substitutable by each other and within each other. The process has four possibilities: capital for labour; capital for capital; labour for capital; and labour for labour. In the context of food and beverage operations capital means machines, equipment and fabricated materials. The tools which management have in this respect are design and process design. Process here does not means a total systems approach but something less ambitious, namely, production and service processes seen through the eyes of resource allocation, that is in terms of how much capital and how much labour is required in the context of the substitution principle and substitution possibilities.

Just as there is a dilemma over markets and productivity there is also a design dilemma in that the whole concept of the restaurant (the intended market, the design and layout, the décor and the concept of the menu) are all part of the initial design idea but once the operation is up and running only the layout and the concept of the menu play a part in subsequent productivity. Furthermore, of these two only the menu concept is easily adaptable. In other words, the main factors in operational productivity are first the concept of the menu and secondly, the layout of the kitchen and restaurant. What both these two factors actually do is to determine the amount of work required from labour and the amount of work required from tools and machines in the kitchen and restaurant.

The concept of the menu will be the result of the marketing strategy. From this a set of decisions follow which will include: type of dishes; range of dishes; rate of item change; pricing policy; quality; merchandising and menu design. Once this menu concept has been fixed it decrees the degree of complexity of production and service. It is this degree of complexity that will largely determine productivity because it is the complexity of the menu which forms the objectives and challenges to production and service process design.

At one level of analysis we could simply say that the simpler the menu the simpler would be the production and service processes and consequently productivity will be high because it will be easier to meet productivity aims (1) and (2) above. It could also be argued that simplicity would make for greater flexibility and therefore it would meet the third productivity aim. The fast-food industry might justify this notion. The reverse implications would apply to complex menus. By this argument à la carte haute cuisine menus would make for low productivity. However, restaurant concepts are not necessarily at these extremes nor should the assumption of these polar extremes be taken for granted. Simple production systems might be inflexible to customer demand as anyone who has waited in a fish and chip shop queue might appreciate. Similarly, there is no prohibition on Taylorism in the kitchen, nor any logical reason why haute cuisine should be inefficiently produced. The 'partie system' was, in its heyday, an efficient production system.

Process design and menu complexity

Given any level of physical design efficiency (often referred to as productivity without customers) the determinants of productivity are the stochastic nature of demand and the complexity of the menu. Demand is a matter for marketing and merchandising strategy but it is its stochastic nature together with the concept of the menu that form the real context of operational productivity. The appropriate design tool available to management is process design. Process design is a means by which management specify the kitchen production processes and the service delivery processes in a coherent way which optimizes resources and maintains the quality intended. In action, design processes perform a maintenance function in respect of strategic goals and an adaptive function in relation to contingency.

In productivity terms, these design processes are no different in food and beverage operations than any other business – they are about the options of deploying amounts of capital or amounts of labour. In most circumstances the objectives of process design would be in line with the first two aims of productivity described above, so that they would focus on efficiency and cost minimization. However, the third aim requires that resources must also be judged by their responsiveness to changes in demand.

Any resource can be regarded as responsive if it meets any or any combination of the following criteria:

- the degree to which it is more sustainable and less perishable (able to be stored);

- the degree to which it is has more than one purpose (flexible utility);

- the degree to which it only incurs costs if used (e.g. casual labour);

- the degree to which it is substitutable (cooking skills for the equivalent bought-in prepared food and vice versa).

Judging a resource by its responsiveness, as distinct from its cost, focuses attention on the performance of the resource but this is not implying that costs are secondary to efficiency nor that cost considerations are not a full part of valuing a resource.

Figure 9.1 describes the relationship between the two determinant variables – demand and menu complexity – and the capital and labour variables which can be manipulated through process design. The main focus is on labour substitution both by capital in the form of machines and within itself by different levels of human capital. Human capital should be seen as the sum of a person's education, training, experience, knowledge and information. In this framework, capital is

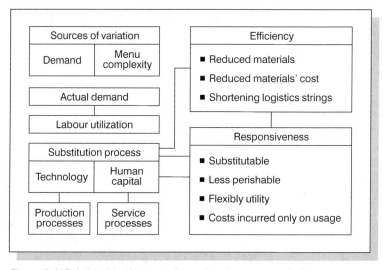

Figure 9.1 Relationships between demand and menu complexity

represented by the terms 'technological intervention' which can mean substitution by machines and augmenting by machines, and by the term 'fabrication' which here means pre-prepared and bought-in materials. A key element of the framework is the distinction between 'pure efficiency' and responsiveness. Pure efficiency is about shortening the length of the logistical string in a process, about reducing the input of materials and about lowering the cost of all inputs but responsiveness is about the ability of the resource to respond to changes in demand. They are not mutually exclusive, but conceptual separation aids analysis.

The key relationship is between both types of labour substitution and menu complexity. The relationship between these three is itself complex but is given coherence if it is seen through the link which all three have with human capital. The assumption that productivity is a function of the relationship between complexity, technological intervention and human capital has a common sense rationale to it. Surely greater simplicity and standardization would benefit productivity just as a wider range of items would adversely effect it? However, given that the range may have a marketing function irrespective of consumer preference, that is, to draw in the customer, there will be effects on productivity. It could be argued that a wide range might require high human capital and standardization low human capital. It is not that simple. Standardization could, for employees, mean a bundle of low skilled tasks. This may require more human capital rather than less. This point was clearly made in a comparative study of UK and German hotels (Prais, Jarvis and Wagner, 1989). Clearly technological substitution and labour substitution are part of resolving this conundrum. It should not be assumed that such intervention necessarily means deskilling. It could equally imply multi-skilling and even enskilling (enhanced skilling). The issues surrounding human capital decisions are complex. The crucial point about increasing human capital inputs is that it not only increases personal output (the straightforward efficiency gain) but also increases the threshold of our ability to substitute labour and therefore increase our capacity to match supply with demand (Brusco, 1998).

Drawing productivity process design back to fundamental notions of substituting capital and labour has the advantage of separating cost from activity. If the substitution is done solely on the basis of cost and output efficiency the result may be a distortion because of the need for resources not just to be cost effective, not just to be efficient in terms of output, but also to be responsive. In other words, there are three criteria for judging a resource not two.

Productivity and cost substitution

The point has been made that the arbiter of capital labour substitution is relative cost. Notwithstanding this issue, it is also worth asking whether cost substitution operates in its own right irrespective of any productivity merits. Judging resources by responsiveness highlights another form of substitution, that of productivity for low labour costs. The restaurant industry often, for a variety of reasons, used more labour than it needs.

It is not unknown for high standard food and beverage outlets to throw bodies at the concept of good service, nor for restaurants to play their part in ethnic enclave labour markets (Wilson and Portes, 1980). What is happening in both these cases is that productivity is deliberately being foregone for perfectly legitimate reasons. In similar vein, the marketing strategy of 'adding value' by including extra products and services always runs the risk of running into this trap. A more serious case is where productivity, and particularly the contribution of capital input, is foregone simply because labour is so cheap. Alpert (1986) found evidence of this but also found sufficient contra indicators to speculate that some American restaurant operators saw the productivity value of higher priced labour. Though not explicit he implies a rationale that labour does at least one thing better than capital – sell!

References

Alpert, W. T. (1986) *The Minimum Wage in the Restaurant Industry*, New York: Praeger.

Baker, M. and Riley, M. (1994) New perspectives on hotel productivity, *International Journal of Hospitality Management*, **13**(4): 7–15.

Brusco, M. J. (1998) Cross-utilization of a two skill workforce, *International Journal of Operations and Production Management*, **18**(6): 555–564.

Gronroos, C. (1984) Service quality model and its marketing implications, *European Journal of Marketing*, **18**: 36–44.

Heap, J. (1996) Top-line productivity: a model for the hospitality and tourism industry, in N. Johns (Ed) *Productivity Management in Hospitality and Tourism*: London, Cassell, **1**: 2–18.

Jones, P. (1990) Managing food service productivity in the long term: strategy, structure and performance, *International Journal of Hospitality Management*, **9**(2): 144–145.

Jones, P. and Lockwood, A. (1989) *The Management of Hotel Operations*, London: Cassell.

Pickworth, J. R. (1987) Minding the Ps and Qs: Linking quality and productivity, *Cornell Hotel and Restaurant Administration Quarterly*, **28**(1): 40–47.

Prais, S. J., Jarvis, J. and Wagner, K. (1989) Productivity and Vocational Skills in Services in Britain and Germany: Hotels, *National Institute Economic Review*, November: 52–74.

Riley, M. (1999) Re-defining the debate on hospitality productivity, *Tourism and Hospitality Research: The Surrey Quarterly Review*, **1**(2): 182–186.

Wilson, K. L. and Portes, A. (1980) Immigrant enclaves: an analysis of the labor market experiences of Cubans in Miami, *American Journal of Sociology*, **86**(2): 295–319.

CHAPTER 10

Why are there so many celebrity chefs and cooks (and do we need them)? Culinary cultism and crassness on television and beyond

Roy C. Wood

Cookery and food programmes on television have a popular niche (see Chapter 6). There are lots of them, formats are varied (albeit only slightly) and many of the chefs and cooks who appear on them if not already 'celebrities' or at least household names, stand a very good chance of achieving such distinction. Moreover, the activities of chefs and cooks, in a cross-media environment with an insatiable desire for news, are frequently reported, not only in features but in the news sections of our daily papers. Cookery books authored (or at least compiled) by these chefs and cooks sell in their thousands – sometimes – particularly if they are the 'book based on the popular television series' as the standard advertising-speak usually has it. Cookery and food programmes form part of what has become known as 'lifestyle television' (see Ferguson and Zukin, 1998) whereby popular hobbies and pastimes, relatively 'normal' in character are made to acquire a sub-obsessive status. Thus, in addition to cookery and food we have a burgeoning television output in gardening; DIY programmes (with an emphasis on decoration); programmes about pets; and antiques programmes. Good, healthy interests that allow television companies to argue that they are reflecting broadly distributed societal interests. Imagine the reaction if there were four or five programmes a week on train-spotting or taxidermy broadcast on terrestrial television, never mind cable and satellite.

Even among the relatively 'normal' list of interests cited above, chefs and cooks stand out like a sore thumb, or so this chapter will argue. The reason for this is that cookery television trades far harder on the personalities of the exponents, the 'personalities' of the chefs and cooks, than other types of television. In general, the 'personalities' of gardening, antique and pet programmes do not receive as much cross-media interest in their other activities (unless it includes something prurient). What is cookery television for? Why are there so many television cooks and chefs – and do we need them? And what is culinary television like? Unsurprisingly, diverse commentators have had quite a lot to say on these subjects.

Chefs and cooks

What is a chef? What is a cook? These are further examples of these common sense questions of which this book has rather made an issue. In the real world, the appellation 'chef' is usually attached to a male cook in charge of a kitchen producing meals for diners in the public world outside the home. A laboured sociological definition, but an important one, the term cook historically having some tradition of attachment to (subordinate) women in the world of public cooking or to women cooking in the home (Chivers, 1973). Think of 'celebrity' chefs on television or in other media and most are male. Gaskell (1997: 21) offers a journalistic investigation of the absence of women from restaurant kitchens. Given that 95 out of every 100 meals in the UK are prepared by women, why, he asks 'are the flashy male efforts so highly regarded by television producers and the publishers of restaurant guides . . . ?' Several reasons are evinced. Interviewed by Gaskell, Raymond Blanc offers up the observations that it is a very demanding occupation physically; it is probably a question of DNA as women have been so subservient to men for so long that they can cook for duty not pleasure; that women tend to follow recipes slavishly where 'The men will always add something personal. Something creative'; and that in commercial kitchens men and women often find their partners and, as relationships develop, men emotionally blackmail their female partners out of their job.

Before the politically correct reach for their nutcrackers, it should be noted that Raymond Blanc is really articulating common sense views that abound in the industry. Indeed, in the same article, one half of television's two fat ladies, (the now deceased) Jennifer Paterson attributes male dominance to the requirement for physical strength and stamina. Her partner, Clarissa Dickson Wright is cited as disagreeing: she instead blames the French system of culinary training. To be credible as a chef you must acquire experience working in a French restaurant, working in a French restaurant exposes women to chauvinism, they are treated badly and, by implication, give up. *Quad erat demonstrandum.* Women chefs interviewed by Gaskell are sceptical of such arguments. Juliet Peston observes that 'most women who cook to work also look after the home and work longer hours. The idea that women aren't strong enough or lack the stamina is nonsense.' The husband of the then one-starred (by Michelin) Hilary Brown notes that others in that illustrious category all work in small kitchens on their own, a notion that resonates with certain (isolationist) strands of feminist thinking.

There are no doubt many good sociological reasons to explain the absence of large numbers of women from senior positions in commercial cookery. Without wishing to trivialize these, for the purposes of this chapter it is more germane to explore the male chef/female cook distinction as it currently appears. One caveat to this, however, is to observe that in the case of television, this distinction reflects societal stereotypes, if not roles. In other words, despite the growth in the number of male chefs seen on television, this is still seen as socially anomalous, if only mildly so. We expect to see women, in the kitchen, cooking. Despite the rhetoric of the last thirty years about greater equality between men and women, social research still reveals that a dispropor-tionate of domestic management falls on the female of the household, including meal preparation. Men in the television kitchen, cooking, is still in some way perceived as unusual. The degree of abnormality is substantially reduced, however, as many successful male chefs on television are successful chefs *per se* – that is, they are involved in the restaurant business as chef or in some other capacity.

Chefs on television and beyond

Reflect on the social characteristics routinely attributed to (male) chefs – how do we think of them? Chances are that a few moments reflection will yield a useful stereotype of chefs as being one or more exceptionally creative; eccentric; short-tempered and even more sophisticatedly temperamental; stern and perhaps even bullying; and (if you're British) maybe foreign – especially French or Italian. Stereotypes are poor guides to reality but they often serve a useful purpose in pointing towards how, as observers, we can investigate reality. For those to whom the stereotype applies, the supposed elements of the stereotype also serve a useful purpose, specifying others' expectations of the person or persons filling the stereotyped role as well as providing a useful set of near-mythological characteristics to manipulate to advantage in the performance of that role.

This latter point is particularly important for sometimes the impact of a stereotype upon those persons thus characterized can have far reaching consequences, not just for individuals but for the whole occupation. For example, the laws of probability mediate against the possibility that all chefs are *exceptionally creative* (or even creative) yet the stereotype prevails. In most commercial cooking, the work of chefs has been heavily deskilled and there is little scope for creative working in restaurants that rely heavily on technology and standard recipes. Yet creativity and artistry are values which chefs cling to as intrinsic to their occupation. Similarly, the laws of probability forbid us to believe that all chefs are temperamental in the sense of being highly volatile, or short-tempered, bullying and prone to harassing others (despite a growing body of evidence to support this latter view – see, for example, North, 1997; Golding, 1997a, 1997b; and most importantly Johns and Menzel, 1999).

The whole of 'foodie' culture revolves, of course, around chefs and yet remarkably little is known about chefs as an occupation, nor the aesthetic values that drive chefs (but see Wood, 1991, 1995). As Fine (1985: 5) puts it in his study of trainee chefs, socialization into an occupation consists not only of acquiring techniques for task performance but taking over particular standards, beliefs and moral concerns: students are not concerned with efficiency alone but with ensuring that tasks are done well. In this sense, Fine argues, they 'develop a concern for form as well as with function'. Fine goes on to argue that cooking is not typically regarded as one of the fine arts but argues that food is judged by its sensory components and 'the higher levels of the occupation do merge with the fine arts' (Fine, 1985: 6, we shall consider these arguments in greater depth in the later discussion of food as art – see Chapter 11). Students entering chef training programmes are largely unaware of what is involved in the occupation and have only a vague knowledge that there is an aesthetic associated with professional cooking. They are taught the techniques that, Fine (1985: 11–12) suggests, 'contain within them the aesthetic rules that students must generalize to related tasks'. He goes on: 'Although students are exhorted to make their food look appetizing, because "people eat with their eyes", this *bon mot* tells students little about how to achieve this goal.' Interestingly, the aesthetic rules are potentially more complex than in other productive activities because cooking appeals to at least four of the five senses – sight, taste, texture and smell – even sound can be aesthetically important. Despite all this, the visual component has first priority in the 'aesthetic concerns of food preparation'.

As part of the learning process, students are taught tricks of the trade (e.g. adding red colouring to bring out the colour of cherry pie) and constantly reminded that they are cooking for customers of whose taste they are unaware and which, as a consequence, must involve them compromising their standards in an effort to hit the midpoint of taste'. Fine (1985: 13) goes on '... cooks are constrained, however they might personally feel, to strive for the lowest common denominator – that level of food taste that will appeal to all of their customers. This assumes implicit knowledge of the tastes of their audience – tastes that will differ in different establishments.' Much of the aesthetics of cooking is directed to visual appeal because there is more consensus on what looks nice than on what tastes good. In the classes that Fine studied, instructors showed slides of the work of previous students, often to the amusement of their current charges but, more importantly, concern with the visual aesthetics of food applied to everyday issues of food preparation and not just elaborate 'special' foods. Aesthetic issues are always related to economic ones – the cost of the object influences the amount of work and the quality of materials put into it – 'cooking is not art for art's sake, but an occupation that needs to produce a marketable commodity for its not always sophisticated public' (Fine, 1985: 15).

The emerging aesthetic awareness of students is reflected in the expansion of their culinary tastes. Most students have limited previous experience – many had never tasted middle-class staples like avocados and artichokes which are not part of the

Hospitality, Leisure & Tourism Series

taste repertoire of working class Americans. A latent part of the education process is to introduce students to those foods. They also have to learn how to make food taste right even when it tastes wrong to them – this they do by learning the appropriate standards of taste through the reactions of their tutors. As their aesthetic judgements increase in sophistication, they become increasingly critical of food that is poorly prepared. Despite their trade orientation, cookery students know they must be artistic to some degree, recognizing that the taste, texture, smell and looks of food are in their hands, their responsibility. Recipes are never used as exact measures, only as guidelines, and students are expected to add approximate amounts of ingredients especially herbs and spices – forcing students to make creative decisions (Fine, 1985: 19–24).

Although students learn an acknowledged aesthetic consensus in cooking, they also learn that this consensus leaves room for some individuality – indeed, the use of judgement and discretion is important to successful cooking in a technical sense. Fine (1985: 25) argues that:

> We must not overemphasize the aesthetic qualities of professional cooking or of the training that students receive. Much of the cooking that these students will be expected to do will not be recognized as artistic in either form or content. No matter how aesthetic a cook may make his or her product, in a matter of minutes it will be consumed and destroyed. Cooking is an activity that captures the moment, presenting food during that short period it is at the height of perfection. Because cooks typically work in a backstage area, one cannot even claim that cooking is a 'performance art'. The art in cooking is at best evanescent.
>
> An equally important constraint of the aesthetic valuation of cooking is that one must please an audience, not one's peers. This paying audience may not share the cook's aesthetic standard, and may not even understand it, as these students did not before they entered the program. Cost often takes priority over the aesthetic niceties. Cooks may become frustrated with the 'inappropriate' demands of their customers, as when customers ask for ketchup.

Peterson and Birg (1988: 67–68) questioned 120 chefs in Chicago receiving 62 returns of which 14 per cent were in hotels; 29 per cent in restaurants; 23 per cent in country clubs; and 16 per cent in corporations. The majority of all respondents – 92 per cent –

claimed they were artistic, with corporate chefs considering themselves least so and restaurant chefs, country club chefs and hotel chefs most so. A clear contradiction in expressing personal style was the professional occupational ideology emphasizing constancy of taste. For respondents this problem was perceived to be resolved in creativity, 98 per cent considering themselves creative. The authors note that 'A generalised conclusion is: chefs strive for expression of a personal style and the development of new products, while placing requirements on their staffs for the execution of consistency in their individual style' (1988: 69). The creativity of chefs involves, according to Peterson and Birg, aspects of performing and non-performing arts – the 'showing' of the artist is matched by the 'presentation' of the chef. Some 95 per cent of chefs in the sample considered presentation either essential or important to their work. Support for the importance of the presentation is found in the occupational role of the portfolio which contains photographs of selected presentations, and themes revealing individual specializations – e.g. chocolate, sugar work and ice carvings. Other props supporting the chefs' reputations are awards – plaques, medals – the former usually displayed, the latter kept in drawers to avoid accusations of immodesty. The majority of chefs in the authors' sample – some 68 per cent – had created a named dish and 93 per cent had written their own recipe, with hotel and restaurant chefs most likely to have done so (1988: 69–70).

What these studies show is that the ideology of the occupation of chef as reflected in training raises clear expectations in those who choose this career. Fine, and Peterson and Birg, focus on what might be termed the 'reasonable' aspects of creativity showing how the creative, aesthetic sense is developed in chefs. Perhaps, then, it is reasonable to assume that, even if not all chefs are 'creative' or 'exceptionally creative', in a precisely defined manner all have potential in this regard. The stereotype of the creative chef transcends aesthetics, however, although aesthetic ability in an intensely visual world is clearly important. The argument can take bizarre twists, though. It has been suggested, for example, that a mark of exceptional creativity is a disposition to dyslexia. Huddart (1998: 32–34) cites anecdotal evidence to the effect that chefs are more likely to be dyslexic than would be expected from the incidence of the disability in the wider population. Of course, until evidence permits an accurate view this possibility must be cautiously allowed. But does this mean that chefs are more prone to be bullies, to be temperamental and volatile, or eccentric? Or does the socially current stereotype merely facilitate or allow chefs to behave in this way?

The point about stereotypes is that they are constituted by interrelated elements. Thus, in our case, 'creativity' can be used to try and explain or excuse bullying, volatility and eccentricity. In the world of the celebrity chef this is all too easy to see. Temperament and volatility can lead to bullying – of staff *and* customers. In respect of customers, some evidence from the world of celebrity chefs suggests temperament and volatility can mutate into arrogant disregard for the customer and a self-belief, such that not only is the customer not always right, they never are. Examples of chefs (and restaurants more widely) behaving badly (or not, depending on your point of view) abound. In the early 1990s as a restaurant reviewer for *The Sunday Times*, film director Michael Winner was reportedly barred from several establishments (Anon, 1994a: 8).

More recently, another food 'critic', A. A. Gill also of *The Sunday Times* was ejected by chef Gordon Ramsay from the latter's Chelsea eatery. So much of a *cause célèbre* did this become that *The Independent* newspaper (14 October 1998: 3) allowed Ramsay a 'right of reply':

> Celebrity chef hits back
>
> I think food critics in this country are seriously influential individuals and that's fine as long as they discuss what is on the plate rather than the person who is cooking it.
>
> I lived in France for three years where they don't have an abundance of food critics with celebrity status. It's a very professional tight ship out there and the critics don't make vindictive, personal remarks. They don't get close to chefs out there in the way that they do in this country. I stay at arm's length distance from food critics because all my customers are critics. I don't get involved with any of them for professional reasons. I can't be seen to be involved with any of them because it then becomes an unbalanced article.
>
> A. A. Gill is a very witty writer and I don't want to be personally criticised by him for the next 10 years. If it's a constructive point of view then I will accept what he writes but if it becomes personal I'll close my doors to that. Personal attacks and insulting my staff is something I'm not putting up with . . . I have made it quite clear that he is not welcome (at my restaurant, the Aubergine). I don't respect him as a food critic and I don't have to stand there and cook for him. Being rude to staff is something I object to. My staff were deeply upset by the unprofessional behaviour from a respected food critic.

There is some small irony in a chef such as Ramsay who enjoys a high degree of media exposure criticizing Gill for his 'celebrity status'. Various other feelings were elicited by Harmer (1998: 60) for the trade magazine *Caterer and Hotelkeeper*. Interviewing a number of chef proprietors she found:

> The general feeling is that chefs should be able to accept criticism of their food and restaurants, and it is only when published comments become spiteful that they believe there is a justification for asking a critic to leave.

Quite so, although a number of chefs contacted did feel that when a critic's comments become personal, ejecting them from the restaurant was justified, Michael Roux jnr having ejected Michael Winner from his establishment. Winner was also recorded as being *persona non grata* at Anthony Worrall Thompson's and Paul Heathcote's restaurants. Restaurant critics are not, of course, ordinary members of the public but Harmer found that chefs also felt that ejecting 'difficult' and 'awkward' customers was quite legitimate which begs the question of what kind of behaviour categorically constitutes 'difficult' and 'awkward'. The dangers are various. Here is Nico Ladenis (1997: 15) for example:

> Imagine getting really excited about something you have created. You have spent time and energy, researching and working to perfect it. Then you finally present it to another person and they say 'This is all very nice – but I want something different'.
>
> That is how I feel about customers who bring their diets into my restaurant. By definition, a diet is personal and should not be imposed on anyone else.

Whereas, of course, a celebrity chef's menu should be. To be fair, Ladenis does go on to note that at this level of *haute cuisine* it is difficult to comprehend why customers select a restaurant with a clear reputation for its chef in high gastronomy if they wish to eat foods that do not fall into that category. Also, he does not state whether committing such a *faux pas* constitutes an 'ejection' offence but the warning signs are there! As they are (or were) with chef 'superstar' Marco Pierre White according to Green (1997: 19):

> His kitchen was the toughest in the business, the commis chefs who couldn't chop fast enough, take blazing heat from the range, and work from six in the morning to

midnight were 'useless . . .'. If Marco bullied his brigade, and he did, he kicked harder at authority. He offered the editor of the *Good Food Guide* a loan to fix his teeth . . . and rang at least one restaurant critic (me) screaming.

The message of all the above seems to be that (celebrity) chefs at least are equally unpleasant, temperamental and bullying (all in the name of creativity of course) to employees, customers and critics. They are, apparently, not much nicer to each other. To conclude this discussion, we can refer to John Walsh's extended discussion of a book of interviews by Bob Mullen with celebrity chefs (Walsh, 1998: 5):

What does Tom Aitkens (of the hugely expensive Pied-à-Terre restaurant) . . . think of Nico Ladenis's establishment, Chez Nico? 'A pile of shit.' What does the grand, world-conquering Marco Pierre White make of Pied-à-Terre? 'Shit. The cooking falls apart.' How does Michael Roux, sainted foodie doyen . . . regard the views of Mr Ladenis? They're 'bollocks with a capital B'. What does Nico think of Mr Roux? 'He is like a dead sheep.'

Let us now contrast the enlightened attitude and behaviour of celebrity chefs with those of celebrity cooks.

Television cooks

In the early days of television, cookery programmes fronted by the likes of Philip Harbin and Fanny Cradock had a mission to explain, to educate and to exemplify – not only cookery techniques but 'taste' and 'behaviour' appropriate to cookery and food service in the home (Cradock was particularly hot on this). They no less traded on the personality of their presenters, and their presenters traded on the programmes – Fanny Cradock with ever-present (at least in the latter days of her television career), paramour and consort Johnny, became a 'celebrity' on the back of her television fame and so, to a lesser degree, did Harbin. Cookery programmes were very much oriented to the home, to domestic food production for ordinary and special occasions, on a world still feeling, if not experiencing, the trauma of the Second World War and rationing. How little has changed – and how much. In the 1990s this style of cookery programme is dominated by one person, Delia Smith, who generates among those who can be bothered to care equal amounts of plaudits and brickbats. Close study of Delia Smith is (all too believably) instructive for the purposes of this discussion.

The strange case of Delia Smith

During the latter half of 1995 and first part of 1996, the television cook Delia Smith was subject to an almost unprecedented proliferation of profiles in the 'serious' press. The hook on which this coverage was hung was the sales success of Smith's latest book, and a television tie-in to her series *Winter Collection*. The main theme of much of the coverage was the power and influence of Delia Smith over the population at large. Thus Sylvester (1995: 12) reported that Smith had the power to increase sales of ingredients by as much as 2000 per cent. In the present case, cranberries were a feature of Smith's cooking and featured on her book's front cover photograph. As a result, Sylvester reported, cranberry stocks were low. In 1990, the article noted, a similar phenomenon had been Smith's recommendation of liquid glucose for use in making a truffel torte. Available for the most part only from pharmacists, most shops had allegedly sold out in days. Further, upon the publication of Smith's *Summer Collection* in 1994, there was a subsequent lime and coriander famine resulting from the recommended use of these ingredients. Somewhat breathlessly, Sylvester goes on to note that Smith's *Winter Collection* television series had, in the week before 22 October 1995, attracted 4 million viewers, fairly high figures for a BBC2 programme. At the same time, by the same point in October a million copies of her book had been sold and printers were reported to be running off 35,000 copies a day in order to keep pace with demand, a demand that Smith's publishers (BBC Books) expected to lead to a further million sales before Christmas.

Why is Delia Smith, in the words of 'Marco Pierre White, the notoriously uncharitable award-winning chef', 'a phenomenon' (cited in Sylvester, 1995)? Most of the journalistic commentators of the time converged on similar factors. First, is Smith's ordinariness. She is 'unpretentious', 'unintimidating' (Sylvester, 1995); 'she is entirely sane and endearingly normal ... she wouldn't know glamour if it came topped with breadcrumbs and baked golden brown', and she is 'not like other foodies who pontificate and preach from the safety of their pulpits ... she is one of us' (Richardson, 1995: quotes from pages 127 and 128 respectively).

This 'one of us' remark (ironic perhaps in featuring in an article contained in a magazine aimed primarily at homosexual men) is the second factor to be considered, for 'one of us' is not simply a paean to ordinariness but to English nationalism. She 'is proud to be British [sic] – the woman who first started cooking because she thought, "why should everything be French"' (Sylvester, 1995).

This does not mean, however, that her recipes lack sophistication: Delia Smith does not attract (entirely) the kind of aloof ridicule with which foreigners are supposed to view English cooking. Indeed as Rose Shepherd (1995: 19) puts it:

> Many of her recipes are exotic, but they are passed through the filter of her Englishness, becoming in the process just like mother makes. She is doing more than anyone to demystify foreign cuisines – which is fine if you don't relish the mystique. In Delia's capable hands, Libyan Soup with Couscous comes to seem as homey as one presumes it is in Libya itself. There is no escapism here, no appeal to the senses other than to a kind of atavistic love of hearth and home and England and St George. Even in her summer collection, she does not trade on images of luscious figs on marble tabletops on sun-drenched Tuscan terraces, or of the vine-clad hills of Provence.

A third and entirely practical reason explaining Smith's success is, according to much of the press coverage reviewed here, the fact that her recipes 'work'. Shepherd (1995: 19) notes that: 'Her recipes are sound: good results are almost guaranteed. She is accessible to beginners.' Richardson (1995: 128) is a little more circumspect, noting that: 'The Delia Smith legend says that her recipes always work: this may or may not be true, but the important thing is that Delia always makes you *believe* they'll work, which is practically the same thing.' Richardson's remarks are, in fact, among the most perceptive commentaries on the Delia Smith phenomena in this period (but see Box 10.1). In pointing to the possibility of the observation that Delia's recipes 'work' is part of the Smith mythology, Richardson moves us into the realm of discussing those features that lend *credibility* to Smith as a cook. It is this perceived credibility that is at the heart of her success. How is such credibility established? Richardson offers further clues. The first of these concerns what may be called, following similar debates in heritage tourism, 'authentic simplicity'. Thus, in Richardson's (1995: 127) words: 'Her manner is cordial, all-girls together, like women's mag on legs; but there is also a half-bossy air of professionalism' and 'Her gospel is simplicity, enjoyment and no messing about' (Richardson, 1995: 128). This 'authentic simplicity' is not simply a focusing of Delia's 'ordinariness' but a transformation of that ordinariness into a confidence that communicates itself to her audience. The second point here is that the confidence comprises both didacticism and reassurance: the latter is often missing from the presentations of those chef 'superstars' who offer the television public their overwrought and pretentious insights into cooking and cookery. Yes, Delia has an air of professionalism, yes she is for 'no messing about' (by which we construe at least a rationalistic orientation to the view that 'funny foreign food' need not be mystifying once it is subjected to a good dose of English rationalism) but she is not puritanical. Richardson (1995) again: 'She has the charmingly petit-bourgeois fondness for "popping" things into other things, for adding "a touch of luxury" and "spoiling" yourself . . .' In other words, Delia exhibits many of the qualities that the English like to think of themselves as possessing: a largely utilitarian

---

Box 10.1

In a tongue-in-cheek article, Eric Griffiths, a Fellow of Trinity College, Cambridge, seeks to place Delia Smith in a literary and philosophical context. Griffiths (1996: 20) writes that 'Delia and her cooking transcend sensuous immediacy . . . In her shows, she eschews the pandering to the audience's taste-buds so deplorable in other exponents of the edible. She never tastes her own food on screen. Cooking Green Thai Curry for us, she remarks, "The aromas are just indescribable, so I won't try to describe them".' Delia's cooking is characterised by calm, says Griffiths, quoting Kafka to the effect that 'Calm without envy at the sight of other people's deight' is an important element in true aesthetic pleasure (which, says Griffiths, is why Hegel would have liked Delia). The calm of Delia's work is, for Griffiths, manifest in 'her over-arching and point-instant grip of time'. She is 'so narrative', saying 'and then' seventeen time when demonstrating one recipe. In her books, this narrative asserts itself with a vengeance – 'Her recipes do not just begin, they tell you they are beginning.' Furthermore, her instructions are 'ticked off' as the recipe develops – when, now, next – and so on until we reach 'finally'. Her favourite verb is 'pop' – 'popping' things in the oven, she has 'regal self-control' and dowdy reticence' (1996: 21).

Griffiths argues that cook-books are faity-tales for grown-ups – 'We love the ones we first heard and want to hear them told to us again', much cookery writing is 'greatly silly'. He concludes by referring to Mary Douglas' view that the rules of the menu are no more or less social than the rules of verse and says: 'But a menu says nothing . . . it is a nonsense poem. And this is generally true of the discourse of cookery, written or pictured, in its negation of matter, its spree from the real.'

Eric Griffiths (1996) 'Hegel's Winter Collection', *Times Literary Supplement*, March 8, 20–21.

approach to food and eating predicated on predictability and moderation but with an occasional capacity for a more sybaritic pattern or patterns of behaviour.

Now, there is much to be said for not taking this argument too far. After all, we do not wish to mythologize Delia any further. However, the case made above 'holds'. Smith's credibility as a cook derives from all the features mentioned and as Richardson (1995: 127) notes, Smith is the most bought and most published food writer alive. It is an accepted wisdom amongst many in the publicity and food-writing trades that Smith's books are purchased as gifts but this by no means diminishes the view of Delia as a popularist writer. Furthermore, Smith's perceived credibility is clearly linked to her wholesomeness (indeed, critics may argue, piousness). As Richardson (1995: 127) puts it '. . . the odd thing is that the people who own these books not only use the recipes but know *interesting things* about their author'. One such 'thing' is that Delia apparently prays before starting a dish. Her religious ideals are generally widely known and there is no prima facie case for assuming that these are anything other than sincerely held beliefs whose air of wholesomeness is incidental. Indeed, a central tenet of simplistic Christianity as with other religions is humility and Richardson (1995: 128) reminds us that much of Delia's cool efficiency and wholesomeness is fixed in the mind of her audience together with a knowledge that she also likes to admit her own weaknesses – in the culinary sphere at least.

The price of this kind of success can be considerable, however. In April 1996 *The Independent* newspaper (Anon, 1996: 3) reported that the 'popular food writer Delia Smith has been snubbed by the foodie "Oscars". Neither her best-selling book Delia Smith's *Winter Collection*, nor the BBC television programme of the same name have been short-listed by the prestigious Glenfiddich Awards.' Instead, *The Independent* noted, the four judges had selected more 'obscure' foodie names. A Glenfiddich spokesman was quoted as observing that Smith had 'won a special award last year for services to the world of food writing'. Like the actor, then, who never wins an Oscar for an actual film but gets a special lifetime achievement award, Smith's success as a populist is grudgingly marked in a manner that places her outside the group of fashion-conscious and élitist obscurantists who promote the largely ill-judged 'concept' cooking that currently defines *haute cuisine*.

This tension surfaced in Smith's career in 1998, when her latest *How to Cook* television series, a 'back to basics' course of programmes supported by a hefty book, was aired on BBC2. In one programme, Smith demonstrated how to boil an egg. This led Gary Rhodes, a well-known media chef, to accuse Smith of insulting the intelligence of her audience. In a trenchant commentary on the spat, Bell (1998: 3) noted recent survey evidence that suggested a decline in knowledge of basic cookery skills among the young (36 per cent of those who said they cooked nominated sandwich making as their particular skill). Bell observed that few people would regularly cook at home the kinds of dishes for which Rhodes and his fellow media chefs were noted in their television programmes. Indeed, she argued, Rhodes and friends should admit that their programmes are 'principally about entertainment'. The drift of Bell's argument thus appeared to be implicitly supportive of the Smith approach.

However, it is at this point worth noting that whereas Delia Smith is typical of television cooks (as opposed to chefs) in one important regard – she is a woman – she is not necessarily typical of television cooks as a whole. In fact, when considering terrestrial television, it is currently difficult to think of any cooks – especially female ones – who enjoy the same status as male chef counterparts or indeed Delia Smith – the 'two fat ladies' Clarissa Dickson Wright and the late Jennifer Paterson, and Madhur Jaffrey would probably qualify. This raises an interesting – and at this point largely unanswerable – question similar to that implied by Bell (1998: 3), namely whether, in the end, it is entertainment that always triumphs over instruction and learning. If this is so, then the proliferation and predominance of male celebrity chefs on television and beyond could be seen as an extension of what used to be called 'variety' or 'light entertainment' television. In other words, the dominance of male chefs is as much a part of the institutional traditions and inequalities of television culture as it is of the culinary world. The parallels bear some scrutiny. For every Morecambe and Wise that 'light entertainment' television produced there were at least a dozen lesser players, even mediocrities, many refugees from the days of theatrical revue and working men's clubs. Many had their own personas (indeed many *only* had their persona) on which they traded for their 'fame' – whether this persona was a sophisticated roué; an inebriated tramp; a cheeky cockney chappy. If those stereotypes ring any bells, perhaps you are watching too many television cookery programmes.

Having said all this, television chefs and cooks share a good deal. Most significant is the already noted 'through media' nature of their work; television is, as it were, only one part of the product. Associated with the programmes are the inevitable cookery and recipe books. More informally, any television cook or chef worth their salt will acquire the (at least occasional) status as media pundit. Many will have regular columns (often 'ghosted') in newspapers and magazines offered as a result of their celebrity but keeping their name in the public eye. There may be product endorsements and advertising opportunities. There will be 'public appearances' (opening fêtes, supermarkets and the like) and after-dinner speaking engagements for societies and organizations. There will be the inevitable video of the television programme and perhaps more besides. Television chefs may even continue to cook in a restaurant – their own or somebody else's – whilst television cooks will write for supermarket magazines and be a football club director (Delia Smith); or run a bookshop and write for provincial newspapers (Clarissa Dickson Wright). For all this, do we need these people? Do they serve a useful purpose? Or an innocent but futile one?

The triumph of the new vulgarity

The case for the defence can be marshalled from a variety of sources. An anonymous 'Comment' writer in *The Sunday Telegraph* (Anon, 1995: 21) newspaper is a useful starting point. The author begins by noting that 'it has become a commonplace observation that the British, who used to be notorious for the awfulness of their food, have become rather obsessed by it'. The writer continues by saying 'among the chattering classes, much of the credit for this culinary transformation is given to Elizabeth David [.] . . . But this influence, though profound, was limited to the literate upper-middle-classes.' According to this commentator, television has acted as the catalyst for widespread interest in food and eating and in particular the activities of television chefs and cooks: 'The British have been taken gently from dried eggs to truffled eggs by a long course of small-screen education, and the pomposity and snobbery of *haute cuisine* have been deflated by enthusiasm.' The author notes that several famous television chefs and cooks, including Delia Smith, Philip Harben, Fanny Cradock and Graham Kerr were/are all self-taught. The writer of the *The Telegraph* piece does not pursue this theme but in the case of Delia Smith in particular suggests that 'Her success derives from her absence of condescension (another self-taught cook, she does not mind giving viewers the simplest and most obvious information) and the absolute dependability of her recipes; a Delia dish which didn't come off would seem like a crime against nature'. According to this argument, then, Smith's success, is in demystifying the 'art' of cookery according to this writer and her treatment by the Elizabeth David camp is summed up in the comment: 'Currently the Foodie Establishment, possibly out of envy or snobbery, are dismissive of her. *The Foodie Handbook* . . . couldn't bear to mention her.'

Of course this writer is talking of television cooks, what they would make of television chefs is another matter. The idea that television cookery programmes in general have benefited culinary standards in Britain is taken up by Sutcliffe (1996: 8) who begins by observing that the proliferation of daytime TV cookery programmes is due to the fact that they are cheap to make. He goes on to argue that in general, cookery and cooking remains a minority social interest and cookery programmes a niche market. This latter is, Sutcliffe (1996: 8) argues, an argument for rather than against these programmes' beneficial influence because: 'By and large, these programmes are watched by an aspirant, self-educating audience and, however ham-fistedly, however half-heartedly, the techniques and recipes shown on television are likely to find their way into domestic kitchens.' He goes on to suggest that this leads to a trickle-down effect – 'Culinary standards in Britain haven't been magically transformed by the increase in cookery programmes but they are indisputably moving in the right direction' (1996: 25).

Sutcliffe also comments on the argument that the celebrity chef series dangles unattainable pleasures in front of people whose budget does not extend to some of the ingredients. Parallels with the argument of Griffiths (see Box 10.1) about food writing as fantasy are apparent in Sutcliffe's agreement with the proposition that one does not watch a programme about cars and expect to own a Ferrari – but one indulges one's dreams while watching such a programme. Indeed, Sutcliffe (1996: 25) argues, 'You would have to be priggishly censorious to let the wealth of the cook put you off the food he or she has cooked'. Sutcliffe concludes that many programmes on cookery are still silly and/or misleading, too many encouraging 'the rigid commandments of the recipe over the creativity of assured technique' and some are 'recklessly tasteless' – 'Floyd's recent series from South Africa, for instance, included dishes that seemed to have been thrown together as edible satire or gourmet experimentation'.

Similar arguments for the benefits of TV chefs and cooks have been made in terms of the revival of these culinary occupations in Britain. Nick Foulkes (1996: 18–21) argues that the occupation is attracting increasing numbers of middle-class, often public school and university educated men (sic). He quotes Sir Terence Conran's view that cooking has become a cult profession for the 1990s when in previous decades it was hairdressing and the music business (the 1960s); fashion design and opening small boutiques (the 1970s); and bond-dealing and design (the 1980s). Rawley Leigh, a well-known 'Clifton and Cambridge-educated chef' agrees, saying that cooks have a certain chic 'rather like hairdressers and photographers, but no nice, respectable, middle-class family wants their children to become hairdressers' (see Foulkes, 1996: 18). According to Foulkes, Leigh suggests that one attraction of cooking to the 'disoriented' middle class is its hierarchical nature reminiscent of the public school fagging system – 'I think it is a bit like the army now' he is quoted as saying.

According to Foulkes, many of these middle-class chefs have done much to 'gentrify' the profession, they 'have brought in the well-spoken young man with floppy hairdoes', a contrast to the past according to Terence Conran: 'In my youth', he says, 'cooks were cooks [are they no longer?], they worked bloody hard, smoked a hell of a lot of cigarettes and after work either went to the pub or straight home to bed' (1996: 20). There is more than a hint of mythologizing cant contained in Conran's remarks as there are in another chef quoted – one Eddie Baines (who, we are told, recently cropped up on a list of eligible bachelors in *Tatler*) who is recorded as observing that 'in England, we have never had chefs, only cooks, and it was only in the Eighties that it become an exciting career' (1996: 20–21). In translation, this rather obviously inaccurate statement means (a) chefs were essentially proletarian prior to middle-class annexation of the profession (a fairly small-world view as, of course, the vast majority of chefs still come from working-class backgrounds and do not run their own bijou restaurant but work for others in the industry who do); and (b) only the middle-class presence has made the job of cook 'exciting'.

Such an inaccurate conceit can perhaps be best understood in terms of the issue that Foulkes does not tackle, namely that there has always been a small cadre of middle-class cooks and chefs working in the hospitality industry. Their greater visibility in recent years then requires some justification of the kind offered by Foulkes if it is to be understood by a middle-class audience supposed to be in a state of induced anxiety that some of their number are apparently settling for jobs and careers which one or two generations ago was something that the children of those from other classes did. Sure enough, Foulkes (1996: 21) sets out such justification in a crudely inaccurate way. Thus we have:

> For the middle classes entering the career market, cooking offers a living with a certain amount of creativity and such is its popularity that there are already kitchens where not to be middle class would set one apart from one's fellows. 'Everyone in the kitchen I am working with is middle class' says one arts administrator-turned-chef, who declines to be named.

I bet. For creativity, read in 90 per cent of cases, 'inventiveness'. In fairness to Foulkes (1996: 21), he also captures the essential vulgarity of these new middle-class cooks when he notes:

> As in many middle-class fields of endeavour, the feeling of superiority of the educated amateur is beginning to surface. 'I think catering college is bad for you' is the uncompromising verdict of the same former arts administrator: 'If you turn up at a restaurant aged 26 having done art history, you have a pretty good idea what you want. There are people who come into the industry as trade and there are those who come into it as foodies.'

In other words, there'll always be an England of such pomposity that it would be tragic if it were not so risibly comic.

It is not only among the middle-class that the image of chef as a career has seemingly been improved. In her report, O'Brien (1997: 3) reports the Head of the Hotel School at Westminster College as saying 'Celebrity chefs are making the industry popular' – his own School seeing a rise in applicants that year and reaching 155 chef students compared to the targeted 90. Mention is made of the highly pressurized nature of kitchen work and the high drop out rate among young chefs, as well as the shortage of talent because of the growth of 'vast, glitzy restaurants'. Drop out rates are influenced by unsociable hours, difficult conditions and often exploitative low pay, leading *Time Out*'s food critic, Caroline Stacey, to remark that 'People think it's more glamorous than it really is, they see the top of a very grungy iceberg'. She goes on to lament the invisibility of women in the profession: 'As usual it's the pushy men who hog the headlines. More women are becoming successful chefs, but they don't get the stardom!'

Yet in Scotland, Fraser (1999: 9) reports that the cult of celebrity chefs on TV has seen a revival in interest of school home economics – among boys. Overall, standard grade entrants to examinations in home economics rose by 16 per cent in the five years to 1998 whereas for the higher examination the figure was 25 per cent. It has even been suggested that television chefs noted for their seafood cookery have led affluent middle-class foodies to purchase more fish, leading to the first rise in fish sales for many years (Rowe, Prestage and Cook, 1999:7). Despite this, a report in *The Economist* (Anon, 1998: 40) noting that the number of restaurants in London has doubled in the last fifteen years claims that there is a shortage of skilled chefs in Britain with one London-based chain having to recruit from Germany and France.

Conclusions

Where does this leave us? In many respects, the arguments considered in the last section and the chapter more widely suggest that at best, our increasing obsession with celebrity chefs and cooks is harmless. Indeed, a number of plausible insights suggest that celebrity chefs and cooks do some good, or at least do no significant harm. If the activities of these groups encourage the wider acquisition and enhancement of culinary skills and an informed interest in food, then like motherhood and apple pie, we should surely embrace and applaud our protagonists' efforts? There is, however, a darker side to this picture.

First, it is by no means clear beyond the power of anecdote that celebrity chefs and cooks do perform the positive roles as described. Second, if these individuals are role models, what kind of role models are they? Behavioural considerations apart, fashion dictates that the kind of people described in this chapter constitute a minority at the (supposed) apex of their profession. The difficulty is that there is no clear correspondence between excellence and achievement or, put another way, we cannot be sure that chefs and cooks are successful in the media because they are good chefs and cooks or because they are good media chefs and cooks. The majority of young chefs or cooks embarking on a culinary career are bound to risk disappointment if their aspirations tend to running their own restaurant, appearing in their own television series and achieving celebrity. Most are going to pursue careers in more routine culinary environments, far from the fine dining restaurants of a Gordon Ramsay or a Raymond Blanc. Even if we were to assume that celebrity chefs and cooks owed there celebrity to culinary excellence, then the question arises as to how is such excellence established in the first instance. Zeldin (1997: 7) has noted that restaurant critics and commentators in the public news-sheets and other media have become more skilled and knowledgeable (and, one might add, more numerous), with a tendency to indulge in arguments about who is 'the best'. If (particularly as far as chefs are concerned) excellence is established by a combination of the third-party championing of individuals combined with the self-promoting activities of the individuals themselves, then this is hardly a reliable guide to real quality. As Zeldin (1997: 7) pithily observes, 'A nation cannot be judged simply on the reputation of a few famous heroes, fighting for yet more reputation'.

To this we can add a further observation. Recalling from Chapter 2 Chaudhuri's (1999) observations concerning the extent to which in even the most fashionable restaurants, menus can acquire a sameness as a result of dish design resting on some lowest common denominator determined by market research, Fearnley-Whittingstall (1999: 28) goes one step further. Focusing on many of the currently leading 'celebrity chefs', he observes that most can trace their gastronomic lineage back to a small group of like pioneers in the 1980s:

> At the beginning of the Eighties there were five chefs [sic]: two Roux brothers, a Mosimann, a Blanc and a Ladenis. Between them they taught dozens of young chefs how to cook serious French food, of whom a clutch became the next generation of stars (the names White, Novelli and Ramsay spring to mind). This second generation has itself now spawned a third, even fourth generation of protégés. Result: there are now probably close to 200 chefs running British restaurant kitchens who can trace their tutelage, directly or indirectly, back to the Big Five.

Fearnley-Whittingstall argues that one positive outcome of this has been an improvement of standards. On the downside, however, it has promoted what he terms a 'mediocrity of excellence', whereby food produced is of a high standard but 'when experienced on a regular basis, tends towards uninspiring homogeneity'. Of course, Fearnely-Whittingstall is talking only of élite dining but there is again the suggestion of standardization and indeed, trends that are far from the self-image of chefs and those of their promoters considered earlier in the chapter. Homogeneity is not obviously compatible with creativity and innovation, the virtues that are meant to characterize the cookery profession.

And herein lies the makings of a paradox. Far from representing the apex of culinary achievement there is the suspicion that the cult of celebrity among chefs and cooks has merely generated a torpid parody of excellence in cuisine, one that owes more to the influence of fashion and the insatiable appetite of the media for visual excitement and entertainment. This phenomenon is not sustained by evolutionary processes in cuisine but by the demands of celebrity itself. We hear little at present of 'nouvelle cuisine' which has been a recurring phenomenon in the history of French and English gastronomy (Mennell, 1985; Wood, 1991). The most recent incarnation of nouvelle cuisine (in the 1970s and 1980s) coincided with the rise of celebrity chefs and cooks on any scale. Yet even the culinary profession itself was moved at the time to differ-

Hospitality, Leisure & Tourism Series

entiate between nouvelle cuisine that represented the evolution of tradition and that which represented chefs jumping on the gastronomic bandwagon with ill-conceived offerings (Wood, 1991). This capacity for self-appraisal has now all been lost or submerged in the unseemly and Gadarene rush for celebrity. In postmodern terms, anything goes that can be sustained by reputational and promotional devices. When the Channel 4 television company broadcast a programme in 1994 in its provocative documentary series *J'accuse* suggesting that chefs should stay in the kitchen and keep off the television screen, the screams from the culinary profession could be heard across the land (e.g. Anon, 1994b). If Fearnley-Whittingstall (1999) is right, then the cuisine of most of the country's top chefs is little more than the McDonald's of the chattering classes – safe, samey and predictable. Such food is the fish and chips of the bourgeoisie (Wood, 1991), a tasteless and vulgar simulacrum of culture and refinement that owes more to the traditions of crassness associated with media cults of celebrity than it does to culinary intellectualism and skill. Celebrity chefs – who needs them?

References

Anon (1994a) Winner receives public banning, *Caterer and Hotelkeeper*, 18 August: 8.

Anon (1994b) A panning chefs don't deserve, *Caterer and Hotelkeeper*, 3 March: 9.

Anon (1995) Profile: television cooks: cuisine on the screen, *The Sunday Telegraph*, 1 January: 21.

Anon (1996) Cooking queen out of favour, *The Independent*, 10 April: 3.

Anon (1998) The great chef shortage, *The Economist*, 9 May: 40.

Bell, A. (1998) Storm in an egg cup as Gary says Delia's cookery advice is 'insulting', *The Independent*, 27 October: 3.

Chaudhuri, A. (1999) Choice is off the menu, *The Independent on Sunday*, 29 August: 14.

Chivers, T. (1973) The proletarianisation of a service worker, *Sociological Review*.

Fearnley-Whittingstall, H. (1999) Setting an example, *The Independent on Sunday (Review)*, 29 August: 28.

Ferguson, P. P. and Zukin, S. (1998) The careers of chefs, in R. Scapp and B. Seitz (Eds) *Eating Culture*, New York: State University of New York, 92–111.

Fine, G. A. (1985) Occupational aesthetics: low trade school students learn to cook, *Urban Life*, **14**(1): 3–31.

Foulkes, N. (1996) The man who would be Marco, *The Sunday Telegraph (Magazine)*, 7 January: 18–21.

Fraser, S. (1999) Cult of TV chefs fires more boys' ambition to put on a pinny, *Scotland on Sunday*, 24 January: 9.

Gaskell, J. (1997) Sex and the Michelin men: the kitchen – no place for a woman? *The Sunday Telegraph*, 26 January: 21.

Golding, C. (1997a) Industry bullying is 'part of the job', *Caterer and Hotelkeeper*, 11 September: 12.

Golding, C. (1997b) Harassment still not an issue with some bosses, *Caterer and Hotelkeeper*, 9 October: 9.

Green, E. (1997) The screaming success, *The Independent*, 10 August: 19.

Griffiths, E. (1996) Hegel's Winter Collection, *Times Literary Supplement*, March 8, 20–21.

Harmer, J. (1998) Ejection seating, *Caterer and Hotelkeeper*, 5 November: 60–61.

Huddart, G. (1998) Too gifted for words, *Caterer and Hotelkeeper*, 2 July: 32–34.

Johns, N. and Menzel, P. J. (1999) 'If you can't stand the heat!' . . . kitchen violence and culinary art, *International Journal of Hospitality Management*, **18**(2): 99–109.

Ladenis, N. (1997) Defender of the chef's Maginot line, *The Times*, 6 May: 15.

Mennell, S. (1985) *All Manners of Food: Eating and Taste in England and France from the Middle Ages to the Present*, Oxford: Basil Blackwell.

North, S.-J. (1997) Beyond a joke, *Caterer and Hotelkeeper*, 14 August: 30–32.

O'Brien, L. (1997) Catering: the new media studies, *Independent on Sunday (Real Life)*, 16 November: 3.

Peterson, Y. and Birg, L. D. (1988) Top hat: the chef as creative occupation, *Free Inquiry in Creative Sociology*, **16**(1): 67–72.

Richardson, P. (1995) It's delicious! It's delightful! It's Delia!, *Attitude*, **20**: 126–129.

Rowe, M., Prestage, M. and Cook, E. (1999) TV chefs and their seafoodie fans rescue Britain's fishermen, *The Independent on Sunday*, 15 August: 7.

Shepherd, R. (1995) Delia runs wild in the bookshop, *The Independent*, 17 October: 19.

Sutcliffe, T. (1996) Do we need TV chefs?, *The Independent (Section Two)*, 1 July: 8.

Sylvester, R. (1995) Delia's feast spells a famine, *The Sunday Times*, 22 October: 12.

Walsh, J. (1998) A real kitchen-sink drama, *The Independent*, 14 December: 5.

Wood, R. C. (1991) The shock of the new: a sociology of nouvelle cuisine, *Journal of Consumer Studies and Home Economics*, **15**(4): 327–338.

Wood, R. C. (1995) *The Sociology of the Meal*, Edinburgh: Edinburgh University Press.

Zeldin, T. (1997) Good news for frogs and snails, *The Observer (Review)*, 18 May: 7.

CHAPTER 11

Is food an art form? Pretentiousness and pomposity in cookery

Roy C. Wood

What do we mean when we say food is an art form? More to the point, what do other people mean when they say this, especially those cooks and chefs who with varying degrees of modesty admit to their work having the qualities of art, and the critics and other social commentators who frequently lend their support to such perceptions? Let there be no doubt that this is the case, as Lupton (1996: 145) notes: 'In contemporary western societies there is a gourmet culture among the economically privileged in which "artistic", "refined" and "innovative" cuisine is valorized, both when dining out at expensive and fashionable restaurants, and preparing special meals at home.'

There are dangers for the non-specialist seeking to explore these issues, if only because professional scholars in the philosophy, aesthetics and history of art have difficulties enough of their own in defining the right questions, let alone agreeing upon common ground. Furthermore, as Zolberg (1990: 3) observes, 'social scientists who turn their attention to the arts in society are treading on dangerous terrain . . . [.] They earn resentment from specialist in the arts who question the legitimacy of their endeavour.' It is possible to sympathize with such a reaction: who in their right mind prefers a careless and potentially dangerous amateur to a professional? And yet, the diversity of views among 'the professionals' as to the nature of art, how art should be defined, and what should be excluded or included, is perhaps more deep than wide. Thus, while even a modest dip into the literature on such matters reveals numerous battlefields, these are quite well defined. A cautious amateur can thus give a flavour of the parameters of the more important areas of interest and examine the implications of these for 'food as art'. To begin this process, it is as well that some precision is lent to the question that frames this chapter. When we ask 'is food an art form?' in a food and beverage context we do not mean food in its natural state, but in the state achieved by the processing (in the 'systems' sense of the term) of food. This raises an immediate difficulty, because the act(s) of processing, which in an elemental sense include preparing, treating and cooking food, perhaps even bringing into being that food, becomes part of what we are seeking to evaluate – i.e. is food an art form? Put more simply, we must at the first keep in mind a preliminary distinction between art as process and art as product. It is this thought, for reasons which shall become apparent, that will guide the following discussion.

Defining art

As intimated earlier, defining what art is (or is not) remains a central feature of specialized academic scholarship and debate among philosophers, historians, aestheticians and sociologists of art and others. We can gain only a flavour of these debates here and focus on the principal and recurring themes and issues in the literature.

First, we can note that art tends to be conceived of in terms of extremes – this is art, this is not; this is good art, this is bad art and so on. In more refined views, art is conceived of as a plurality of forms placed on a continuum. Thus, Gans (1974) in exploring the aesthetic qualities of popular culture distinguishes between high and popular culture; the former achieved on the artist's terms alone while the latter is on terms dictated by the audience. Gans proposes various 'taste cultures' – high culture; upper-middle-class culture; lower-middle-class culture; and working-class culture. High culture is the smallest taste culture but the one that has the highest profile by virtue of its adoption and promulgation by influential élites. It is the culture by which all other taste cultures are judged. As one progresses from high culture to popular culture via upper- and lower-middle and working-class taste, audiences are found to be less concerned with the creative process and artistic form and more with content, action and plot. This is a grossly simplified perspective on a series of complex arguments, but it serves to emphasize two points. The first is that art can and is frequently considered without reference to type – painting, sculpture, film and so on. The second point is a corollary of this and is that in discussing 'art' as a generic phenomenon, there is a tendency to differentiate not only in terms of type but in terms of relative value and worth. The two concepts do overlap, or rather fuse, as it is frequently implied and often explicitly argued that there is a hierarchy of artistic types. Allusions to distinctions between 'fine art' and 'craft', or 'pure art' and 'applied art' abound in both popular and academic literature. Where they are all admitted as types of art, painting, sculpture, 'literature', theatre, classical music and opera occupy elevated positions in this hierarchy of types compared to photography, film, television, popular music and 'musicals'. It almost goes without saying that within each of these types, there are further hierarchies of value.

Second here, some definitions of art insist, to the distaste of writers like Young (1995: 330), that: 'something is an artwork if and only if arthood has been conferred upon it by appropriately qualified members of the artworld'. An element in what is known as the institutional theory of art (Warburton, 1995; Young, 1997) in one sense this appears an élitist view, reserving definitions of art to only the appropriately qualified. However, the 'appropriately qualified' need not be so in a formal academic or experiential sense, only in matters of taste, and taste is of course subject to fashion. A variation on this view but with a very different tenor and implication for defining art is to conflate the process of producing art with the art (end product) itself. Crudely expressed, this is the view that something is a work of art if it is defined as such, particularly (but not exclusively) by the artist. The late critic Peter Fuller (1993: 35) fulminates on this point:

> A 'painting' these days tends to be identified with the mere presence of paint as a substance. A 'sculpture' can be anything. In a pamphlet accompanying the Hayward Gallery's despicable 1983 Sculpture Show, Norbert Lynton [a leading art scholar] declared that 'sculpture is what sculptors do. No other definition is possible.' This is

ludicrous. After all, sculptors get up in the morning, read the paper, take the dog for a walk, and so on. None of this is necessarily sculpture, although it's possible that it could all be designated as such.

Following this line of argument, one can suppose that artistic value and worth are to some degree dependent on the ability of artists and others to persuade a wider constituency that the work of artists is indeed art. It is a view rejected by those of Peter Fuller's disposition. Fuller (1993: 34; see also Sewell, 1994; 1995 who, as art critic of the *London Evening Standard* is perhaps the current most articulate critic in this vein) laments 'works of art':

> which apparently embody no imaginative, nor indeed physical, transformation of materials; no sense of belonging to any of the particular arts, such as painting, sculpture, drawing and engraving; no sense of tradition nor of skill. Such works possess no identifiable aesthetic qualities and offer, in my view at least, no opportunity for aesthetic experience or evaluation.

More specifically, in the case of painting, arguments similar to those of Fuller are often placed in the context of those who broadly favour the view that representational art (as opposed to abstract art) is the true standard by which painting should be judged. The philosopher Colin Radford (1996: 174–175) identifies abstract art as one form of painting that has 'produced incomprehension and fury in laypersons, critics and indeed in other artists'. Radford speculates that this is due at least in part to the scale of intellectual and perceptual disturbance caused by the shift from looking at something which is readily identifiable, to something which is not. In abstract art, for example, there are none of the usual tests of competence by which to judge a work. Thus, a portraitist can be judged according to the quality of the likeness (where this can be verified); a painter of animals by how much their picture of a sheep approximates to a real sheep. With abstract art, Radford (1996: 175) argues, meaningful tests of competence are suspended: 'there is virtually none of this, no demand on, or test of, draughtsmanship, verisimilitude, mastery of perspective, or many of the dimensions that contribute to the composition of representational painting – no wonder David Hockney gave up painting abstracts because he didn't find it interesting'.

Third, and following from the above views, we can discern another quality to art namely the role of skill in artistry. We are returned to the issue of the role of process in art identified in the opening paragraph of the chapter. Fuller and Radford both point to the role of skill or technique in determining whether something is a work of art. However, skill and technique are not usually regarded as qualities sufficient for making such a determination. Armstrong (1996: 381) makes precisely this point in the context of what constitutes artistry in painting when he notes that 'on its own, the ability to render a likeness or to have superb control over the medium and instruments of painting is not a sufficient condition for the creation of an artistically valuable picture'. He goes on to point out that the concept of 'artistry' is not equivalent to skill although skill (in the sense of technical mastery) is a part of it. Rather artistry is the combination of skill and imagination to endow some object with aesthetic interest. This aesthetic interest is a form of 'added value', a concept not unfamiliar to management students, whereby the artist endows an object with qualities for which the object can be valued over and above its utility.

Fourth, one view of how art should be defined insists that all genuine art produces an aesthetic response or emotion in the person(s) contemplating it. Most associated with the work of art critic Clive Bell (Warburton, 1995: 149; see also Fuller, 1993), such emotions are created because all works of art share a common feature, so-called 'significant form', which is a set of relations between parts of an artwork which are integral to the structure rather than content of that work. This 'significant form' is intuitively recognized by the sensitive appraiser or critic of art but significant form itself, precisely because it consists of interrelated abstract relations, cannot be more concretely defined. It requires no genius whatsoever to realize that, as with elements of the institutional view of art referred to earlier, there is a certain élitism at work here. Those members of the elect who can appreciate 'significant form' are in possession of a gift that others lack (it seems unlikely that a person can be taught to appreciate significant form – one either has the power of recognition or one does not). As Warburton (1995: 150) notes there are two other objections to 'significant form' theory. The first is that as a theory, it is highly circular. An aesthetic response is caused by an aesthetic response-making quality of which little or nothing is known. Also, this theory of art cannot be refuted, i.e. it cannot be subjected to conventional notions of proof.

Finally here we must briefly consider one other 'theory' of art that has some bearing on the question at hand. Associated with R. G. Collingwood as presented in his book *The Principles of Art* (1938), so-called idealist theory argues somewhat radically that a work of art is non-physical but exists only in the mind of the artist as an idea or emotion. These ideas and emotions are given physical expression as the artist becomes involved with their particular medium but such expression is merely the shadow or shade of the artwork which remains firmly fixed in the artist's mind. Idealist theory offers another take on the skill/artistry dichotomy referred to earlier, notably in the distinction made between art and craft. Such distinctions, while not confined to idealist theory, are important because of the concept of utility (see Warburton, 1995: 151; Armstrong, 1996; Slater, 1997). In idealist terms, works of art serve no functional or practical purpose whereas craft objects have precisely such purposeful function-ality and utility. Art may contain elements of craft but art is 'for itself', rather than a means to end.

Food and art: what we already know

In this section, we will consider some of the more important contributions to the small but interesting literature on the nature of food as art. The estimable social anthropologist, Mary Douglas (1982: 106) begins from the proposition that food is eaten for partly instrumental and partly aesthetic reasons. In other words, there is a biological necessity to eating but also a minimum aesthetic (in the sense of 'artistic') present in the selection, preparation, presentation and consumption of food. According to Douglas, the instrumental/aesthetic dichotomy places food as an applied art form with clothing, architecture and utensil design rather than a pure or fine art such as music, sculpture or the visual arts. Having said this, Douglas points out that in most of the applied arts there is a tension between requirements of function and requirements of design: clothing, buildings and utensils are rarely designed without a function or functions in mind. The same is not always true of food where it is possible that functional (i.e. biological) requirements are sometimes distorted by an overemphasis on the aesthetic. Food, Douglas (1982: 107) argues, can be produced entirely for display. When it is, the aesthetic qualities of food, now separated from biological imperatives, have a close association with decorative arts such as flower arranging and painting. The latter is a 'pure' or 'fine' art in Douglas' own terms, a confusion she does not appear to recognize and one compounded by her view that the artistic qualities of food are subject to pattern-making rules as is the case with poetry, music and dance (one of which at least – music – she also classifies as a 'pure' art).

Douglas' lack of consistency in the employment of these various definitions should not detract from her efforts to establish whether food is an art form. A number of 'tests' can be proposed in this regard, first of which is examination of whether the rules that govern the presentation (patterning) of food are similar to those in other applied arts. An important element in this analysis concerns temporal rules. Here is Douglas (1982: 108) in full flow:

> Does the food system unfold the rules which make its patterns in a short or long time? How quickly does the pattern repeat itself? Is it more like a poem consisting entirely of rhymed couplets with a fixed metre? Or does it develop like a great epic poem, with galloping rhymed couplets when the narrative is jolly, blank verse when the theme deepens, and all the chapters symmetrically concluded with sonnets in the strict ab ba form?

Douglas argues that food develops its rules over the course of a day, as do the rules for clothing which are also subject to rules related to seasonality. However, food can develop its sequence and display its structure over time both more rapidly and more slowly than clothing, the real sequence of food patterning only being concluded at the end of life itself 'when we have moved from the christening cake, to the wedding cake, to the funeral baked meats' (Douglas, 1982: 109). Denuded of its social anthropological opaqueness, what Douglas appears to be arguing is that yes, food shares temporal patterning rules with other applied art forms, but these rules applied to foods are infinitely more flexible than in these other applied cases (caution is required here since it is quite possible to argue using similarly opaque social anthropological phraseology that the real sequence of clothing is similarly concluded only at the end of life as we move from christening gown to wedding clothes and ultimately, funeral shroud).

A second set of tests applied by Douglas (1982: 109–110) to the issue of whether food is an art form relates to the rigidity and simplicity of the rules of a food system. Such questions as 'what range of materials are permitted'; 'what elements of the system are stable and which open to experimentation'; 'what are the rules governing the visibility of food preparation'; and 'what are the rules for food processing in the home and outside the home' are all critical here. Finally, Douglas' third area of concern is whether food shares the same sensory (texture, colour and smell) rules as other art forms. This, she believes, is a possible area of difference with other art forms, food having an autonomous system of rules with regard to permitted combinations of texture, colour and smell, and combinations thereof. Whether or not there are differences between food and other art forms, it is certainly the case that texture, colour and smell can influence perceptions of the likely palatability of food. As Fieldhouse (1995: 196) argues, colour can constitute an index of normality in food based on expectations. Colour can also influence perceptions of sweetness. Texture and smell act as signals of deterioration and appropriate cooking technique. Many people, especially children, often refuse to eat preferred foods because of deficiencies in appearance.

Quinet (1981) focuses on the problem of function in discussions of food as art. Beginning with the art/craft distinction (briefly touched upon in the previous section) she suggests that if we mean by art that form of art which is craft, it is still possible that some culinary products are 'works of art' in an aesthetic sense. Objections to regarding culinary products as art rest on notions of function. A work of art is generally viewed as something to be appreciated for its own sake rather than as something with any particular utility or function. Its central 'function' is thus as an object of appreciation. In contrast, the central function of food is, variously, to provide something to eat, or taste, or nutrients for the sustenance of life. One way round this objection is to view the products of culinary skill as works of art in their own right, ignoring the functional properties that render them as foodstuffs. In this context, food is appreciated primarily as a visual display, as in the case of the wedding cake (see also Charsley, 1992). Such an argument is, Quinet observes, unsatisfactory for a variety of reasons, not least that ignoring a feature or features of an object does not make them any less significant.

A second objection to viewing food as art is that aesthetic appreciation is appreciation of an artwork for its own sake, that is for its intrinsic qualities. Thus, that eating and tasting lead to the destruction of the object of aesthetic consideration hardly seems easily reconcilable with a concern for the object for its own sake. One might add, though Quinet makes little or nothing of it, that most things regarded as works of art are defined in terms of their possessing some temporal permanency. The primary function of food as something to be ingested denies such permanency. Some products of culinary practice are, of course, not meant to be eaten and are (or were) produced entirely for aesthetic purposes. Quinet (1981: 164) relates the well-known example of the French chef Careme:

> The great French chef Careme was said to have had incredible facility with pastry and sugar and to have constructed fantastic structures out of them as well as from other materials. He wrote that 'the Fine Arts are five in number: Painting, Music, Sculpture, Poetry and Architecture – whereof the principal branch is confectionery'.

After an exhaustive and complex (but immensely rewarding) series of arguments, Quinet (1981: 169) concludes that the non-aesthetic functionality of culinary products may actually contribute to the construction of an art object. Put another way, the argument appears to be that there is no *de facto* reason for believing that the intended functionality of culinary process and products need exclude such products from being works of art, although this does not mean 'that *any* combination of aesthetically relevant food-properties will in fact yield a work of art, any more than will any combination of aesthetically relevant colour qualities'. This is a useful though not uncontentious conclusion in that while it permits of the logic of the case that some culinary products can be viewed as works of art, the question is left open as to those qualities that differentiate art from 'not art'.

In probably the most recent extensive discussion of food as art, at least from the standpoint of the philosophy of aesthetics, Telfer (1996: 44) concurs with Quinet that food (and indeed drink) might sometimes constitute artworks. Indeed, Telfer is emphatic that there can be aesthetic reactions to tastes and smells as there can to the visual appreciation of the appearance of food. That there can be aesthetic, non-instrumental, reactions to food also means that judgements are possible as to the objectivity of such aesthetic qualities. That is, the claim can be made, or argument put, that certain aesthetic reactions are ones that people ought to recognize and like. Telfer (1996: 47–49) further rejects the notion that food is 'just' a craft and not art at all. Art and craft are distinctions between different elements of an artist's work which may be represented in differing proportions in any one work. That something, some object, has a usefulness or utility value does not prevent it from being a work of art.

Telfer is concerned with the issue of whether food and drink can ever be considered as 'works of art'. The phrase 'work of art' used in a classifying sense says something about how an object is regarded, whereas an evaluative statement is concerned with the merit in labelling something a work of art. To say something is a work of art in a classifying sense is to accept the artist's and/or exhibitor's implied (or sometimes explicit) claim that an object presented is meant to be considered aesthetically, that is, as a work of art. There is, however, a second sense in which we can speak of a work of art in a classifying sense and this applies to all those objects which, though not intended, originally, by their creators to be works of art, have in the eyes of society become so – for example, religious buildings. Use of the term 'work of art' in an evaluative way directs attention to the extent to which an object merits that particular label. Thus, the intentions of the artist or exhibitor that we should regard something as a work of art can be rejected – a dead sheep preserved in formaldehyde may be intended as a work of art but many people reject such a notion. Furthermore, in describing a work of art in an evaluative sense, one may accept that something is a work of art without necessarily regarding it as particularly good.

In discussing classifying and evaluative aspects of works of art, Telfer (1996: 46) also draws attention to what kind of 'thing' art 'is' – i.e. what kind of existence art enjoys. This, she argues is problematic. It is also relevant to understanding whether food can be considered as art. Telfer's main concern here is to point out that many works of art exist as physical entities (buildings, pictures) but some do not. Using the example of Beethoven's *Moonlight Sonata*, Telfer points out that if the original manuscript of this piece as written by Beethoven is destroyed, there still remains in existence something called the *Moonlight Sonata*. At the same time, Telfer notes, it would be wrong to identify this piece of music with its performances because of both the plurality of possibilities (different musicians may interpret the piece in many different ways) but because the piece would still exist as a work of art even if it had never been performed.

The relevance of the distinction between classifying and evaluative senses of the term 'work of art' are important, Telfer (1996: 45–46) argues, because some dishes do clearly represent works of art in a classifying sense, though it can be asserted that dishes do not constitute works of art in an evaluative sense. Thus, what she calls 'run-of-the-mill' food cannot be regarded as art as it is not meant primarily for aesthetic consideration. Many meals are intended by their cooks to be regarded aesthetically however and it these that must be treated seriously in respect of claims to the status 'works of art'. Similarly, if the distinction between art and craft is essentially an artificial one, then some foods can still be treated as art. Telfer (1996: 49) further notes that:

> recipes are sometimes treated as works of art, of a kind analogous to musical compositions. The cook who creates such a recipe is a creative artist. A cook can also create recipes by producing variations on someone else's recipe or on a traditional one, like a jazz composer arranging a standard tune or a classical composer arranging folk song: cooks who do this are also creative artists.

However, Telfer adds, those who actually produce the dishes may or may not be artists. They may be 'technicians' following the exact orders of a chef. In most cases, however, the imprecision of cooking as a set of processes, and the frequent vagaries of recipes ('add a pinch of', 'season to taste') allows the scope for creative artistry such that 'a particular cook's version of a recipe is an interpretative work of art'. Thus, the creator of a recipe can be compared to a composer and a cook who follows a recipe to a performer.

In addressing questions of the kind of existence enjoyed by works of art, Telfer (1996: 50–51) notes that there are difficulties in accepting both (some) recipes and dishes as works of art. In the case of recipes, she remarks, how are we to view the superb pie created by the Marks and Spencer chef then turned out in thousands? Can each pie be a work of art? In a qualified and classifying sense, Telfer thinks so, the process being analogous to the production of many copies of engravings or prints. In the case of dishes, the problem is deeper. Food is prepared for consumption, but, as Telfer (1996: 50) asks: 'how can there be works of art which are destroyed by the very activity, eating, which is necessary for contemplating them?' One way round this and related issues, Telfer argues, is to note that it is not the physical structure of a dish that is aesthetically contemplated but the combination of flavours which are present throughout the dish. The problem with this view of course is that Telfer already accepts odours as an essential part of food aesthetics, to which one can add appearance: elements which are undoubtedly destroyed or reduced, or at least irrevocably altered by the process of consumption.

Telfer (1996: 58–60) concludes that the art of food is a simple and minor one. Three reasons are advanced for this. The first is transience. Transience means that food can neither be contemplated for any length of time nor acquire the stature of a long-lived work of art to 'speak' to multiple generations (i.e. be contemplated over time). A recipe is not in itself transient (if written down) but the problem is that a recipe can never be precise enough to speak across generations. Recipes can also be undermined by changes in the nature of ingredients, changes engendered by advances in technology. Similarly, pursuing the composer (recipe) and performer (realizing the recipe) metaphor, the performance of recipes is transient and can never be completely recorded because the end purpose of the activity is consumption of the artwork. The second reason why food is a minor art form, Telfer argues, is because its artistic meaning is restricted. Food does not represent anything else whereas many representational arts are intended to do just this, to make us see ourselves and our experiences in particular ways. Of course, art is not always representational, non-representational art does, however, express emotion which, Telfer argues, food does not. Emotion may be put into the preparation of food but this cannot be expressed in the end product itself. Finally, Telfer claims that food cannot move us in the same way as other works of art, in the sense of shaking us fundamentally.

To round this discussion off, we will briefly consider some views on the food-as-art debate closer to the foodservice industry, or at least more distant from the philosophical/sociological debates reviewed thus far. In Chapter 10 we examined Fine's (1985) work on the aesthetic training of chefs. That chefs develop some aesthetic sense is not in dispute. How, if at all, this leads chefs to regard themselves as artists, or at the very least involved in the production of art, is unclear. Peterson and Birg (1988: 70) note that societal conventions are such that fine artists such as painters and sculptors regard the public as irrelevant to the creative enterprise and often complain of the visual illiteracy of the self same public. In the authors' study, 45 per cent of their sample of chefs believed that the public had uneducated palates, with restaurant chefs least likely to believe this. Some 52 per cent of respondents also felt their patrons appreciated the presentation more than the taste of food. This may go some way to explaining the emphasis on presentation that has grown as part of the movement to present chefs as artists. Peterson and Birg (1988: 71) also point out that artists and writers do not know their publics at the time they create their products and their creations occur almost exclusively backstage, whereas chefs execute their performance both front- and backstage relative to their guests, and obtain more immediate feedback from their guests than artists and writers.

Evidencing a clear grip on many of the issues discussed earlier in this section, that doyen of food writers, Egon Ronay (1987) asks rhetorically whether cooking is an art. The answer is:

> Certainly not. It is a skill . . . [.] Yet once in a blue moon, a true artist can elevate a skill, like cooking, to the level of the fine arts. But generally speaking, you cannot apply the words 'artists' and 'art' to chefs and cooking.

The basis for this assertion is that an artisan, whatever their trade, is concerned with directing their skills to a utilitarian or functional purpose, an artist 'uses his [sic] talents for an aesthetic purpose, even if his creations are eventually used for utilitarian purposes?'. Ronay implies a distinction between 'true' artists and others (unspecified). In the culinary world, chefs who are 'true' artists possess certain qualities: they are obsessive, extremely sensitive, highly strung and creatively self-indulgent 'to the point of other-worldliness'. Ronay develops his argument in a manner which verges on self-contradiction. He asks whether cooking can be bracketed with painting, sculpture or music. Again, the answer is 'yes' because 'the fine arts are concerned with the beautiful: visual, verbal and auditory'. But loose-talk must be guarded against. Ronay accepts that some cooking and some food is art, but not that food which is lauded 'because it looks beautiful, not because it tastes so'. He points out that artists require an audience for their work, suggesting that lack of an appreciative audience in the UK is one reason why British cuisine remains underdeveloped. In echoes of Telfer (1996), Ronay remarks that:

> Paradoxically, the appreciation of art-level cooking, of all the fine arts, is arguably the least subject to opinion: artistic creations in other fields are only appreciated properly if one's perception and impression corresponds with that of the artist: never more so than in modern art. Culinary works of art have an instant impact on the palate (of those who have one); they don't have to be interpreted. For their enjoyment you don't have to harmonise with their creators.

He concludes:

> Cooking is the only tragic art form in the sense that a culinary work of art is completely ephemeral. There is no way of recording it. Taste cannot be relived, only recalled.

Food in art: a brief detour

Before trying to make wider sense of the discussion thus far, it is worth noting that food has long been subject of 'works of art' and, further, the notion of food as an art form seems to have gained wide credence among the 'arts establishment' in recent years. Space does not permit an extensive discussion of the role of food in art, especially painting, but from still life to surrealism and pop art, food has proved a popular subject matter, so popular in fact that in 1997 the Towner Art Gallery and Local Museum in Eastbourne ran a Sainsbury's-sponsored exhibition entitled 'Wait and see (what's for dinner?)' complemented by a series of events including a 'food film season'. In 1999 Glasgow ran an exhibition 'Food: Design and Culture' as part of its celebrations at being chosen as UK City of Architecture and Design (Catterall, 1999). During the heyday of the new wave of *nouvelle cuisine*, several 'food in art' coffee table books were produced, most notably Clifton (1998). One rather bizarre variation on this trend was the production of an English-language version of Marinetti's *The Futurist Cookbook* (Chamberlain, 1989). Marinetti, was a futurist 'artist' (futurism, crudely defined, was a modernist artistic movement at the start of the twentieth century that rejected the romanticism of the century before in favour of a technology driven view of art, one that glorified speed and conflict). *The Futurist Cookbook* is now generally regarded as an elaborate intellectual joke. The book contains commentary and recipes, the latter never less that arresting as in 'A simultaneous dish' (Chamberlain, 1989: 142):

Chicken aspic, half of it studded with squares of raw young camel meat rubbed with garlic and smoked, and half studded with balls of hare meat stewed in wine.

Eat this by washing down every mouthful of camel with a sip of *acqua del Serino* and every mouthful of hare with a sip of *Scirà* (a non-alcoholic Turkish wine made with must).

A moment's pause for reflection yields the idea that, from the viewpoint of the beginning of the twenty-first century, and knowing all that has happened 'in art' since Marinetti put pen to paper, *The Futurist Cookbook* is not perhaps as much a joke as some commentators have suggested. After all, in an era when an animal preserved in formaldehyde constitutes art, why should not the dishes proffered by the futurists be accorded similar status? That in general they are not seems to indicate another reason why food is not an art form. This is that the combination of foods (the artistic media) are much more closely regulated by convention, and by more diverse conventions, whether on a local or global scale. This does not mean that taste is static or unchanging, merely that at any moment, the potential for the cook as artist to indulge the avant-garde is more constrained.

A corollary of this view is that food can be presented in a manner to mimic various artistic styles – for example in painting. Thus one might have dishes presented in an impressionist or surrealist manner. This view has been explored at some length and persuasively by Steel (1985) and despite the underlying seriousness of the suggestion, is a view cruelly mocked. In a commentary playing on this general notion the humorous columnist Miles Kington (1996: 14) managed to hit both food-as-art pretensions and postmodernism in a single shot. A man staying at a seaside hotel finds from the breakfast menu that he can have 'eggs – any style' and each morning for the next fortnight tests the waiter and the kitchen with demands for eggs representative of different artistic styles and historical periods,

Art deco	A boiled egg in an art deco cup with a long 1920s spoon
Neo-classical	A plate of scrambled eggs arranged under a palladian arch of toast
Fauvist	A plate of loosely cooked eggs dyed purple and red and smeared across the plate (inedible)
Celtic revivalist	Coddled eggs in a nest of seaweed
Jazz age	Eggs with gin

Table 11.1 Artistic eggs (after Kington, 1996: 14)

some of which are shown in Table 11.1 together with responses. On the final day, the guest asks for eggs in the post-modernist style to which the waiter replies 'We at this hotel do not think that post-modernism is worthy to be called a style, sir', adding 'It is merely a ragbag of cultural mannerisms'.

Conclusions

Having offered a somewhat streamlined view of the core issues attendant on answering the question 'Is food an art form?' the time has come to try to resolve the matter. The essential issues in defining art can be even more crudely summarized as follows.

- Conceptions of art have often been in terms of degree ranged on continua, for example from good art to bad art; high culture to low culture. Onto such continua are grafted assumptions about the possibility of making generic statements about art irrespective of form (for example, high culture embraces 'classic literature', opera, the theatre) and these statements are invariably cast in terms of the value or worth of art (high culture is valuable and worthy, low culture less so).

- Some views of art advocate definitions in terms of whether particular works are defined as art by cognoscenti in the art world, including those who produce such works.

- For many, meaningful definitions of art must separate the process and materials that go into making a work of art from the end product itself. These need not, ultimately, be evaluated separately, indeed there is some question as to whether it would be possible to do so. Rather, in this view, the application of 'artistic' materials, techniques and processes does not guarantee that the final object or work of contemplation is a work of art.

- There is a strong tradition in art criticism that a work of art is defined in terms of the aesthetic response it elicits in the persons who view it. This response is seen as integral to the artwork and appreciation of it is inherent to those with an artistic temperament. Thus, all who possess this temperament will recognize a work of art and works that are not art, almost intuitively.

- Yet another view of art is that 'the work' originates and remains in the mind of the artist who gives it physical representation. This representation, however, is a mere shadow of the idea of the artwork which is not therefore entirely accessible by the non-artist.

Clearly, some of these views of art are difficult to reconcile meaningfully. In the food as art debate, the following issues emerge.

- Douglas (1982) concentrates on what type of art food and cooking might be, seeking comparisons among related art forms. In doing this, she explores the patterning of food systems and seeks to establish whether there are like patterns between the food system and other artistic systems. She concludes that food does share certain patterning rules with other art forms but for food, these are more flexible. She does not develop, however, this argument in any detail, save to speculate that it is the textures and flavours of food that may confirm distinctive artistic qualities on food.

- Quinet (1981) focuses on the issue of the functional in cuisine versus that of aesthetic appreciation of the intrinsic qualities of the artwork. In the conventional discourse of art criticism, this relationship is problematic because many would argue that the functional and impermanent nature of food means that it cannot have a lasting aesthetic quality. Quinet, however, concludes that it is the very functional qualities of food that may contribute to the construction of an art object. Value judgements are still required though because not every combination of food will lead to the construction of an artwork.

- Telfer (1996) builds on Quinet to reject the distinction between art and craft, aesthetics and functionality, in art. Both are to be found in the processes and end products of artists' efforts. Telfer also dwells on the problems inherent to the debate between those who see art as being defined by the artistic community alone and those who determine art on the basis of some set of values relating to worth. For Telfer, the tension between these two positions is a critical one. Some food is intended to be art and is art, some is not. Some food (routine food) irrespective of the artist's intention is never art. The difficulties in resolving these issues can to a degree be illustrated through the medium of the recipe – the superb Marks and Spencer pie, the original an artwork, reproduced in thousands, can be a work of art in a classifying sense. The problem for Telfer is that in destroying (consuming) food, we destroy the very physicality that gives other art works a necessary permanence. Telfer gets around this by arguing, like Douglas, that it is perhaps the essence of food that defines its artistic quality – texture, aroma, and flavours. Telfer's conclusion is that food is a minor art form because it is transient, does not represent anything (notably enduring truths and emotions) and is incapable, like most art, of really moving the art consumer.

One issue not considered in the literature reviewed here concerns the extent to which common sense notions of the 'artistry' of chefs and cooks and the artistic status of their food have become absorbed into culinary culture to the extent that in a very loose sense, producers of food consciously begin to experiment with food as if it *was* an art form. The recent trend towards 'fusion' cooking whereby foodstuffs from two or more distinctive national styles are combined in a single dish could be regarded as just such an example of artistic experimentation (see Holland and McCool, 1994). Against this view is the more deterministic pronouncements of writers such as Ravel (1992: 147) who complains of the tendency for consumers (and by extension, chefs and cooks) to confuse gastronomy and exoticism. For customers, he argues 'the dish that is special is an exotic dish'. This type of dish is least likely to be prepared successfully he argues, leading chefs and cooks to disguise lack of competence by the use of myriad devices such as flaming food, or serving dishes with inappropriate sauces that mask flavour. Experimentation, in short, is not reliable, and it is not art. Anderson (1995: 42) in choleric manner, agrees, arguing that 'We need inventive cooks about as much as we need contemporary experimental composers ...'. For Anderson, creativity and innovation in food as a *modus operandi* means that many of the chefs and cooks lauded by the 'foodie' establishment have never mastered, or have forgotten or neglected what Anderson calls 'the old good dishes'. He concludes:

> Food is still a chore for the masses, and a hobby and a talking point for a few foodies. The idea of novelty and creativeness attracted the chatterers. Not only does it make food 'arty', it hides their failure to pursue the true virtues of the kitchen – perseverance, hard, often boring work, daily good habits and the obedience to great traditions. Bugger inventiveness.

Once again, we must ask where this leaves us. On the assumption that we do not adopt a thoroughgoing relativist approach to the question 'Is food an art form?' whereby anything can be called a work of art, then the weight of reasoned commentary seems to admit to food and cooking as an art form. In many ways this is a pleasing and apposite conclusion and one which, with some irony, is better than denying that food is an art form at all. It places the modern cult of the chef with its associated hyperbole, arrogance and pomposity in some kind of rational perspective and allows us to see cooking, stripped of all pretentiousness, in a naturalistic state, for what it is: a joyous, artisanal and evolving craft with its roots firmly in an experimental tradition and not a failing culture of taste predicated on impulse, fashion and ill-conceived aspirations to some phoney grandeur.

References

Anderson, D. (1995) Food: whatever happened to our testicles?, *The Spectator*, 30 December: 42.

Armstrong, J. (1996) Artistry, *British Journal of Aesthetics*, **36**(4): 381–388.

Catterall, C. (Ed) (1999) *Food: Design and Culture*, London: Laurence King.

Chamberlain, L. (Ed) (1989) *Marinetti – Futurist Cookbook*, London: Trefoil Publications.

Charsley, S. R. (1992) *Wedding Cakes and Cultural History*, London: Routledge.

Clifton, C. (1988) *The Art of Food*, London: Windward.

Collingwood, R. G. (1938) *The Principles of Art*, Oxford: Clarendon Press.

Douglas, M. (1982) Food as an art form, in *In the Active Voice*, London: Routledge and Kegan Paul, 105–113.

Fieldhouse, P. (1995) *Food and Nutrition: Customs and Culture*, London: Chapman and Hall, 2nd edition.

Fine, G. A. (1985) Occupational aesthetics: low trade school students learn to cook, *Urban Life*, **14**(1): 3–31.

Fuller, J. (1993) But is it art?, in J. McDonald (Ed) *Peter Fuller's Modern Painters: Reflections on British Art*, London: Methuen, 34–48.

Gans, H. (1974) *Popular Culture and High Culture*, New York: Basic Books.

Holland, M. A. and McCool, A. C. (1994) Cross-cultural cuisine: long-term trend or short-lived fad, *Florida International University Hospitality Review*, **12**(1): 17–30.

Kington, M. (1996) Eggsistential guide to eating your art out, *The Independent*, 11 September: 14.

Lupton, D. (1996) *Food, the Body and the Self*, London: Sage.

Peterson, Y. and Birg, L. D. (1988) Top hat: the chef as creative occupation, *Free Inquiry in Creative Sociology*, **16**(1): 67–72.

Quinet, M. (1981) Food as art the problem of function, *British Journal of Aesthetics*, **21**(2): 159–171.

Radford, C. (1996) *Driving to California: An Unconventional Introduction to Philosophy*, Edinburgh: Edinburgh University Press.

Ravel, J.-F. (1992) Cuisine and Culture, in D. W. Curtin and L. M. Heldke (Eds) *Cooking, Eating, Thinking: Transformative Philosophies of Food*, Bloomington and Indianapolis: Indiana University Press, 145–152.

Ronay, E. (1987) Strokes from the palate as fine art, *The Sunday Times*, 25 October: 72.

Sewell, B. (1994) *The Reviews That Caused the Rumpus and Other Pieces*, London: Bloomsbury.

Sewell, B. (1995) *An Alphabet of Villains*, London: Bloomsbury.

Slater, H. (1997) Art and aesthetics, *British Journal of Aesthetics*, **37**(3): 226–231.

Steel, J. (1985) *The Nature of Prescription in Cuisine*, unpublished PhD thesis, Glasgow: University of Strathclyde.

Telfer, E. (1996) *Food for Thought: Philosophy and Food*, London: Routledge.

Warburton, N. (1995) *Philosophy: the Basics*, London: Routledge, 2nd edition.

Young, J. O. (1995) Artwork and artworlds, *British Journal of Aesthetics*, **35**(4): 330–337.

Young, J. O. (1997) Defining art responsibly, *British Journal of Aesthetics*, **37**(1): 57–65.

Zolberg, V. L. (1990) *Constructing a Sociology of the Arts*, Cambridge: Cambridge University Press.

CHAPTER 12

Is there such a thing as beverage management? Drink and the food and beverage consumer

Joseph E. Fattorini

Introduction

Over the past twenty years or so, consumers' enjoyment of alcoholic drink has become more sophisticated. The so called 'wine revolution' in the UK and other countries has been led by consumers who want to get more out of a bottle of wine. They want to know where it comes from, how best to drink it and what to eat with it. This has been accompanied by a number of other smaller revolutions in consumer (drink) interest. Concern with real ale and speciality beer is now more than a rearguard action against what was seen in the 1970s as the dominance of poor quality keg lagers. New markets enjoy Scotch whisky and other spirits. Even coffee has moved from being a standardized commodity to being a differentiated, premium product.

But in the midst of a drinks revolution, beverage management has been left behind. That is not to say that there are not some outstanding examples of innovative, exciting and consumer centred beverage management, there are. But beverage management as a discipline needs to catch up. The evidence for this comes from various sources and this chapter will identify some of the aspects of beverage management that need to be researched, adapted into workable models and systems, and then taught to practising and aspiring beverage managers. Clearly beverage management must be customer centred and this chapter examines the habits of the beverage consumer for clues as to what might make for effective beverage management. Finally, it is worth noting that this chapter deals primarily with alcoholic drink. In the past beverage management has been a proxy for 'wine management' and even sometimes just 'wine knowledge'. Consumers, as well as becoming more knowledgeable about wine, have become more confident in experimenting with other drinks at mealtimes and asserting their own tastes over convention. This is not solely a consumer-led function. Beer and spirit producers clearly wish to encourage consumers to enjoy their drinks in a variety of settings. Wine appears well established as the principal drink to accompany food, and much of the chapter necessarily concentrates on wine. But other drinks may suit certain foods better, either because of taste or theme, and were beverage management to adopt a more innovative approach to food and drink matching, benefits to customers and restaurant would be sure to follow.

What is beverage management?

Like most hospitality management disciplines, understanding what beverage management is means reading textbooks and research reports, watching what is taught in colleges, and approaching practitioners. Unfortunately there are only a very limited number of texts that deal with beverage management exclusively. Durkan and Cousins (1995) and Fattorini (1997) both deal with the topic in some detail, although both adopt a wine-centred approach. Other information can be found by looking at more general food and beverage texts that include sections on the subject, for instance Buttle (1986), Lillicrap and Cousins (1990) and Davis and Stone (1991). There is also some limited research on the topic. There have been articles that explore wine marketing (Fattorini, 1994b, 1996), sales (Dodd, 1997) and wine pricing (Barrows, 1996), but overall, research remains limited and eclectic. So what does the aspiring food and beverage manager learn about alcoholic drink? The answer appears to be either too much or too little. Most beverage learning concentrates on three areas: control, service and product knowledge.

Control

Control is the most straightforward and least complex of these. Drinks are generally simpler to control than food, but the systems that are used to ensure adequate control are much the same. The process of receiving, storing, issuing and ordering should be very similar to that for food, if perhaps less frequent. Although much is made of how wines should be kept at the right temperature and in tightly controlled storage conditions, the parameters are far more flexible than they are for dairy products or other perishable foods. Unfortunately where problems do arise in the control function of beverage management it is (almost paradoxically) because it is seen as nothing more than a simpler subset of the food control process. Barrows (1996: 164) notes 'Not nearly enough attention is paid to the pricing of wines ... wine pricing is still in its infancy when compared to the current information that is available on menu pricing'. Pointing out that most restaurateurs adopt the percentage mark-up of wine pricing he goes on:

> Unfortunately, in this way, it is being treated as a mere extension of a restaurant's liquor offerings, which are often priced in the same manner after the operator has targeted a desired liquor cost percentage. Whilst this approach could be appropriate for pricing spirits in some cases, it may not always be appropriate when pricing wines, particularly at this time when consumers are extremely price sensitive. Overall, the restaurant industry may actually be discouraging wine purchases because they are terribly over priced.

Barrows notes a number of alternative approaches such as the sliding scale. This marks up less expensive wines more than more costly wines. This way reasonable margins are maintained on more expensive wines, whilst at the same time making them relatively more attractive to customers. In the case of one wine style – Champagne – such a system has been used for many years. Champagne has often been marked up using a lower percentage than that used for still wines because in restaurants with an otherwise modestly priced wine list, the high price of Champagne marked up at a flat rate can seem excessive, so restaurateurs have been more modest in their pricing.

Whether this variable mark-up rate is used solely for Champagne or for all wines over a certain price, the approach is not consumer based. Such a system presumes that price is the only variable when customers are choosing a bottle of wine. Yet, as any wine bore will tell those unlucky enough to be seated next to him at a dinner party (and it usually is a him), wine is an enormously complicated product, and matching it to food is a complex task. Not only is wine a complex product, the restaurant-going public also now better understands it. Customers, who know either a wine style or even an individual brand from retail wine shopping resent spending twice or three times what they paid in the shop for the same wine. This has been recognized by restaurateurs who may insist that their wine merchants supply only wines that are unavailable to the off-trade. Yet even this does little to prevent moderately knowledgeable customers from calculating the general retail cost of a bottle of wine. The issue has been exacerbated in recent years in the UK by the consolidation of the wine trade. First Quench, the UK's largest high street wine merchant is part owned by Whitbread. One of the synergies that benefits Whitbread is the cost savings made on centralizing wine purchasing and supply to its off-licences and restaurants, so that the wines that appear in Whitbread's managed pubs and restaurants are also the 'own label' lines of its wine shops.

To overcome some of these problems, Barrows (1996) suggests a more sophisticated, market-oriented wine pricing process in restaurants. This is based on the menu engineering techniques of Kasavana and Smith (1982). This will be familiar to food and beverage practitioners and involves constructing a matrix based on the contribution margin of different products and their menu mix percentage. The items (originally menu choices, in this case wines) are then classified into one of four groups. 'Stars' have a high contribution margin and high demand. Puzzles also have a high contribution margin but low demand. 'Plowhorses' have a low contribution margin with high demand. Finally, dogs have a low contribution margin and low demand.

For a fuller discussion of the techniques of menu engineering, readers should refer to the original texts or one of the many discussions on the merits of menu engineering that have emerged since. For wine list evaluation there are several points to note. Despite the apparent precision implied by the term 'engineering', drawing up the matrix cannot turn a poorly performing wine list into a profits engine overnight. Rather, this should allow managers to look at their wine list in a more sophisticated way. Kasavana and Smith (1982) and Barrows (1996) also suggest action to be taken in the case of each of their four classifications. 'Stars' should be monitored closely as they clearly play a key role in the restaurant's profitability. These are the wines that should be highlighted on the menu or wine list. Barrows suggests that unlike food stars, which Kasavana and Smith felt should be tested for price elasticity, wine stars which are so much more price sensitive should be left alone. Instead he feels they are best promoted through by-the-glass sales. 'Plowhorses', Barrows suggests are best promoted as 'recommended wines' on the menu to go with specific choices. Alternatively, a way to capitalize on the popularity of these wines is to offer them as half bottles, or even magnums, to capitalize on the fact that customers are clearly comfortable buying these wines, but may buy a different (and more profitable) bottle size to suit their circumstances. 'Puzzles' are difficult on wine lists in that they involve tying up money in stock but provide good returns when they are sold. These are often wines that are held for special occasions or for the prestige of keeping certain wines on a wine list. The precise remedy for these wines is dependent on the restaurant. Provided there are not too many of them, they may create the impression of a distinguished or superior wine list and in that sense they can confer cachet on the business. Some writers (for instance Shoemaker, 1994) suggest that they provide the role of 'decoy', drawing favourable attention to less expensive wines although this may lead to the overall impression of a costly wine list. A more honest approach is to review these wines, ensuring that their unpopularity is based on poor recognition among customers rather than high price or poor quality. For example, unusual grape varieties, producing regions and wine styles can all be off-putting to restaurant customers. Staff, particularly those with a responsibility for advising on wine choice, should then be well briefed on the wines and aware of the need to promote these. Finally, with regard to 'dogs' some suggest that these should be removed from the menu or list. Barrows (1996: 176) suggests that if these are the most expensive and exclusive wines they should be taken off the main list and put on 'the "Captain's List" which is a wine list made available to customers only upon special request'. Aside from the rather trite name suggested by Barrows, restaurant customers are now well enough acquainted with wine to be underwhelmed at the thought of choosing from a hallowed prestige wine list. If there are wines that are not popular and have no other redeeming features, it is probably best to remove them.

Service

Wine service is here used to mean the rather broader subject of wine marketing in restaurants. Yet this is not the case in much existing training practice in food and beverage management. Wine service has often meant simply that. Students and staff in training have been taught rigid, formal forms of wine service.

Textbooks describe the steps of presenting the bottle, opening, decanting, and presenting the wine to the host to taste and then pouring for each customer in turn. There are several issues here. First, little attention is paid to the process of helping customers choose suitable wines or other drinks to go with their meal. Some texts merely catalogue some well known wine producing nations and some of their better known wines, and then draw up a matrix showing so-called 'classic' food and wine combinations. The second issue is that the traditional, formalized approach to wine service that these texts or training courses describe is one that is widely disliked by customers. It is in that sense the very antithesis of a customer centred approach. Few customers know why they 'taste' the wine, what they are looking for when it is presented, and in what circumstances they may send the wine back. What is needed instead is an approach to wine and drinks service that is broader in its approach and less constrained by formal process.

Several researchers have suggested improvements. In his study Dodd (1997) shows that restaurant wine purchases were to a large degree impulse purchases. The most efficient way of increasing wine sales was through merchandising, particularly on the menu. Placing wines on the menu had a significant impact on total sales. Dodd (1997: 72) also speculated that suggesting specific wines with menu items could increase this effect still further, noting that:

> There may be several reasons for the increase in wine sales with the inclusion of wine on the menu. It is possible that the inclusion on the menu provided a stimulus in the environment that led to an increase in impulse purchases. Additionally, having the wine list already in front of the consumer may have reduced the need for information search.

The notion that providing a stimulus in the environment can increase wine sales has been further explored by Fattorini (1996). Borrowing from Campbell-Smith's (1967) *The Marketing of the Meal Experience* Fattorini suggests that a route to increased wine sales lies in addressing three themes used by Campbell-Smith: food and (more importantly) drink; service; and atmosphere. Each of these has to complement the other, in an integrated approach. Fattorini suggests that food and beverage managers can turn burgeoning interest in wine to their advantage. Rather than using the mystique of wine in attempts to charge a premium price, restaurants should provide a 'wine experience' that capitalizes on the consumer's interest. In terms of the drink itself, this means selecting more innovative and less well known wines for the wine list, and importantly wines that provide excellent matches for the food served. Alternatively, if particular beers, spirits, sake or other drinks suit the food better, then they are the more proper matches and must be listed. Service also means having staff that can be confident when talking about the wines and other drinks listed and advising customers. They must also be unobtrusive and unfussy in their wine service techniques. In less formal high street restaurants, pompous wine service is out of place and may well conflict with the restaurant's theme, and staff must be confident in providing a level of wine service that matches the restaurant's style. Finally, the 'wine experience' must consider atmosphere. Given widespread consumer interest in the wine trade, in some cases borrowing props from the trade could present an image of wine expertise and interest that give customers the confidence to spend more money. For instance, the retail trade has borrowed heavily from the props of wine manufacture with half barrels, cases, decorative or branded wine case ends and even replica whisky stills to give their shops the look of an 'oenological Disneyland' (Fattorini, 1994b). Where appropriate such an approach may reap dividends in the on-trade too.

Finally, service does not extend only to wine. Interestingly Dodd (1997: 71–72) notes that the results from his experimental study indicate:

> attempts to stimulate sales of a specific type of beverage will not carry over to all other beverages that the restaurant sells. However, it does appear that sales of these other beverages didn't decline because of the emphasis on wine. Consumers didn't seem to be making substitutes, they were just increasing their purchases of the product (wine) that was being promoted.

Outlets specializing in drinks other than wine have often pioneered innovative beverage service and marketing. Micro-breweries in the UK capitalize on the manufacturing of drink that takes place often only feet from diners. Many use glass partitions between the brewery and the restaurant so that diners can see the brewery at work and in some cases design the restaurant/brewery building to maximize consumer contact with the brewery.

Where several beers are made on site, tasting 'paddles' are often used. These look rather like a large table tennis bat with 4–6 holes drilled through to hold 1/3rd pint samples of all the beers. Alternatively tasting mats are used to allow the customer to try each one and read tasting notes printed on the mats. These can prove very effective in promoting additional purchases. Also because of customers' unfamiliarity with for instance 6 1/3rd pints (only 2 pints in total) a premium price can be charged for the tasting selection.

Similarly, coffee service has developed a great deal in recent years. Many textbooks go no further than suggesting names for Irish style coffees with different spirits added. Coffee suppliers will often supply equipment to make Italian coffee on many different bases and some even provide training on the use and service of different Italian coffee styles. Similar examples of innovation in drinks service can be found in outlets serving sake, (warmed by specialist equipment or chilled) to accompany fusion dishes, or even spirits.

Product knowledge

Product knowledge for the restaurant sector has until recently been little more than an extension of the product knowledge taught to the off-trade. Even in off-trade merchants the relevance of some of what is taught to sales staff has to be questioned. The main provider of much wine and drinks training (either formally through their courses or informally through in-house training that borrows from them) is the Wine and Spirit Education Trust (WSET). The WSET examinations, the basic certificate, slightly more challenging higher certificate and demanding diploma, have been the benchmark of UK wine and spirits education for some time. However these examinations were designed to teach the trade, not the restaurant sector and are consequently ill-suited to many in the restaurant business.

The courses often concentrate on the variables of production, soil, grape types, climate, production methods and so on. But this is of limited, if any, use in a restaurant where the pertinent information is whether the wine goes with the food. The courses are also comprehensive. This is very useful to the wine trade where even the most basic shop may have several hundred lines and may extend to several thousand. Restaurant wine knowledge however needs depth on a limited range of products. Finally, the courses, perhaps by historical accident, perhaps because of the interests of the course designers, often stray into areas that even the most knowledgeable wine merchant could put to little use. Vine pests and diseases are undoubtedly a very important topic for wine makers, but they are a subject of limited use for restaurant waiting staff for whom certain types of customer perhaps require a different kind of pest control! Yet several general food and beverage management texts contain sections on the effects and cures of mites and fungal growths.

This begs the question, what knowledge should staff have? One strategy that has been introduced into the training courses of the Scottish Chefs' Society has been to treat wine as just another ingredient. Each wine has certain qualities that make it suitable to be used in a particular context and the chef and waiting staff should understand these. But superfluous knowledge takes time to learn and the staff has little motivation to apply themselves to this learning because they cannot see the point. This is demotivating and pointless and is thus left out. Waiting staff in particular should spend time applying themselves to learning things that might help them sell wines better. One strategy suggested by Fattorini (1997) is that staff learn narratives about the wines on their lists. Discussions with wine merchants and producers often reveal that the best selling wines are those with a story attached to them. For instance, narratives about wines may include historical associations, associations with famous personalities, or associating wines with particular emotions or experiences. Piper Heidsieck Champagne often point out that their wine was a great favourite of Marilyn Monroe and is served at several film awards ceremonies, associating the wine with the glamour of the movies. Customers, who cannot taste the wine to confirm they like it until they have bought it, take the wine on trust, on the basis that film moguls and stars would be unlikely to favour a poor wine. It also confirms the wine's status as a premium product, giving the customer the confidence to spend more money.

The most important factor in staff product knowledge is that it should move away from the thinly spread, comprehensive approach necessary for those who work in the off-trade, to a focused, in-depth approach that concentrates exclusively on the wines that are carried by the restaurant. This allows the staff the knowledge to sell wines well enough to give the customer confidence to spend their money. The process also works the other way too. As will be discussed shortly, consumers have never been so well informed about the wines they know about and enjoy. To give staff the confidence to sell to well-informed customers, staff need to feel they are masters of their own wine list but without having to devote several years of hard learning to the task. An approach to product knowledge based on the needs of the restaurants in which they work helps to achieve this.

What does the beverage consumer want?

In asserting that customers in restaurants are better informed about drinks than ever before, it is necessary to establish whether such a broad statement stands up to scrutiny. In particular, it would be useful to know whether customers' increased knowledge of wines and drinks has a material impact on what they want from beverages in restaurants.

The archetypal knowledgeable drink consumer in the popular imagination in the UK is the so-called 'wine snob'. This sorry character has provided hours of easy laughs for (both professional and amateur) comedians for many years. Yet there is a paradoxical attitude to wine knowledge in the UK and other countries because in certain circumstances considerable wine knowledge is highly regarded. In the cinema, wine knowledge in the hands of James Bond is used as shorthand for sophistication and suave confidence, and on at least one occasion saves the secret agent's life. At the very least this suggests that the simple characterization of two groups, the wine buffs who know a great deal about wine and are 'snobs', and the rest of us, is at best a caricature. Consumer attitudes to drink of all kinds *are* more complex, and the beverage management of a restaurant can have a significant impact on how consumers perceive the outlet, and thus upon their behaviour. We can explore this issue under five headings as follows.

The 'professional consumer'

Fattorini (1994a, 1994b) explores the notion of 'professional customers', defined as those who work in middle-class, professional occupations, but who are keen to associate themselves with the wine and restaurant trades. Suggesting, 'these consumers wish to be seen to have affiliations with a business they perceive as romantic and glamorous whilst retaining the security of their other life' (1994b, 7) Fattorini notes that media representations of chefs and hospitality entrepreneurs frequently appeal to the lack of creativity and self determination in their own work. For the British middle class (and this is undoubtedly the social group to whom these comments apply), the wine trade is particularly highly regarded. The nature of wine trade work ensures that its members are knowledgeable about wine (itself a desirable social trait), and work with it everyday. It has long been considered the 'acceptable trade' (not least among academically poor public school boys) and popular images of the trade suggest long buying trips to middle-class holiday destinations such as France and Tuscany. Fattorini (1994a) expands on this theme and explores ways in which media representations of work in the hotel and catering trades encourages the belief that work within the hospitality industry is a middle-class paradise.

One indication of the desire of so many to be associated with the wine trade is the increasing numbers keen to take the trade's examinations. The Wine and Spirit Education Trust's basic certificate and higher certificate examinations have long been studied by those with an amateur as well as professional interest in wine. But the Trust's challenging two-year diploma has been designed particularly for those in 'a managerial position or (who) may be under consideration for promotion to such a position' (Wine and Spirit Education Trust, 1998) within the wine trade, as recommended by the Trust's prospectus. Yet very large numbers of amateur enthusiasts also take this demanding examination each year, in some cases with the majority of candidates coming from outside the trade.

Such consumer enthusiasm is to be applauded, but undoubtedly this interest, albeit among a small, if keen, group of restaurant goers, must have implications for restaurant staff. One consequence noted by Fattorini (1994b) was that some professional pride in achieving this prestigious qualification might be diluted by the recognition that a significant minority of ordinary consumers also achieved the accolade merely as a hobby. To remedy this managers must work hard to ensure that all staff feel they are in command of their own wine list. This may be through tastings, opportunities to learn more about the wines carried, or most importantly, an emphasis during in-house training on the wines and other drinks carried by the restaurant, not on wines and other drinks in general.

A more important consideration for the food and beverage manager is how this extensive knowledge among some consumers can be harnessed to the restaurant's advantage. Wine consumers keen enough to take a couple of months of night classes let alone a two-year diploma have to enjoy their hobby very much. Some, many even, can become bores. Staff must feel able to 'converse with the inner bore' when consumers want to discuss the restaurant wine list. They must feel confident in talking about all the drinks carried. By engaging the consumer's interest they will find opportunities to suggest additional drinks such as pudding wines and aperitifs and to recommend more expensive bottles.

The 'media educated'

While they may be significant in terms of the numbers taking the examinations of the WSET, those consumers keen enough to take wine classes remains a relatively small proportion of total restaurant goers. But whilst the 'ordinary' restaurant customer may feel that they do not have an extensive wine knowledge, it is larger now than ever before. Food, cookery and wine all feature heavily on television and radio schedules as well as in newspapers and magazines. There are also a considerable number of books aimed specifically at non-expert wine consumers. As a result it is almost impossible to avoid learning something about food and wine just by reading the paper and watching a little television. These features are also quick to pick up on new trends, and beer, sake, spirits, fortified wines and drinks like coffee and tea have all received extensive coverage in the media in recent years. As a consequence, restaurants must presume that even those least motivated to learn more about drink will have at least some knowledge of the subject. The practical use of this knowledge is limited, however, and consumers who may recognize names or grape varieties will still need help to make the best choice of drink.

The influence of retailing

The practical use of knowledge picked up from media features may be limited, but one other source of information can prove very troublesome for restaurateurs. In post-war Britain many people only drank wine in restaurants. But today many millions purchase wine to drink at home every day, and as a consequence have become aware of the brands, styles and more importantly the prices of the wine they buy.

This causes problems for restaurateurs when customers recognize wines on a list that they have enjoyed at home, only to discover they are several times more expensive in the restaurant. The wines they recognize need not be exactly the same brand either. There are certain expectations about how much basic Chablis, Chianti or Australian Chardonnay should cost, so that irrespective of the brand, customers feel that they are being 'ripped off' by restaurants. There is perhaps no solution to this problem. Restaurateurs' protestations about the economics of running a restaurant cut little ice with sceptical customers. As far as they are concerned they have paid ten or fifteen pounds to have someone pull a bottle off a shelf and take out the cork.

Pressure from consumers may become more intense on this matter in years to come. But clever food and beverage managers and restaurateurs may find some help from selling other drinks. Customers are less aware of the 'right' price for a bottle of sake. Premium beers from unknown breweries if properly sold can earn a significant margin. Coffee and speciality teas are not only staggeringly popular, but also staggeringly profitable for those who sell them well. But these recommendations come with a caveat.

The quality aware consumer

The preceding remarks should not be interpreted as meaning simply that great margins can be earned by selling overpriced sake, beer and soft drinks to customers. They do not. Consumers will pay a significant premium for quality, and they are increasingly adept at grading quality for themselves.

The success of coffee shops in the UK in the late 1990s has not been because there was nowhere that served coffee before. They have been successful because they have provided a high quality product in an innovative manner, and in fashionable surroundings. The same will be true for those who maintain significant margins on the drink products sold in restaurants. Wine by the glass can no longer be from a three-day-old bottle of house red at the back of the fridge if it is to keep customers happy. An interesting selection, kept fresh by modern technology and served by knowledgeable staff is what customers have come to expect. Coffee should be properly made using the correct equipment with trained staff. Restaurants that claim 'an extensive selection of whiskies' must have more on offer than the half-drained connoisseurs' selection on a plastic stand provided by the wholesaler. To convince customers to buy pudding wines will need more than a tired old Vin Doux Naturel on the list for several pounds a glass.

The 'semiotically aware' customer

The unfortunate title of this last section indicates simply that customers feel they know what drinks mean. In that sense the wine snob has not disappeared, they have simply become more widespread and their snobbery takes a different, subtler form. Such a shift has been hinted at in several forms by a number of writers. Barr (1988) suggests that a new snobbery of 'lightness' in drinks had replaced the earlier snobbery of knowledge or brand. In the late 1990s the snobbery is more complex and driven by awareness and a desire for quality products.

But how does this desire for quality permeate even the mundane purchase of drinks? A number of writers and commentators have suggested the rise of an 'experience' lifestyle over the previously dominant 'acquisition' lifestyle. Now, rather than owning a prestigious brand of car or watch, consumers want to be able to collect experiences: a trip to Bali; driving a tank; bungee jumping; or a weekend at a health spa. The suggestion is that this 'experience' lifestyle permeates down to the everyday. To eat at the best restaurants, drink interesting or rare wines, have an interesting flavoured latte at lunch. The evidence is mixed but encouraging. During a recent promotion, Oddbins, a major UK wine retailer, stocked a series of beers, described by the buyer as 'beers for wine lovers'. They were marketed as limited availability stock that had been bought only after much haggling by the buying team. Although tasty they were not significantly different from many widely available brands. However, they sold far better than their everyday counterparts on the basis of their limited availability. Customers appeared to be motivated by the idea that there was only a limited time that they would have the opportunity to enjoy these prestigious, if cheap (less than £2.00) products.

It was important for these consumers to have enjoyed these drinks, or served them to their friends, because it demonstrated that they 'had their finger on the pulse' of contemporary beers. In this small way they had collected an experience that demonstrated who they were and in a small way what they valued. This is a similar process to that of those who bought certain brands in order to demonstrate something about their personality.

How do we satisfy the new beverage consumer?

A crude (true-life) example demonstrates how some of the discussion above can be put into practise in a food and beverage environment. At an (unnamed) restaurant, a clerical error led to twelve cases of an expensive red Burgundy being delivered rather than one – far more than the restaurant might sell in a year. Rather than attempt to send the wine back the *sommelier* tested his selling skills. Whenever there was a table where the food chosen would have been a good match for the wine and the customers appeared open to suggestions, he recommended this wine, on the basis that it was 'like driving an Aston Martin for an hour'. The twelve cases were sold in a month.

Modern restaurant customers are no fools when it comes to drinks of all kinds. In the example above, many asked questions about the vineyard, producer and wine style, all of which the *sommelier* could answer. But consumers are not coldly objective either. They like to be associated with desirable experiences and products just as much as any previous generation, only often in more subtle ways. They may seek these associations through inverse snobbery – going for the little known artisan producer, rather than the big brand or a pint of beer rather than wine. They may seek such associations through coffee, tea, or spirits that in the past have always been commodity drinks, not usually known for connoisseurship. In such an environment beverage management can be crucial in ensuring a restaurant remains competitive. By dismissing it as frivolous wine tasting and the preserve of the resident wine buff, restaurants run the risk of failing to anticipate and satisfy consumer needs. Hopefully, those who practice, teach and train in this area will continue to recognize its growing importance.

References

Barr, A. (1988) *Wine Snobbery: An Insider's Guide to the Booze Business*, London: Faber and Faber.

Barrows, C. W. (1996) Evaluating the Profit Potential of Restaurant Wine Lists, *Journal of Restaurant and Foodservice Marketing*, 1(3/4): 161–177.

Buttle, F. (1986) *Hotel and Food Service Marketing: A Managerial Approach*, London: Cassell.

Campbell-Smith, G. (1967) *The Marketing of the Meal Experience: A Fundamental Approach*, London: University of Surrey.

Davis, B. and Stone, S. (1991) *Food and Beverage Management*, Oxford: Butterworth-Heinemann.

Dodd, T. H. (1997) Techniques to Increase Impulse Wine Purchases in a Restaurant Setting, *Journal of Restaurant and Foodservice Marketing*, 2(1): 63–73.

Durkan, A. and Cousins, J. (1995) *The Beverage Book*, London: Hodder and Stoughton.

Fattorini, J. E. (1994a) Food Journalism: A Medium For Conflict, *British Food Journal*, 96(10): 24–28.

Fattorini, J. E. (1994b) Professional Consumers: Themes in High Street Wine Marketing, *International Journal of Wine Marketing*, 6(2): 5–13.

Fattorini, J. E. (1996) The Marketing of the Wine Experience: An Innovative Approach, *Proceedings of the International Conference on Culinary Arts and Sciences (ICAAs) 1996*, University of Bournemouth, 1102–1112.

Fattorini, J. E. (1997) *Managing Wine and Wine Sales*, London: International Thomson Business Press.

Kasavana, M. L. and Smith, D. I. (1982) *Menu Engineering*, Lansing, MI: Hospitality Publications.

Lillicrap, D. R. and Cousins, J. A. (1990) *Food and Beverage Service*, London: Hodder and Stoughton.

Shoemaker, S. (1994) A Proposal to Improve the Overall Price Value Perception of a Product Line, *Journal of Restaurant and Foodservice Marketing*, 1(1): 98–101.

Wine and Spirit Education Trust (1998) *Annual Prospectus*, London: WSET.

What are the implications of tourism destination identity for food and beverage policy? Culture and cuisine in a changing global marketplace

Michael J. Riley

Introduction

In a sense, the menu is the beginning, middle and end of the restaurant business: image, marketing quality and production all stem from its composition. In creating a menu or a set of menus, food and beverage managers and chefs rarely start with a blank sheet of paper. For one thing, the concept of the restaurant itself, whether it be stand alone or within a hotel, implies a style of menu. Whilst the creative process remains relatively open to the knowledge and inspiration of management and chef, their thinking can rarely be immune from the influence of the context in which they operate. Menus are there to attract customers and to satisfy their needs and expectations, and best-guessing these needs and expectations is a key success factor. Best-guessing might of course involve serious market research which, at the very least, should answer the primary question, 'who is going to eat here?'. If the answer is 'tourists', then the food and beverage strategy may have to accommodate, and perhaps complement, the region's tourism strategy, the rationale being, simply, that the antecedent expectations of tourists may be influenced by a number of sources related to tourism and to 'being' a tourist. These could include the role which food plays in the image of the hotel; the identity of the destination, region or country; and in the selection criteria of the destination. However, this could be problematic because tourists are unlikely always to be the sole customers. There is also the local population.

The question of whether food and beverage policy has a single or dual focus is a strategic issue. If it comes down to appealing to both tourists and the local population then issues of the food and beverage concept, marketing, and pricing have to take cognisance of divergence of taste and expectation between those of the indigenous population and those of the tourists. The key issues here are the distinct possibility that tourists and locals will have different frameworks for evaluation of the food and perhaps more importantly, different concepts of value for money. Evaluation, appreciation and value for money are culturally determined. Furthermore, any strategy has to also consider how to be competitive through differentiation between establishments in the market. The demands of appealing to a dual market and the demands of competition may not always be easily reconciled. On the one hand, the hegemony of tourism may demand a convergence of menu types in conformance with the destination image but, on the other hand, the demands of competition may push for divergence in the marketplace. In strategic terms there is a friction between the need to differentiate in the local market and the need to conform to expectations encouraged by tourism images.

The purpose here is to explore the relationship between the concept of 'national cuisine' and tourism in order to develop a framework by which their mutual influence can be understood. One of the consequences of the growth of tourism is that it has led to tastes becoming mobile across national boundaries. Tourism has acted as an engine of cultural dispersion. One way to look at this process is to see it as the globalization of national cuisine and to see the hybrid phenomenon 'international cuisine' as the early expression of this isomorphism. The trouble with this proposition is that it could be accused of carrying pejorative undertones in that it pits cuisine, as an attribute of indigenous culture (and therefore good) against wicked mass tourism with its powers of cultural dispersion and dilution. This type of argument is not helpful. The tourism-environment debate, for example, has, to an extent, and to the detriment of the real issues, fallen into this trap. The arguments which follow make no value judgements about tourism or cuisine but attempt to devise a framework in which some of the pragmatic issues can be addressed. In passing, it is worth noting that the extensive sociological literature on food is not helpful. Studies of the connections between food, culture and tourism are conspicuous by their absence (Reynolds, 1995). Similarly, the tourism literature relegates food and cuisine to a minor role in tourism development despite its commercial value (Riley and Davis, 1992). The literature notwithstanding, the issues that lie at the heart of the tourism-cuisine relationship are, first, a concern with the place of cuisine in social culture and the associated issue of whether or not this matters to tourism marketing; second, the nature of the adaptation processes caused by tourism importing and exporting tastes; and third, on what basis is cuisine evaluated?

Logically the first stage of connecting cuisine to tourism in any country is to establish whether food and eating is part of national culture. If it is a cultural entity, then it follows that like any other cultural entity it is subject to adaptation processes. However, even if food and eating is part of national culture, it does not follow automatically that it will be a conspicuous or prominent part and therefore the second stage would be to connect food and eating to national identity. If it can be so connected then it is possible for it to play a role in the tourism destination image of the country. It then comes within the range of tourism marketing. A quite distinct consideration here is the case of international cuisine. Accepting the existence of such an entity raises questions as to its role. Is it an output of the relationship between national cuisine and tourism or an intervening concept it its own right? To take cuisine first into culture and then into tourism destination image whilst simultaneously establishing the role of international cuisine requires connecting three sets of argument. The first concerns the cultural analysis of cuisine, that is, its relationship to national culture. The second concerns the processes of adaptation that social cultures and cuisine go through, and the third concerns the role of marketing in the adaptation process.

How national is national cuisine?

The nature of 'national' cuisine is a curious one. It is maintained by a dependence on home grown foods, a reputational process which is reinforced by the media, the degree of association with national culture, and is subject to a process of adaptation which produces a degree of divergence and convergence within the national cuisine.

Home produce

To an extent, despite modern advances in food distribution, agriculture dictates that every country should have a set of specific foods which are native to that country. They may even be unique. However, even allowing for the power of agricultural science, advances in food distribution and changes in food economics to alter the ethnocentric properties of food, it is still possible for a country 'to be famous for' a particular food even if it is widely available elsewhere.

The degree to which cuisine is embedded in national culture

Within the sociology of food literature two themes suggest that food is linked to social culture. The first relates food and eating to social relationships (Visser, 1981; Finkelstein, 1989, Wood, 1995). The second establishes food as a reflection of the distribution of power within social structures (Mennell, 1985). However, establishing a role for food in personal relationships and social structures is not a sufficient argument to place food at the centre of national culture. To do that it is necessary to prove a degree of embeddedness. It would be appropriate at this point to consider the nature of culture. The distinction made by Pierce (1991) between a behavioural contingency and a cultural contingency is crucial to our understanding of culture. Whilst a piece of behaviour may take place very often, involve a network of people, and be reproducible by other networks who do not know each other, the meaning of that behaviour does not go beyond the activity itself. A cultural practice, however, contains and represents 'meta-contingencies' that is, behavioural characteristics and activities that have a social meaning greater than the practice itself and which, by their nature, reinforce the culture which houses them. Celebrating birthdays is a cultural practice not because everybody does it but because it has a religious meaning. Contrast this with the practice in Britain of celebrating 'Guy Fawkes' Night'. It is essentially an excuse for a good time but if fireworks were banned, the occasion would probably gradually die away altogether or might end up as a cult in California! A smaller scale example might be more useful. In the British context, compare drinking in pubs with eating fish and chips. Both are common practices yet the former reflects something of the social fabric of the country, particularly family, gender, class and age relationships whilst the latter is just a national habit. In other words, a constant, widely practised pattern of behaviour is not necessarily cultural. However, it is also clear that a cultural practice needs behavioural reinforcement.

Social culture is not immortal

Finkelstein (1989) argues that 'dining out' is simply action which supports a surface life (see Chapter 3). For her it is the word 'out' that disconnects food from culture. This view of culture and food places the 'home' as the cultural centre. Continental European eating habits may contradict this notion by their general acceptance of eating out as part of family life. Following the principle that culture needs behavioural reinforcement, if every-one 'eats out' on a regular basis, irrespective of social and economic differentiation, then this might constitute behavioural support for cuisine being part of social culture. That aside, the significance of a behavioural practice being embedded in culture is that it naturally maintains an approved and accepted way of life and therefore has a tendency to resist change.

The thrust of the argument is that countries differ in the degree to which their food and eating habits have a social and cultural meaning beyond the behaviour itself. This argument, however, could be interpreted to imply that the country with the greatest proportion of meals taken outside the home would be the one in which the national cuisine is more embedded in social culture. This is a difficult position to maintain because it would bring America, with its fast-food culture, to the fore. The fast-food culture of America raises the issue of whether there are qualitative criteria for the concept of cuisine. The key issue is not the extent of the common behaviour but whether or not it has a function in maintaining social cohesion and is appreciated and valued through social norms. French cuisine and 'going down the pub' are strange bedfellows but bedfellows nevertheless.

How homogeneous is national cuisine?

Like language, cuisine is not a static entity and whilst its fundamental character is unlikely to change in the short run it may evolve in different directions. Just as in a language there are dialects so in a cuisine there are variations. The two principal sources of diversity are the physical geography of the country and its social diversity.

The geographical dimensions work through agriculture to particularize and to limit locally produced ingredients. Ethnic diversity in the population works through the role of cuisine in social identity to create ethnically distinct cuisine which may not converge into a national cuisine. This raises the question of how far a national cuisine is related to national borders. To an ethnic group their cuisine is national. The greater the division of a society into classes, castes and status groups with their attendant ethnocentric properties, of which cuisine is a part, then the greater will be the diversity of the cuisine.

However, there is a case for convergence. Both these principal sources of diversity are, to an extent, influenced by the strength of their boundaries and the willingness of society to erode them. It is a question of isolation and integration. Efficient transport and the application of chemistry can alter the agricultural boundaries to make a wider range of foods available to a cuisine. Similarly, political and social integration can erode ethnic boundaries. However, all these arguments mean nothing if the cuisine is not embedded in social culture. Riley (1994) argues that when a cuisine is not embedded in social culture it is susceptible to novelty and invasion by other cuisine.

How global is cuisine?

Whether or not there is such a thing as 'international cuisine' it is undoubtedly true that there are certain dishes and drinks which are mobile across national borders. International tourism is the vehicle for this cultural dispersion. The mode of this dispersion comes in two forms which are, on the one hand, the actual exporting of units of national cuisine and culture for example, English pubs abroad, or the assimilation of national cuisine into a hybrid 'international' one. This hybrid has evolved through the practices of hotel food and beverage managers and marketing managers who have created a set of dishes which appear safe and reassuring to travellers. In character they tend to typify national cuisine.

This hybrid entity has a technical dimension. There is the question of how national cuisine accommodated the demands of international cuisine. Whilst it is reasonable to imagine that national and regional cuisines share technical continuity, this may not be so with national and international cuisine. There are implications here for the training of cooks. However the important questions in connecting cuisine to tourism lie more on the demand side than the supply side. The comparative merits of the unknown, and therefore less safe, national cuisine and the known and therefore safer, international cuisine intervene in the role cuisine plays in the attractiveness of the tourism destination. It cannot be assumed, as some of the literature on sustainability would argue, that tourists are interested in authenticity in cuisine (Reynolds, 1993). If this is the case and the tourist is attracted by the traditional, but to them, new and unknown, then to foster international cuisine could be a case of killing the goose. On the other hand, a degree of safety may be the very impetus to travel in the first place. In these terms international cuisine, like all inclusive packages, makes perfect sense. The third argument would be that international cuisine is a transition mechanism taking people from the familiar to the unfamiliar.

Evaluation and marketing

It has been suggested that logically the connection between a national cuisine and tourism is based on the degree to which the cuisine forms part of social culture and is therefore part of national identity. Tourism marketing can, in such circumstances, use cuisine as a destination attraction. However, there is no reason why cuisine should not be exploited irrespective of its place in national culture. Cuisine may be dragged into service in the pursuit of added value. If cuisine is used in tourism marketing then it could be expected that that would influence the evaluation process through the creation of expectations (Man-fredo, Bright and Haas, 1995). However, it could be argued that it is impossible to escape from the embeddedness argument precisely because of evaluation processes. If a cuisine is part of local culture, the critical reception of performance will be by consensual standards. People who are not part of that culture, say, tourists, will not share the indigenous population's schema for appreciating the cuisine. It is then most likely that tourists will have to use some other form of comparison. The usual suspects as points of reference would be the tourist's own national cuisine and/or the expectations created by marketing. However, the alternative to both is to relate their experiences of the cuisine to value for money. When circumstances exist in which a cuisine is evaluated locally by quality standards imbued by culture, but is at the same time being judged by tourists through value for money, a tension is created which can only be resolved by change. This little tension between social culture and tourism represents the wider argument about the globalization process. That process would clearly benefit from the hegemony of value for money over other evaluative criteria.

References

Finkelstein J. (1989) *Dining Out: A Sociology of Modern Manners*, Oxford: Polity.

Manfredo, M. J., Bright A. B., and Haas, G. E. (1995) Research in Tourism Advertising, in M. Manfredo (Ed) *Influencing Human Behavior*, Illinois: Sagamore Publishing, 327–368.

Mennell, S. (1985) *All Manners of Food; Eating and Taste in England and France from the Middle Ages to the Present*, Oxford: Blackwell.

Pierce, D. (1991) Culture and society: the role of behavioural analysis, in P. Lamal (Ed) *Behavioural Analysis of Societies and Cultural Practices*. London: Hemisphere, 13–34.

Reynolds, P. C. (1993) Food and tourism: towards an understanding of sustainable culture, *Journal of Sustainable Tourism*, **1**(1): 48–54.

Reynolds, P. (1995) Culinary heritage in the face of tourism, in C. Cooper (Ed) *Progress in Tourism, Recreation and Hospitality Management, Vol 6*, London: Bellhaven Press, 189–196.

Riley, M. (1994) Marketing eating out: the influence of social culture and innovation, *British Food Journal*: **96**(10): 15–19.

Riley, M. and Davis, E. (1992) Development and innovation: the case of food and beverage management in hotels, in C. Cooper (Ed) *Progress in Tourism, Recreation and Hospitality Management, Vol 4*, London: Belhaven Press, 201–208.

Visser, M. (1981) *The Rituals of Dinner*, London: Penguin.

Wood, R. C. (1995) *The Sociology of the Meal*, Edinburgh: Edinburgh University Press.

CHAPTER 14

Are restaurant dress codes in decline? The ever-changing nature of food snobbery

Matthew J. Alexander and Erwin Losekoot

Introduction

Like the poor, the many snobberies attendant upon food and eating are always with us. Talking or writing about snobbery in any explicit manner is, for many, a dubious social practice in its own right. Little has been written on food snobbery (but see Wood, 1996). A 'snob' is defined (in the Oxford Quick Reference Dictionary, 1998) as a 'person who despises those inferior in social position, wealth, intellect, taste, etc.'. The 'etc.' is tantalizing, as is the revelation that the origin of the term is, officially, 'unknown'. The use of the term 'despises' is also strong stuff. When we hear from time to time of the 'politics of envy', it is usually in the context of the more disadvantaged expressing concern about the privileges of the more advantaged. Some of the former undoubtedly despise the latter: the majority are probably more simply outraged. Snobbery does not exist solely between broad social groups or classes, but also within such groups (Veblen, 1899; Bourdieu, 1984). Nor is snobbery simply about individual or group dispositions towards others. Snobbery is about actively constructing beliefs, perceptions, views and tastes that differentiate one group from another. These beliefs, perceptions, views and tastes all point in the same direction of distinction – they are designed to reinforce a sense of social and cultural superiority. It is logically inevitable therefore that such 'refinements' are wholly artificial and can be sustained only for so long as there is complicity on the part of those intended to be excluded that any mark of distinction is indeed just that.

Food snobbery

Food markets – and notably eating-out markets – are mass markets. This is an inescapable feature of food production and provision and the presence of niche markets – for *haute cuisine* or specialist dining – does not undermine the mass market but rather emphasizes its ubiquitousness. As noted briefly above, this is clearly reflected in food commentary where the mass market is referred to for the most part only to criticize it. For much of 1995, the broadsheet press took an unedifying pleasure in the trial of the two defendants in the McDonald's libel case. The fast-food giant had taken exception to certain allegations made by the defendants about the quality of the firm's products and practices. The main aim of food commentators is to deride and denigrate popular taste except where the 'popular' suggests other useful culinary or societal myths such as the sanctity of the family and family well-being (as in certain magazines where food commentary tends to be of the 'recipe' kind and is directed towards women who 'have' to cater for the jaded tastes of their spouse and children) and the ideas of health, naturalness and the rediscovery of forgotten tastes (a popular leitmotif throughout the 1980s and 1990s).

The mass market is, however, small fry compared to the battle for good taste that rages at the 'élite' end of the food commentary market. Here, there have been some interesting developments of late. From a reading of any food journalist's output during the 1980s and early 1990s it would have been possible to derive an impression of a social cadre at peace with itself. Every development in whatever passed for *nouvelle cuisine* was recorded. Chef-gurus were cultivated and like so many serial killers, profiled (in that dreadful journalistic misuse of the word). Restaurants where an 'average' dinner for two cost £140 (with wine) were reviewed, as were the pitiful outpourings of those chef superstars whose managers and PR agents, complicit with an adoring press, managed to con(vince) certain sectors of the book buying public that possession of a text of artistic photographs and elegantly presented recipes that parodied food would place them among the culinary cognoscenti (see also Chapter 10). Within this fantasy world, food journalists performed a promotional task but also the task of charting the vicissitudes of reputations – of restaurateurs, of chefs, of other food commentators. A cosy inclusivity of that to be considered worthwhile was established and indeed was reinforced by the growth of food commentary itself, for example in the so-called Oxford Symposia which, led among others by the estimable Alan Davidson, produced a small journal (*Petit Propos Culinaires*) and annual symposium proceedings. Such a phenomenon as the creation of a Guild (sic!) of Food Writers who awarded an annual prize sponsored by Glenfiddich confirmed the practice of food writing as a somewhat schizoid craft, torn between bourgeois gentility and the crass practices of journalism. This self-confidence spurred food commentators to ever greater and more stylized excesses.

Excess, though, is always dangerous, and invites a backlash. In the 1990s, a new and almost strident style of food commentary has developed. With varying degrees of explicitness, it has represented the predominant style of food writing as vulgar – and by extension the culinary practices of the last decade or so as similarly tasteless. These attacks have come in various forms. Take the journalistic response to the 1994 *Good Hotel Guide*. Nicholson-Lord (1994: 5) notes that the Guide criticized 'pretentious, "over the top" menus' and writes more generally that 'Some British hotels are too sophisticated for their own good, according to the latest issue of the *Good Hotel Guide* . . . They are catering too much for gourmets and "foodies" and not enough for people with more simple tastes.' As examples, Nicholson-Lord quotes the Guide's identification of a £29.50 dinner menu from an expensive country house hotel which included:

- a rich liver parfait with a seed mustard crust, laid on a port and redcurrant coulis and accompanied by toasted brioche;
- slivers of smoked beef laid on salad leaves mixed with mango and cashew nuts served with a blue cheese dressing;
- breast of corn-fed chicken laid on buttered leaf spinach with a Dijon mustard sauce and wild mushrooms.

In a more direct attack on food snobbery, Jane Jakeman (1994: 19) argues precisely that dinner party culture is moribund but persists because of the illusion of family life it creates, and because of snobbery. The family meal, she argues, is an oppression 'that forces us all to consume the same kind of food in the same way at the same time, regardless of differences in appetite, digestion and taste'. Despite its persistence, she argues, the meal is under attack as most people revert to the human 'norm' of grazing and snacking (see Chapter 2 for a critique of this view). She suggests that the purchase of street food is heir to our eating history and that the private dinner is a seventeenth century creation growing out of the bourgeois family house and protestant concept of family government which 'saw the dinner table as a battleground for discipline and a means of enforcing codes of behaviour' – thus servants and children, with no rights, were excluded; and women's inferior status was signalled by their leaving before the port.

Turning to the present, Jakeman argues that 'In the same way that the literary world ostracizes the popular novel, thereby ignoring the reality of what most people actually read, food writers ignore the reality of what they eat'. She goes on:

> Perhaps a sense of impending doom has stimulated the desperate search for novelty . . . and the gastronomic tourism in which we indulge. It is significant that the very societies whose dishes are extolled most by British food writers are the keenest to embrace the new go-as-you-please food culture. Where do Italians go to eat? Not those trendy little places . . . sought out by affluent middle classes . . . from northern climes . . . [but] . . . in nightclubs or steakhouses, or, glory of glories, the marble-panelled McDonald's that are now the focus of youth and style in most Italian cities.

The same is true, she says, in Spain and, to a degree, France. But, she writes:

> . . . the British middle classes abroad never notice what the locals are really eating. They construct in their minds an entirely fictitious diet of mouth-watering Mediterranean delights based on the myth of foreign food as regularly presented to them in the foodie press.

Jakeman argues that dinner table culture at home and abroad is important to social classes A and B because like other aspects of culture it provides a vocabulary for asserting superiority over the lower social orders. To reinforce their own values, the middle classes reserve their real loathing and disgust for lower-class Britons openly enjoying themselves, 'Having cheeseburgers and fries in the land of olive oil! How crude and tasteless! Look, there's someone eating chips and tomato sauce – ooh, aren't they fat and flabby! And there's someone over there who can't understand a menu in French!'. Jakeman concludes that for the middle classes 'food remains either a symbol of a totally phoney past devoted to a mythic warm family life, or else a vital part of the semiotics of snobbery . . .'.

The point that Jakeman misses is that food commentary in the 'quality' press – both newspapers and magazines – almost entirely involves the commentators talking to themselves. The vast majority of food writers write about what is of interest to only a minority (including themselves) thus actively and consciously distorting public discourse on food. There is something distasteful about the choices made by food writers in respect of what they write about, as well as the journalistic system that supports such choices. Thus it is that the interests of a tiny élite can be expressed almost side by side with reports of third-world famine and its consequences. As thousands die of starvation (as reported in the newspapers' international sections) the food pages are full of reviews of expensive *nouvelle cuisine* restaurants, notifications of exotic ingredients and their potential use, and commentaries on five-star chefs with Napoleon complexes. Like most forms of snobbery, food snobbery and its articulation by food commentators involves a pernicious and grotesque distortion of reality, in this case the reality of the mass food markets of the developed world and the mass starvation that is to be found in so many parts of the less developed world. Snobbery is also, of course, almost entirely concerned with the trivial, for it is the trivial niceties of social behaviour that, when codified, serve to act as a form of social differentiation.

Dress codes

One of the most interesting areas for the study of snobbery in food and beverage operations lies in the area of restaurant dress codes. A periodic preoccupation of the hospitality trade press (the UK's leading organ, *Caterer and Hotelkeeper*, has published at least two reports in the last decade, see Jones, 1992 and Webster and Fox, 1996) the imposition of dress codes by restaurants (and indeed hotels) is still common in the UK and elsewhere and brochures for certain types of holiday (especially cruises) offer gentle reminders of the need to pack evening dress for formal dinners. Furthermore, many banquets and other special meals still specify dress requirements and these are frequently couched in gender-specific language – for example, black tie, white tie, lounge suit. Occasionally female attire is additionally specified (e.g. 'Ladies – cocktail dress') but otherwise invitees who are female are intended to read the dress code and extrapolate. The Chancellor of the Exchequer, Gordon Brown, caused a stir in 1997 when he refused to wear evening dress to the annual Lord Mayor's Banquet.

The message of all this is not just that certain dress codes still matter, but that they are both sexist and, to use the wretched terminology of the political left, classist, that is, cultural assumptions are made about an understanding of clothing terminology (black tie, white tie and the differences therein) and an onus is placed on those who do not own their own attire to hire the same – which assumes they can afford to do this. The persistence of routine dress codes in many restaurants act to exclude, differentiate and distinguish, but this begs the question as to why they are deemed necessary and how reasons for retention are justified.

Jones (1992: 28) in her report for *Caterer and Hotelkeeper* states with confidence that most 'restaurateurs and hoteliers who enforce a strict dress code, say they do so to protect the interests of the majority of their clients'. Thus a Savoy spokesperson is reported as arguing that 'What many people simply don't realize is that dress codes are made for the other guests and not for hoteliers'. The rationale for this, and similar, assertions, is, in the words of the same spokesperson, that 'People love to dress up, it's part of the whole charm of the place' (Jones, 1992: 29). This journalistic investigation also turned up a good many critics of dress codes, varying from those who accepted the principles behind such codes but were angered at the lack of consistency in their application, to industry professionals who rejected outright the whole notion of dress codes as, variously, 'crass nonsense', 'stuffy', and 'ludicrous' (Jones, 1992: 29–30). In expressing his opposition to dress codes, one respondent sought to explain their persistence thus (1992: 30):

> The British are intimidated by restaurants. They don't seem to have the confidence to wear what they feel like wearing. In Europe people go out to restaurants to enjoy themselves. But dining out in Britain, it is considered to be a special occasion and the restaurant is looked upon as a special place.

The *Caterer and Hotelkeeper*'s 1996 survey was of nearly 500 British Hospitality Association (BHA) members. The survey's key results were that (Webster and Fox, 1996: 75):

- 38 per cent of respondents operated a dress code;

- 42 per cent said the code had been relaxed in the last five years;

- 66 per cent said that if they had a dress code, they would refuse anyone inappropriately dressed;

- 5 per cent intended to relax their dress code in the next five years, 50 per cent did not (it is unclear from the report whether this refers to the 38 per cent of respondents operating such a code);

- in an apparently multi-response question, and again presumably pertaining only to the 38 per cent of respondents with a dress code, some 77 per cent said that their code existed to 'maintain standards' and 46 per cent 'because guests want it' (some 17 per cent responded that it suits our particular market).

Webster and Fox's report contains some classic rhetoric from hoteliers and restaurateurs, such as the proprietor of the one-star hotel ('with standards') who said 'This means no T-shirts at dinner, no baseball caps, no drinking out of bottles, and no swearing' or the hotel proprietor who had a policy of 'casual elegance' (sic) and surveying her own guests' demand that 95.1 per cent wanted this casual elegance rule to continue with 38.3 per cent 'wanting the rule tightened to include a jacket and tie for dinner' (1996: 74). The article repays further treats on reading, including one respondent who would not accept '... visible tattoos ... earrings and ... unconventional haircuts' (1996: 75). One can almost hear 'Disgusted of Tunbridge Wells' reaching for their Basildon Bond. At least these ludicrous outpourings are perhaps less serious that the case (in the Virgin Islands) of the night-club guest who, on being refused admission to a night club, refused to leave. The manager instructed a member of his staff to call the police who in turn refused to arrest the guest because they had witnessed no crime. The police did, however, advise the manager that he could make a citizen's arrest of the guest – which he duly did (see McConnell, 1981, for full details of this case)!

Commenting on the BHA/*Caterer and Hotelkeeper*, survey somewhat vitriolically, Levene (1996: 4) notes:

> The trouble with all of these petty regulations is that a dress code is a very crude mechanism for aesthetic control. The three-star hotelier is basically extending a welcome to a Brylcreemed reptile in a nylon shirt and grey shoes while turning away the less obviously smart

punter in the Hermes polo shirt. Not that the latter would be seen dead in such a place. Casually dressed rich people tend to prefer restaurants that don't usually bother with dress codes.

Levene implies that dress codes are both anachronistic and to a degree self-regulating in that 'refined' customers of 'good' or 'proper' taste know how (and where) to behave with regard to the clothes they wear. In other words, knowing how to dress 'properly' is another aspect of how aspirant and actual social élites mark their distinctiveness from the common mass, or *hoi polloi* (we do not have the space here for extensive theorizing: see Gronow, 1997, for a useful general review of the relevant social scientific thinking on these matters and Finkelstein, 1989, and Wood, 1995, for brief insights into aspects relevant to the restaurant trade and food and beverage provision). Having said this, there is, of course, an inverted snobbery associated with dress codes as with other kinds of social behaviour.

In a wry essay Visser (1997: 22) draws on the concept of 'conspicuous consumption' originated by American social theorist Veblen (1899) to point out that over time: 'The modern snobbery system has had time to shift its ground – retaining its authority of course.' What Visser argues is that consumption has long since renounced being overtly conspicuous. With regard to dress codes, 'dressing down' has, at various points in recent history, been a means of making social distinction – torn T-shirts and carefully ripped jeans being among examples cited as having potential 'snob appeal'. The trend towards greater informality among social élites Visser attributes to what she calls 'conspicuous competence'. By this, she appears to mean that success is no longer defined by wealth alone but the role played by wealth in promoting a meritocratic fitness and proficiency – an aura of competence – among élites. Thus, the wealthy élite are wealthy because they are fitter, leaner, meaner and more skilled than the rest of society, and thus more deserving of their status. In Visser's terms, then, 'traditional' restaurant dress codes can be seen as a residual echo of 'old-fashioned' élite values, and their persistence is the equivalent of a desperate death-rattle as the bourgeoisie finally assert their supremacy over the jaded remains of the aristocracy and gentry.

Dress codes – another view

Of course, what Visser and others ignore in their analyses is that there is another side to the dress-code coin. Guest-oriented debates about dress codes obscure the extent to which work-places in general, and the restaurant workplace in particular, regulate and police the dress of employees.

Traditional restaurant 'black and white' is believed to have its origins in the servant system of Victorian aristocratic households (Saunders, 1981). Today there are many variations, and even uniforms that are designed not to look like uniforms! Uniform and dress at work remains, however, a source of employer control, a means of imposing a particular standard upon the workforce – or rather standards, the plural is important because staff dress codes are often highly gendered. In 1994 for example, the Scotrail standards manual specified that women's skirts, when worn, could vary slightly in length 'but should be no more than one inch above or below the knee'. Further, tights had to be 'ladder free' and 'excessive make-up is not acceptable' (Anon, 1994: 7). Writers such as Laurie (1981) (cited in Arkin, 1995: 19) claim that all uniforms serve to stifle individuality. Arkin (1995: 19–20) pursues the view that organizations which place a premium on creativity and innovation often have informal dress codes. One wonders how this squares with the notion of the 'creative' chef (see Chapter 10) although in recent years there has been a notable growth in the range of chefs clothes available compared to a decade ago. More interestingly of course, employee uniforms can be used in certain contexts to convey what employers perceive to be positive images attractive to customers: this normally applies to female employees and male clients alone, however. These aspects of 'aesthetic labour' require further understanding in terms of their consequences for a holistic understanding of the significance of dress codes.

Dress codes in Glasgow

A research project currently in progress to explore dimensions to the 'dress code issue' included a survey of restaurants in Glasgow. The results of the survey are worthy of brief comment here. The survey entailed design of a questionnaire of mainly closed questions on issues related to dress codes and their enforcement and was pilot tested. After revisions, it was sent out by post to sixty-eight hotels and restaurants in the Glasgow city area. The recipients were all listed in the *Yellow Pages* or the *Eating Out* guide of the Glasgow and Clyde Valley Tourist Board. Before sending out the questionnaires, all the establishments were telephoned to make them aware of the research, and the name of the person to whom the questionnaire should be sent was obtained. The initial response at this stage was very positive. The three-page questionnaire was accompanied by a personalized letter addressed to a named manager together with a reply-paid envelope. After a three-week period, a follow-up letter enclosing another copy of the questionnaire was sent to those who had not responded. In it they were requested to return the questionnaire uncompleted if they did not wish to take part in the survey. As a result, the response rate after the follow-up letters was 82 per cent ($n = 56$). This was considered to be a large enough sample to permit coding and analysis using SPSS software.

Some 73 per cent of the sample were independent restaurants, 20 per cent chain restaurants and 7 per cent were hotel restaurants. Asked to define their style of service, 42 per cent of the sample described themselves as brasserie style, 35 per cent fine dining and 15 per cent themed restaurants. A variety of styles of cuisine were distributed throughout the sample, 29 per cent describing their food as 'international'; 16 per cent as Scottish; 9 per cent each for Mexican and Italian; 7 per cent each for Chinese and Indian; and 4 per cent each for American, French, and Greek. Size of restaurant, as measured by seat capacity, also varied. Some 34 per cent of restaurants had in excess of 100 seats; 26 per cent had 76–100 seats; 23 per cent 51–75 seats; and only 17 per cent had 21–50 seats. The average spend in the majority of the sample restaurants was between £10–20 (60 per cent).

The key findings of the survey were as follows. Some 18 per cent of respondents claimed to have a dress code and 82 per cent said they did not, figures at substantial variance with the findings of the *Caterer and Hotelkeeper* survey reported by Webster and Fox (1996). However, when asked if they would exclude customers for wearing one of a list of 'unacceptable items' some 68 per cent of all respondents identified items of clothing which they would not accept in their restaurant. The fact that 58 per cent of these were objections to 'sports team colours' is perhaps to be expected in an area where football rivalries are very strong, and perceived as bad for business.

Nevertheless, given that so many restaurants claimed not to operate a dress code and did in fact do so, if only implicitly, is interesting. At one and the same time it suggests that there is a greater informality in public dining and certain unspoken and variably arbitrary boundaries that cannot be transgressed. The application of dress code rules is seemingly arbitrary in that, in this sample at least, and in some 89 per cent of cases, restaurant management made the decision as to what was 'appropriate' dress. These managers made such decisions for the most part spontaneously – 75 per cent of the restaurants responding that they did not communicate their dress code to customers in any explicit way prior to visiting the restaurant. Some 12 per cent advised customers at the time of making a reservation, and 4 per cent displayed a notice at the restaurant, and a further 4 per cent printed information on their publicity material. It would further appear that customers' ignorance of dress codes is not regarded as an excuse, 64 per cent of respondents claiming that those 'failing' the dress code would be refused entry. Some 20 per cent of respondents would advise customers to change, and only 20 per cent would offer to loan customers an item of clothing which would allow them entry (e.g. a tie). The survey gives a very clear sense that this lack of communication about dress codes is because the regular clientele of restaurants are expected to 'know' what constitutes the 'acceptable'. Further evidence of the arbitrariness (or flexibility) of decisions about dress codes was hinted at by the admission that 18 per cent of managers would waive a dress code for regular guests, and 4 per cent confessed they would admit inappropriately dressed celebrities. However, 64 per cent said their dress code applied to all – without exception. The apparent flexibility, indeed workability, of dress code policies in this sample is reflected in the fact that 62 per cent of respondents said that they had never had to refuse anyone entry on grounds of dress; 4 per cent said they did refuse entry daily; 6 per cent monthly; and 19 per cent recalled refusing someone entry in the past year.

Conclusions

Even given the survey evidence referred to in preceding sections of this chapter, remarkably little is known about the operation of dress codes in the hospitality industry. We can glean enough, however, to realize that sociologically at least, the topic is well placed in the context of debates about snobbery. Snobbery itself is an interesting and under-researched social and sociological phenomenon. In the arena of food commentary, snobbery has a special salience for any attempts at understanding how mass markets for food supply and consumption can be effectively ignored or marginalized in everyday discourse in favour of a focus upon more élitist, socially exclusive concerns. This is particularly evident in commentaries on dining in the public domain. Sociologists have long recognized that food commentary is rarely, if ever, socially neutral. However, they have tended to underplay the extent to which this form of public writing perpetuates a culinary hegemony in which popular taste is, effectively, denigrated and dismissed as culturally inferior.

When it comes to dress codes, different aspects of the same phenomenon are in evidence. The purpose of a dress code, whether for employee or customer, is social control and, by extension, social exclusion. Dress is a convenient shorthand for the wearer, it expresses something 'about them'. Restaurant and hotel dress codes similarly express those institutions' values. Personal dress, its selection and combination, however, allows some scope for flexibility of expression whereas institutional dress codes tend to exhibit a formal coherence and uniformity (sic). Underpinning this formality is, though, a significant degree of (informal) arbitrariness which has its roots firmly in traditional social class concerns (at least in Britain). Whether hotels and restaurants that enforce the tedious 'jacket and tie' philosophy are really acting in their customers' interests remains an open question. It does seem doubtful that the line can be held for much longer. Whatever the case, one can surely continue to rely on the bourgeoisie to mistake style for substance in this and many other regards, for once such perceptions fail, it will be the end of satire.

References

Anon (1994) Watching what you wear at work, *Labour Research*, December: 7–8.

Arkin, A. (1995) Tailoring clothes to suit the image, *People Management*, August: 18–23.

Bourdieu, P. (1984) *Distinction: A Social Critique of the Judgement of Taste*, London: Routledge and Kegan Paul.

Finkelstein, J. (1989) *Dining Out: A Sociology of Modern Manners*, Cambridge: Polity Press.

Gronow, J. (1997) *The Sociology of Taste*, London: Routledge.

Jakeman, J. (1994) How food snobs guard the right to scoff, *The Independent*, 29 July: 19.

Jones, W. (1992) Dressed for dinner?, *Caterer and Hotelkeeper*, 20 August: 28–30.

Levene, L. (1996) Please, no singlets or beer bellies, *The Independent (Section Two)*, 20 September: 4–5.

McConnell, J. P. (1981) When the patron refuses to leave, *Cornell Hotel and Restaurant Administration Quarterly*, February: 21–24.

Nicholson-Lord, D. (1994) Hotels criticised for 'over the top' gourmet menus, *The Independent*, 8 September: 5.

Saunders, C. (1981) *Social Stigma of Occupations*, Farnborough: Gower.

Veblen, T. (1899) *The Theory of the Leisure Class*, New York: Dover (1994 edition).

Visser, M. (1997) *The Way We Are*, London: Penguin, 21–25.

Webster, J. and Fox, L. (1996) Entrée form, *Caterer and Hotelkeeper*, 12 September: 74–75.

Wood, R. C. (1995) *The Sociology of the Meal*, Edinburgh: Edinburgh University Press.

Wood, R. C. (1996) Talking to themselves: food commentators, food snobbery and market reality, *British Food Journal*, **98**(10): 3–7.

CHAPTER 15

Should smoking in restaurants be banned? The debate so far

Dennis P. Nickson

Introduction

This chapter will address the issue of smoking in restaurants by examining the background to the debate, especially the recent Government White Paper (the first ever on smoking), *Smoking Kills*, which provides a commentary on the nature of smoking in contemporary society. Secondly, the chapter will explore the impact that wider societal changes have had on attitudes to smoking in restaurants. This will provide a framework to examine the two most pertinent issues for this chapter: the health and safety of workers; and the potential commercial implications for restaurants of moves to partially or totally ban smoking. Within this discussion cognisance will be taken of the most recent initiatives emanating from *Smoking Kills* and also the Health and Safety Commission's recent deliberations on an Approved Code of Practice for passive smoking in the workplace. The chapter will offer some informed speculation on the likely future changes in the restaurant industry, based on the discussion described above.

One final point of introduction is to recognize that smoking is a very emotive subject that lends itself to propagandizing and sloganeering. Even a perfunctory review of the debate would recognize very quickly the antipathetical attitudes held by bodies such as Action on Smoking and Health (ASH) and Freedom Organisation for the Right to Enjoy Smoking (FOREST). The former organization is at the forefront of attempts to ban or at least severely circumscribe smoking in public, whilst the latter is equally vociferous in their support of smokers' rights. This chapter seeks to navigate a pathway through these extremes and, on a subject that invites polemicism, adopt, as far as possible, a measured review of the debate.

Smoking in broad context

The publication of *Smoking Kills* is part of a broader government initiative entitled Our Healthier Nation, which seeks to improve the health and welfare of the nation. In that vein, the somewhat unsubtle title of the White Paper signals very clearly the rationale and intent of *Smoking Kills*. As the introduction baldly announces 'Smoking kills. Smoking is the single greatest cause of preventable illness and premature deaths in the UK', killing 120,000 people a year, and an estimated 500,000 across the European Union as a whole (Department of Health, 1998: 3). Consequently, the government's intention is to reduce smoking within the UK, including smoking in public places. Nonetheless, despite this intent, the White Paper does acknowledge the continuing relatively high number of smokers within the UK. Indeed, it notes how 'the long downward trend on smoking may be levelling out', with the adult rate of smokers rising for the first time since 1972 (Department of Health, 1998: 4) (see Table 15.1).

Year	Percentage of smokers in UK
1981	39
1990	29
1994	26
1996	28

Source: Derived from Department of Health (1998: 83).

Table 15.1 Adult smoking in the UK – figures for all social classes in those aged over 16

The 13 million or so people that this represents clearly marks an important consideration in relation to any initiatives which may emanate from government to circumscribe smoking in public places. Moreover the recognition that the number of children aged 11–15 who smoke regularly is increasing (especially amongst girls) also suggests that this figure is likely to remain relatively constant, particularly when it is recognized that 82 per cent of smokers who take up the habit as teenagers continue into full adulthood (Department of Health, 1998: 5). It is unsurprising then to find Kettle and Bates (1998: 17) arguing that, 'Between 25 and 35 per cent of the adult population of advanced countries are always likely to be smokers; smoking's attractions for young people are undiminished'. It is clear then that it is unlikely that any governmental initiatives are ever going to wholly eradicate smoking, or even significantly dent the figure of 25–30 per cent. Consequently, despite the government recognizing the financial and health costs of smoking, they concede that 'We do not intend to make smoking unlawful. We are not banning smoking' (Department of Health, 1998: 11).

Nevertheless, *Smoking Kills* does affirm that people are increasingly insisting on a healthier environment and clean air, and that this will impact on businesses, including restaurants, who must recognize the changing public attitudes towards smoking, both from the point of view of employees and customers. For example, the White Paper suggests that 'The vast majority of people agree that smoking should be restricted in public places' and cites evidence that 42 per cent of people take the availability of a non-smoking area into account when choosing a restaurant (Department of Health, 1998: 65).

Smoking in restaurants

The work of a number of authors (e.g. Bojanic, 1996; Cuthbert and Nickson, 1999; and Young, 1997) on the issues attendant on smoking in restaurants reflects an increasing awareness of one of the more challenging issues facing owners and operators in the foodservice industry. Morrison (1993: 28) distils two broad themes from these commentaries:

- The responsibility of the employer to maintain a safe environment for employees and customers.

- The necessity of satisfying the wants of all consumers (i.e. smokers and non-smokers) to remain profitable.

We now consider each of these in turn.

Smoking in the workplace – a health and safety perspective

Concerns about smoking in the workplace are inextricably linked to the phenomenon of environmental tobacco smoke (ETS), or as it is rather more popularly known, passive smoking. As the Health and Safety Commission (HSC) (1999: 1) notes: 'Passive smoking – inhaling other people's tobacco smoke – is a particular issue in the workplace.' Consequently, from a health and safety perspective, the increasingly persuasive evidence of the link between passive smoking and lung cancer, heart disease and more recently strokes (as well as what ASH term 'sub-lethal effects', such as irritating the eyes, affecting the breathing and so on) would suggest that employers would have to be seen to be proactive in responding to the potential threat to their employees' health, safety and welfare (for an overview of the passive smoking debate, see Bosely, 1998, 1999; HSC, 1999; Leah, 1998; Wilson, 1998; and Young, 1997). Indeed, evidence suggests that restaurants are a workplace with a relatively smoky atmosphere, and consequently possibly more damaging to employee health. For example, Young (1997) cites a study which shows that ETS exposure is likely to be at least 1.5 times higher for restaurant workers than for people who actually live with a smoker.

Despite concerns about the deleterious impact of passive smoking, thus far the law in the UK remains rather vague as to what employers might concretely do to protect their employees from the dangers of passive smoking. There are three sources of law which cover the issue of passive smoking. The first is Domestic and European legislation including the UK Health and Safety at Work etc. Act 1974 (HASAWA). Section 2(1) of the HASAWA states 'It shall be the duty of every employer to ensure, so far as is reasonably practicable, the health, safety and welfare at work for all of his employees'. It is widely recognized that the ambiguity of the phrase 'reasonably practicable' means that there is often a tension between the health of employees and the potential costs of any improvements which employers may make to create a safer environment. Indeed, it could be argued that this is particularly true in the case of passive smoking, where it is only relatively recently that employees may consider that they are being subjected to an unnecessary health risk due to their exposure to ETS.

A second regulatory mechanism under this heading is the Control of Substances Hazardous to Health Regulations (COSHH) 1998. These regulations place a requirement on employers to carry out an assessment of risks to their employees from substances identified in the workplace as being potentially hazardous to employees. It may be stretching a point to suggest that these regulations were intended to cover an issue such as passive smoking, but certainly ASH has argued that tobacco smoke should be included in the COSHH list of hazardous substances to clarify employers' duties (Frewin, 1997a).

Finally here, it is necessary to consider European Union (EU) Directives. As from 1 January 1993 there has been a series of Directives emanating from the EU which have sought to make more explicit the duty of employers to protect the health, safety and welfare of their employees. In particular, the Management of Health and Safety at Work Regulations 1992 encourages employers to be more proactive in developing effective managerial control of health and safety in the workplace. This is best exemplified by the notion of risk assessment, where employers are required to identify potential sources of harm, i.e. hazards. Having done this they then have to assess the likelihood or risk that a particular hazard will actually cause harm. Finally, employers have to design, implement or monitor measures to eliminate or lessen the risk. So for the example of passive smoking, the increased acceptance of the potentially harmful impacts to employees from tobacco smoke means that employers are likely to be required to assess the risk of this and consider their responses, such as reducing the time employees may spend in a smoky part of the restaurant.

The second source of law on passive smoking is cases brought through the employment tribunal system. In essence, the legislation described above is likely to provide the context in which any individual cases brought by employees are heard. Warren (1998) has recently reviewed the extant case law in relation to passive smoking. For the purposes of this discussion the most important case would seem to be *Waltons and Morse* v. *Dorrington*. In this case a non-smoker was in an office space shared with seven other secretaries, four of who smoked, although the area was open and well ventilated. Subsequently, she was moved and placed near to rooms occupied entirely by heavy smokers. Despite complaining, the situation did not improve markedly, though the firm did make some effort. Ultimately though Dorrington found alternative employment and claimed constructive dismissal. The decision of the Industrial Tribunal, which was upheld on appeal in the Employment Appeal Tribunal, was that the employer, under the aegis of HASAWA, had failed to provide and maintain a safe working environment that was reasonably tolerable for all employees.

The third and final source of law on passive smoking is cases brought through common law – suing for damages resulting from passive smoking. Despite the above mentioned success through the employment tribunal system, as yet there have been no successful claims for the injurious effects of passive smoking in a personal injury case. Thus, although the law of negligence may potentially allow victims of passive smoking to claim compensation, no employees have yet been successful, although in the early 1990s a local government employee did win £15,000 in an out of court settlement (Morrison, 1993). Despite the lack of definitive case law in this area, a number of people argue that it is only a matter of time before a plaintiff is successful. For example, Warren (1998: 27) reporting on the case of *Sparrow* v. *St Andrews Homes Ltd*, which was heard in the High Court and in which Sparrow lost her claim that the employer had breached HASAWA by exposing her to passive smoking, notes: 'it is feasible that a case with only slightly different facts could result in an entirely different decision'. Unsurprisingly, this view is also held by ASH (1999: 14), who claim that in the Sparrow case the plaintiff won a moral victory, and consequently they believe 'it may only be a matter of time before an individual will be able to prove that damage to their health was caused by passive smoking'.

Current developments

The current impasse in the law is recognized by the HSC, who have been charged by *Smoking Kills* to examine how to address the issue of passive smoking in the workplace. In particular the consultative document, *Proposal for an Approved Code of Practice on Passive Smoking at Work* (HSC, 1991: 1) seeks to address the issue of whether the HSC, 'should take further action to encourage employers to improve employees' health and welfare at work by reducing their exposure to environmental tobacco smoke – and if the answer is "yes", how best to do it'.

At the time of writing, the deadline of the end of October 1999 for comments on the document precludes any definitive analysis of the possible impact of any initiative by the HSC. However, it seems unlikely that the HSC will seek to impose a new law to cover passive smoking. Equally, the HSC is unconvinced that stricter enforcement of existing law is necessarily the best step forward. Instead, they advocate a jointly developed smoking policy between employer and employee as a far better way forward than recourse to the law. As a result the HSC supports the introduction of a new Approved Code of Practice (ACoP), which if agreed upon will be introduced in the early part of 2000. ACoPs have a special status in law, like the Highway Code, and in the case of passive smoking would seek to provide: 'author-itative guidance about the minimum standards employers are expected to reach. An employer who has introduced a smoking policy that ensures employees' health and welfare in line with the ACoP will be doing enough to comply with health, safety and welfare law' (HSC, 1999: 5).

It is interesting to note that the HSC recognizes the particular resonance of these issues for the hospitality industry. For example, concerns as to the commercial viability of completely banning smoking, which is top of a hierarchy of measures that employers may consider taking to ensure employees' health and welfare, would mean that restaurants could consider other measures to protect employees, such as segregation and ventilation, and this issue is further developed below.

In sum, the law presently remains inconclusive, though it does appear that the increasing need for employers to be seen to be proactive in relation to health and safety would point to the need for more comprehensive smoking policies in restaurants. Certainly, Warren (1998: 27) believes that 'it will be difficult (if not impossible) for employers to argue that they were unaware in the late 1990s of the health implications of exposing employees to passive smoking'. A similar line is also taken by the Chartered Institute of Environmental Health (CIEH) who state: 'In the light of [research on passive smoking] the CIEH believes that employers can no longer claim the risks are not high enough to justify the time and trouble to protect staff' (Frewin, 1997b: 7). The increased recognition of passive smoking as an issue would seem to point, then, to restaurants having to consider options other than simply allowing smoking in all parts of the establishment. Therefore, attention now turns to the possible commercial impact of any total or partial ban on smoking.

Commercial considerations – responding to customer wants?

As was noted above, a key theme which underpins government thinking towards smoking in public places is a voluntaristic approach which obviates the need for a universal and legally based ban on smoking. For a government which has suffered many taunts about trying to create a 'nanny state', the refusal to implement an outright ban on smoking in public places, including restaurants, might be considered somewhat surprising. Indeed, compared to many other countries the UK government could be thought of as being relatively 'liberal' in its approach to smoking in public places (see Fox, 1996, for a description of the more rigorous imposition of bans in a number of other countries throughout the world). For example, in America the publication by the Environmental Protection Agency of a report in 1993 on the dangers of passive smoking, *Second-hand Smoking* (cited in Fox, 1996), led to many states, New York, California and Florida among them, banning smoking within restaurants. Indeed, it has been predicted that this trend is likely to snowball in the USA, although Fox's (1996: 63) suggestion that 'smoking will be prohibited in all restaurants in the US by the year 2000' does seem a little premature.

In the past and contemporaneously many UK restaurateurs have had concerns about the imposition of a legally based smoking ban, primarily because of a fear of losing the custom of those who smoke. As noted above, in the UK the approach to the issue has been far less radical, choosing only to comply with the minimal amount of health and safety legislation on the matter. Few British restaurants have been proactive in their approach and have yet to see the benefits of a smoke-free environment on a national scale. The lack of British research on the subject is indicative of this fact. Nevertheless, there is no doubt that the pressure to prohibit smoking in public places has found its way to the UK, as evidenced by *Smoking Kills*. Indeed, even before this in 1993, as part of an earlier Health of the Nation initiative the government launched a campaign to achieve effective no-smoking policies in 80 per cent of public places by the year end (Department of Environment, 1993). This attempt to introduce more effective no-smoking policies would seem to reflect a number of opinion polls which appear to support the circum-scribing of smoking in public places. For example, *Caterer and Hotelkeeper* (Anon, 1998a: 7) reports an ICM poll of 1200 people which found that:

- 54 per cent of people favour bans in all public places;

- 73 per cent of people favour bans in workplaces;

- 64 per cent of people favour bans in restaurants and bars;

- 80 per cent of people favour bans in transport.

It is interesting to note the reaction to such poll findings, with *Caterer and Hotelkeeper*, Anon, 1998b: 12) reporting how ASH felt such figures proved that smoking bans are unlikely to damage trade in restaurants and bars; while FOREST pointed out that the results showed that 46 per cent of people did not support a ban in public places. More recently Golding (1998) notes a similar polarity in the views garnered from a telephone poll of 67,000 people reported on BBC2's *Food and Drink* programme which suggested that 80 per cent of people supported an outright ban in restaurants; this was compared to a Restaurant Association poll, conducted by NOP, which suggested that only 8 per cent of people were in favour of a ban. At the very least, it would appear that there exists some minimum consensus that restaurants should be actively reviewing their smoking policies and be willing to consider a number of alternatives, up to and including an outright ban on smoking.

Smoking policies – the alternatives available to restaurants • • •

Based on *Smoking Kills*, it is possible to identify five broad choices which will inform a restaurant's smoking policy, these being (Department of Health, 1998: 71):

- Non-smoking – No smoking allowed at any time.
- Separated – Smoking and non-smoking areas separated by walls.
- Designated – Areas with spaces clearly defined for smoking and non-smoking.
- Ventilated – Non-defined areas but special ventilation equipment used to improve comfort for non-smokers.
- Smoking – No segregation or special ventilation equipment.

Non-smoking

Despite the concerns of proprietors as to the commercial viability of a total smoking ban, research evidence has generally pointed to this course of action not being financially disastrous for restaurants. For example, Morrison (1993) reports on research which consisted of issuing, between March and May 1990 and again in the same period in 1992, 388 customer questionnaires to patrons of a non-smoking university restaurant. Morrison found that:

- in 1990 74.7 per cent of respondents preferred a smoke-free restaurant, by 1992 this figure had increased to 81.2 per cent;
- in 1990 9.8 per cent of respondents preferred a smoking environment, by 1992 this figure has decreased to 7.18 per cent.

Within the American context, Sciacca (1996) reports a study carried out in 1993 in Flagstaff, the first city in Arizona to prohibit smoking in restaurants. Sciacca hoped to make a comparison of the concerns of restaurateurs both prior and subsequent to the enactment of the ordinance. The main concerns before the enactment included: fears that restaurants would find it difficult to enforce; it would upset customers; it would have negative effects on restaurant employees; and it would be bad for business. After fifteen months, the concerns that had been voiced prior to the implementation were in the most part, not realized. The concern most frequently expressed by restaurateurs, that of implementation affecting business, produced the interesting finding that: '55.9 per cent felt there had been no effect on business, 17.7 per cent believed that it had decreased their business, 17.6 per cent didn't know and 11.8 per cent believed the ordinance had increased their restaurant business' (Sciacca, 1996: 145).

Similar conclusions were drawn from two studies carried out by Glantz and Smith (1994; 1997). They used taxable restaurant sales for fifteen cities where ordinances were in force, as well as fifteen similar control communities without smoke-free ordinances during the period. Their results showed that 'smoke-free restaurant ordinances do not adversely affect restaurant revenues' (1997: 1689). This conclusion is strengthened by the observation that where the opportunity was given to repeal the ordinance in some restaurants, sales either decreased or remained the same, making it clear that the ordinance offered no negative impact on sales. Despite the research that indicates that implementing a no-smoking policy within restaurants would have no negative impact, there has still been strong resistance to such ordinances throughout the industry. The work by Glantz and his colleagues has been questioned in the USA by the National Smokers Alliance (NSA), a group funded by the Tobacco manufacturer's Philip Morris. The NSA believes that the ban is causing 'economic hardship' in restaurants (Drummond, 1999: 12) and there may be some truth in this with Fox (1996) citing evidence to suggest that the New York City smoking ban in restaurants with more than thirty-five seats led directly to the loss of 7806 jobs between 1993–1996, and closures up 25 per cent year-on-year in 1996.

However, the work of Glantz and Smith and others also suggests a positive aspect of 'going smoke-free', namely the potential competitive advantage that could be achieved by opting, through self-regulation, to become non-smoking. In a country like the UK, where very few restaurants have taken this proactive approach, if one were to choose to offer a no-smoking restaurant, customers might actively seek out such establishments. One hotel has made an effective marketing tool out of its smoke-free environment. The Nottingham Moat House chose to advertise their restaurant as no-smoking and found this a very positive influence on business, with weekend evenings fully booked a week in advance with 85 per cent non-residents (Webster, 1994: 36). Cuthbert and Nickson (1999) also report a small-scale piece of research which compares the smoking arrangements found in several restaurants in the UK. Their findings suggest that those restaurants already operating a total ban on smoking may actually be opposed to government legislation banning smoking in restaurants. The reason for this lies in the recognition that it would remove from these restaurants a potential source of competitive advantage. Allied to this the respondents in the research also pointed to the benefits of a cleaner and healthier working environment.

The remaining options

Aside from the final option of allowing smoking in all parts of restaurants, which seems increasingly untenable given much of the foregoing discussion, the sense of choice offered by separation, designation or ventilation is more likely to meet with the approval of restaurateurs. Indeed, a combination of designated areas and ventilation seems to be the preferred choice of restaurateurs, though physically separate areas seem less popular. The attractiveness of designated areas and ventilation is that they offer 'the best of both worlds' to the customer (Lambert, Samet and Spengler, 1993: 1339). For example, the Courtesy of Choice programme is a scheme launched in Britain in March 1995 in the hope of avoiding the disputes that legislation on smoking has caused in the USA. Courtesy of Choice was devised by the International Hotel and Restaurant Association and communications agency Spring O'Brien (and interestingly is funded by the tobacco manufacturers) and has now extended to 3000 restaurants in forty-four countries (Mullen, 1998). The basis of the scheme is to show that smokers and non-smokers can both be accommodated within the same establishment, provided there is good ventilation based on 'the logical and feasible study of airflows' (Baker, 1995: 18).

Indeed, it has been scientifically proven that the segmentation of smoking and non-smoking areas can be done effectively. In 1989, seven Albuquerque restaurants were tested, using scientific apparatus, for the levels of environmental tobacco smoke found in each area of the restaurant (Lambert, Samet and Spengler, 1993: 1339). The results showed that: 'The mean concentrations of respirable suspended particles and nicotine were 40 per cent and 65 per cent lower, respectively, in the no-smoking than in the smoking sections, indicating substantial, but not complete protection against exposure.' The ordinance that was in place in the restaurants was the Clean Indoor Air Act, where it was required that no more than one-third of the seating area was designated for smokers. The report goes on to state (Lambert, Samet and Spengler, 1993: 1341): 'While these types of ordinances do not provide perfect protection, measurements indicate that people sitting in the no-smoking sections of restaurants are exposed to substantially lower concentrations of environmental tobacco smoke than those in the smoking areas.'

Why then, if segregation would seem to hold the key to a harmonious future on the matter, have a number of restaurateurs expressed concerns; and similarly many campaigners insisted upon complete smoking bans and dismissed designation and ventilation as inadequate? With regard to restaurateurs their concern towards designation and ventilation systems lies in the recognition that this may be a costly approach. The HSC, whilst noting that all industrial sectors may be affected by the proposed new ACoP, go on to suggest that the hospitality sector is the most likely to face high costs. This is based on their estimation that over 60,000 hospitality organizations are likely to face potentially major changes from the provision of more non-smoking areas. They suggest that 80 per cent of firms in the sector are likely to respond by introducing designation and ventilation, and this may be a source of some concern for owners and operators. Thus, although Douglas O'Brien of Courtesy of Choice believes that improved air ventilation can be achieved for as little as £500 in a small restaurant, Michael Da Costa, chairman of the Restaurant Association believes that it is likelier to be much costlier and cites the example of his own restaurant where £25,000 was spent installing air conditioning and good ventilation (Mullen, 1998). Indeed, the Restaurant Association have recently argued that small restaurants could face crippling cost to install expensive ventilation systems, with equipment likely to cost at least £3000 per establishment (Anon, 1998c: 6). Clearly, it is remains to be seen what the long-term effects of the costs of providing designated and well-ventilated areas will be, though this option may still be more palatable to restaurateurs compared to an outright ban.

For many of those campaigning for a smoking ban the compromise of designated areas and ventilation may not be enough. They believe that this approach is insufficient to protecting people from the effects of passive smoking (Fox, 1996). Equally the designation of smoking and non-smoking areas may be done in a very haphazard manner. As one report notes (Anon, 1994: 7): 'What is the point of a non-smoker being placed at the frontier of his zone, when the table across the line is occupied by someone, maybe with a dirigible-shaped cigar, the smoke from which might suggest that it was rolled in creosote and soaked in treacle'.

One final aspect to seeking greater to choice is to physically separate different areas of the restaurant. Sustaining this distinction between smoking and non-smoking sections by such separation is a costly, and in many cases, likely to be an impractical suggestion. For example, many restaurants are too small to accommodate this idea both economically and structurally. Fox (1996) reports research by FOREST which suggested that 53 per cent of restaurateurs saw it as impractical and 29 per cent said it would only be possible if their business underwent a complete redesign. Moreover the suggestion to segment restaurants into completely different rooms has been met with much criticism and labelled 'preposterous' (Robinson, Tibbet and Speer, 1995: 30).

Recent initiatives

The discussion thus far signals that an outright ban on smoking in restaurants is unlikely in the near future. Equally, concerns about passive smoking mean that, notwithstanding any extra costs, restaurants will require to be visibly proactive in developing a smoking policy. This point is implicit in *Smoking Kills* and the HSC's proposals for an approved code of practice. Thus, although the essence of the Government's approach is voluntary, in reality the restaurant industry will have to be seen to be taking on board the suggestions contained in the various documents. This is most apparent in the Charter on smoking in public places contained in the White Paper. Although this Charter is a voluntary arrangement for hotel, pub and restaurant owners, it does commit them to a variety of things (see Box 15.1).

The response to the Charter has been interesting. Whilst many in the industry were happy to avoid a legally imposed ban on smoking in restaurants, the duties that the Charter imposes are wide-ranging. The HSC (1999: 6) recognize this in their belief that: 'In some ways the Charter goes beyond what could be required under health, safety and welfare law for the protection of workers, and which would be set out in any ACoP.' Similarly, any sense that the voluntary nature of the Charter means that the industry can use it as an excuse to do nothing is dispelled by Forbes Mutch, who, when Editor of *Caterer and Hotelkeeper*, noted: 'What the White Paper stresses is that the Government is very keen to discourage smoking, and so, if a voluntary code is not acted upon by the hospitality industry, as sure as Woodbines are Woodbines, the next step is likely to be cast-iron legislation' (1998: 13). Indeed, representatives of the licensed hospitality

---

Box 15.1   Public places charter

The signatories of this Charter recognise that non-smoking is the general norm and that there should be increasing provision of facilities for non-smokers and the availability of clean air. The signatories therefore commit themselves in principle to achieving the following objectives in premises for which they are responsible or which they represent:

1 A written policy on smoking, available to customers and staff.
2 Implementation through non-smoking areas, air cleaning and ventilation, as appropriate and whenever practicable.
3 Communication to customers through external signage to an agreed format and appropriate internal signs.
4 Implementation on a rolling basis over a number of years, informed by an initial assessment of the current position, internal monitoring and subsequent independent research to monitor progress.
5 Recognition of smoking policies as a management responsibility to be reflected in general training, qualification and supervision.
6 Support for shared expertise and guidance on commercial and technical benefits of smoking policies and air cleaning.

The Government applauds these aims and will encourage and support the signatories in achieving them.

Association of Licensed Multiple Retailers (ALMR)
Brewers and Licensed Retailers Association (BLRA)
British Hospitality Association (BHA)

Source: Department of Health (1998: 69). Crown copyright material reproduced with kind permission of the Controller of Her Majesty's Stationery Office.

---

trade have agreed, under the terms of the Charter, to make year-on-year improvements in facilities for smokers and non-smokers; and notwithstanding some claims, most notably from ASH, that the voluntary code 'lacks guts' (Golding, 1999: 4), it would seem that it is likely to have a major impact in the future.

Conclusions – the future of smoking in restaurants

The meshing of health and commercial considerations means that smoking in the hospitality industry is a particularly vexed issue. On the one hand, increased concerns about passive smoking mean there are calls for new measures to protect workers from the risks engendered by a smoky environment. On the other hand, the fact that alcohol, eating and smoking is inextricably linked for many people means that employers and their associations fear the possible commercial impact of a partial or total ban on smoking in restaurants.

As Bojanic (1996: 29) notes, thus far: 'The restaurant industry has taken the stance that restaurant owners should be able to make their own business decisions based on the demands of the market.' This view is equally applicable to customers ('if customers are concerned about being exposed to tobacco smoke they will voice their opinions or stop frequenting the restaurant') and employees ('if they do not want to be exposed to ETS, then they do not have to work in a restaurant that allows smoking'). As people increasingly insist on a healthy environment and evidence continues to grow (if it does) of the potentially harmful effects of passive smoking this position is likely to become untenable. In this sense the new Public Places Charter would seem to offer a reasonable compromise to allow restaurateurs to manage the balance between economic rationality and a humane and ethical view of their staff. For once, the restaurant industry may well welcome government intervention in the running of their business as they seek to balance these concerns.

References

Action on Smoking and Health (1999) *Smoking in the Workplace*, London: ASH.

Anon (1994) No title, *The Scotsman*, 2 August: 7.

Anon (1998a) Public smoking ban, *Caterer and Hotelkeeper*, 15 January: 7.

Anon (1998b) BAT denies smoker's bistro plans, *Caterer and Hotelkeeper*, 29 January 1998: 12.

Anon (1998c) Clean air costs could cripple restaurants, *Caterer and Hotelkeeper*, 22 October: 6.

Baker, J. (1995) What cost no smoking, *Hospitality*, June–July: 18–19.

Bojanic, D. (1996) The smoking debate: a look at the issues surrounding smoking bans in restaurants, *Hospitality Research Journal*, **20**(1): 27–38.

Bosely, S. (1998) Smoke gets in your eyes, *Guardian*, 13 October: 19.

Bosely, S. (1999) Passive smoking linked to strokes, *Guardian*, 13 July: 7.

Cuthbert, L. and Nickson, D. (1999) Smoking in the restaurant industry: time for a ban? *International Journal of Contemporary Hospitality Management*, **11**(1): 31–37.

Department of the Environment (1993) *Smoking in Public Places Survey Report and Survey Data*, London: Her Majesty's Stationery Office.

Department of Health (1998) *Smoking Kills – A White Paper on Tobacco*, London: The Stationery Office.

Drummond, G. (1999) Survey says smoking bans don't hurt trade, *Caterer and Hotelkeeper*, 10 June: 12.

Fox, L. (1996) Smoking, *Caterer and Hotelkeeper*, 7 March: 63–66.

Frewin, A. (1997a) ASH warns employers over passive smoking, *Caterer and Hotelkeeper*, 20 November: 18.

Frewin, A. (1997b) EHOs get tougher on passive smoking, *Caterer and Hotelkeeper*, 30 October: 7.

Glantz, S. A. and Smith, L. R. A. (1994) The effects of Ordinances requiring smokefree restaurant sales, *American Journal of Public Health*, **84**(7): 1081–1085.

Glantz, S. and Smith, L. R. A. (1997) The effects of ordinances requiring smoke-free restaurants and bars on revenues: a follow up, *American Journal of Public Health*, **87**(10): 1687–1693.

Golding, C. (1998) Anti-smoking group to police voluntary code, *Caterer and Hotelkeeper*, 17 December: 8.

Golding, C. (1999) Smoking code could prove to be damp squib, *Caterer and Hotelkeeper*, 16 September: 4.

Health and Safety Commission (1999) *Proposal for an Approved Code of Practice on Passive Smoking at Work*, London: Health and Safety Executive.

Kettle, M. and Bates, S. (1998) The billion dollar cigarette war, *Guardian*, 8 July: 17.

Lambert, W. E., Samet, J. M. and Spengler, J. D. (1993) Environmental tobacco smoke concentrations in no-smoking and smoking sections of restaurants, *American Journal of Public Health*, **83**(9): 1339–1341.

Leah, B. (1998) Where there's smoke, *Hospitality*, May/June: 19.

Morrison, P. (1993) A non-smoking hospitality environment: profitable business or financial suicide?, *International Journal of Contemporary Hospitality Management*, **5**(2): 27–31.

Mullen, R. (1998) Filter tips, *Caterer and Hotelkeeper*, 11 June: 58–60.

Mutch, F. (1998) It's time to make that New Year resolution on smoking, *Caterer and Hotelkeeper*, 17 December: 13.

Robinson, J. P., Tibbet, L. and Speer, L. (1995) The air we breathe, *American Demographic*, **17**: 24–32.

Sciacca, J. P. (1996) A mandatory smoking ban in restaurants: concerns vs. experiences, *Journal of Community Health*, **21**(2): 134–149.

Warren, M. (1998) Smokeless feuds, *People Management*, 25 June: 25–27.

Webster, J. (1994) Reading the smoke signals, *Caterer and Hotelkeeper*, 28 April: 36.

Wilson, J. (1998) More smoke equals more cancer risk, *Guardian*, 7 October: 12.

Young, K. (1997) Environmental tobacco smoke and employees, *Cornell Hotel and Restaurant Administrative Quarterly*, February: 36–42.

CHAPTER 16

What lessons can be learned from the history of dining out? Some influences on current trends in the UK

John O'Connor

Introduction

In the prologue to his novel *The Go-Between*, L. P. Hartley observes 'The past is a foreign country: they do things differently there'. If that is true, what lessons, if any, can be learned from the past? Henry Ford thought that history was more or less bunk, but if that view is taken, there is nothing worth learning from history. The problem with attempting to understand current and future trends in dining-out, however, is that one-off market research is just a snapshot: a frozen moment in time. What decision makers require, whether they are hospitality operators or suppliers of materials and equipment to them, is a series of snapshots over time which can reveal changing patterns in food and beverage services supply and consumption. Only when this essentially historical material is available can analysis and interpretation of trends and causes begin. In a very real sense then, history is the raw material from which understanding of the present might be gleaned and from which future scenarios might be constructed.

The last half-century has seen phenomenal developments in dining-out from post-war rationing to the current scene of plenty in which all manner of tastes and appetites can be stimulated and satisfied. The transformation has been extraordinary: profitable for the supplier and convenient and pleasurable for the consumer. Food rationing continued long after the end of the Second World War, while dining out was controlled in two ways: by means of allocations of supplies to caterers based on their trade (Hammond, 1954) and by restricting the price which could be charged for a meal to a maximum of five shillings. This limit was not revoked until May 1950. From 1950 onwards rationing was relaxed by stages, but not until 1954 was the British public free to buy as much as they could afford. Even so, there was no immediate rush to fill the available restaurants as people were concerned to restore, as far as they could, the pre-war pleasures of dining at home. But the British had got used to eating away from home more frequently at one level at least: eating in the office or factory canteen, or at school or college. Mervyn Bryn Jones (1970) showed that between 1950 and 1967 there was only modest growth in demand for meals away from home. The famous 1959 general election slogan of Harold Macmillan 'You've never had it so good' reflected both complacency and awareness of a steady growth in incomes and expenditure. Bryn Jones argued that income was the only factor of importance in determining the national demand for meals away from home, for income contained the effects of many other variables such as social class and the propensity to eat out.

Dining-out in the 1960s

During the 1960s British consumers were beginning to respond to the growth in their incomes by increasing their spending on meals away from home and on the newly discovered delights of holidays abroad. Between 1960 and 1968, expenditure by caterers increased steadily (Table 16.1).

While this growth in caterers' expenditure over the period is modest, at less than 2 per cent per annum in real terms, it is nevertheless real growth. In addition, it is growth in expenditure

1960	1961	1962	1963	1964	1965	1966	1967	1968
524	538	551	567	588	589	592	602	603

*Excluding public authorities
Source: Medlik, 1978 based on National Income and Expenditure data, 1969

Table 16.1 Expenditure on food by caterers* 1960–1969 (£ million) (at constant 1963 prices)

in wholesale prices rather than expenditure by diners. What is of note is that while caterers' expenditure in food was slowly growing, spending on food by households was almost static. Thus caterers were gradually increasing their presence in the food market. By adding value to the raw materials through preparation and service, they were able to maintain their share of consumer spending. But spending on food for home preparation was becoming proportionately less important in the household budget as incomes rose. Between 1953 and 1975 expenditure on food as a proportion of income fell from one-third to one-fifth: a reflection of growth in real incomes as well as a change in spending priorities.

Beneath the surface of this trend, the catering industry was in a state of flux. The face of British high streets was beginning to change. New and less formal styles of restaurant were opening, offering fast food and quick service. At the same time, ethnic restaurants were booming – notably Chinese, Indian and Italian. Most pubs were tied to the breweries and focused on their wet trade. Some offered sandwiches and pies as a convenience to their lunch-time customers.

In 1965, the National Catering Inquiry, sponsored by Smethurst Foods showed that the dominant factor in eating away from home was its association with work. Nationally, four people out of ten ate a meal at work every weekday, either in a staff canteen or at nearby restaurants. A quarter ate out privately at least once a week and a quarter did so at least once a month. The rest ate out less frequently on private occasions, or not at all (Table 16.2). Two-thirds of respondents to this survey would have liked to eat out more often. The main constraint at that time was that customers found dining out too expensive (Smethurst Foods Ltd, 1965).

Even in 1965, over 50 per cent of respondents had visited ethnic restaurants and, of these, six out of ten had visited Chinese

	Daily	Weekly	Monthly	Less often
At work	39	–	18	43
Privately	–	23	24	50

Source: Smethurst Foods Ltd (1965)

Table 16.2 Frequency of eating away from home 1965 (%)

restaurants. By contrast, only 16 per cent had visited Indian restaurants. Chinese restaurants were in the first wave of post-war expansion of restaurants. It has been estimated that there were about 4000 Chinese restaurants in Britain by 1970 out of a total of approximately 32,000. However, the growth of Chinese restaurants levelled out, while Indian restaurants continued to expand to reach an estimated total of 10,000 by 1999.

Eating out in the 1970s

In April 1974 a research project on dining out was commissioned by the Hotels and Catering Economic Development Committee. Its aim was to define the profile of the British diner and to reveal patterns of behaviour and spending on eating-out. The survey, published as *Trends in Catering* (HCEDC, 1976), showed that 44.3 million Britons aged eleven or over consumed an average of 89 million meals a week away from home: this amounted to over 4600 million meals a year in 1975, close to two meals a week for the average Briton. Expenditure on meals, excluding alcohol, amounted to over £2000 million. This was close to 4 per cent of total consumer expenditure. With the inclusion of drink and tobacco sales, the total expenditure on catering services in 1975 was around £55 billion – or 11 per cent of total consumer expenditure. The distribution of expenditure is shown in Table 16.3.

During the following year, expenditure on catering services rose substantially to nearly £7 billion at current prices. Expenditure on meals rose faster than spending on alcoholic drink. Between 1975 and 1976 the British were spending some £30 million a week on personal meals alone and £135 million on all catering services excluding accommodation. The survey showed variation by social class in the number of meal occasions and in expenditure in an average week: (see Table 16.4). Males ate out more frequently than females, accounting for 56 per cent of all meal occasions and 60 per cent of expenditure. Males between

	£ millions
Personal meals	1223
Alcoholic drink (excluding pubs, etc.)	311
Alcoholic drink in pubs, etc.	2440
Soft drinks	38
Hospitals and prisons	139
Residential homes	58
Educational establishments	388
Overseas tourists	125
Tobacco and other goods	774
Total	5496

Source: Hotels and Catering Economic Development Committee (1976)

Table 16.3 Consumer expenditure on catering services 1975 (excluding accommodation)

the ages of 25 and 64 spent 45 per cent of the total while participating in only 35 per cent of the meal occasions. The biggest spenders were men in the 25–44 age group, their female counterparts spent only half as much and ate out half as frequently. The price of a main meal without alcohol in an average restaurant or pub was just under £1. Meals at work were much cheaper. Forty per cent of meals were taken at work but accounted for only 20 per cent of expenditure. Restaurants, cafes and pubs took two-thirds of the expenditure on food.

Spending on eating out showed close correlation with consumer expenditure as a whole during the 1970s. Caterers

Class	Population (%)	Meal occasions (%)	Expenditure (%)
AB	15	18	21
C1	23	24	25
C2	32	35	35
DE	30	23	19
Total	100	100	100

Source: Hotels and Catering Economic Development Committee (1976)

Table 16.4 Meal occasions and expenditure per average week, 1975, by social class

maintained their share of consumer expenditure and were thus able to grow. New styles of dining began to emerge, ranging from the fashionable restaurants offering *nouvelle cuisine* to the popular steak houses and the developing fast-food chains selling hamburgers or chicken. There was also growth in take-away food which was not liable to VAT which had to be applied to restaurants from 1970. As will be shown later, there was an increase in female employment which had a positive effect on demand for eating out.

Trends in the 1980s

By the early 1980s the British had increased the number of meals eaten outside the home to a little over three per week. The highest income group was consuming five meals out per week with the lowest averaging two meals a week (Ministry of Agriculture, Fisheries and Food, 1995). The main determinants of frequency of eating out appeared to be income, age, geographical region and population density in the area of residence. According to the *Family Expenditure Survey* (Central Statistical Office, 1983), in 1982 the average spend of households on meals out was £4.25, but this varied from £1 to £13 according to income group. About 15 per cent of all family food expenditure went on meals out. This was the picture at the time of the 1981 to 1982 recession. Spending in the catering industry suffered a slight decline at this point, while consumer expenditure as a whole stayed level. From 1983 onwards, spending on catering recovered and surged to new high levels as the decade progressed. By 1990, 20 per cent of household food expenditure was being spent on meals eaten away from home, according to the Family Expenditure Survey (cited in Central Statistical Office, 1993). A comparison of all consumer expenditure with that on catering (meals and accommodation) at constant prices reveals the real growth that occurred during the decade (see Table 16.5). Figures 16.1 and 16.2

	1980	1982	1984	1986	1988	1990
Total	195.8	198.0	210.3	231.2	261.3	273.3
Catering	12.9	12.0	13.3	15.2	18.7	20.5

Source: Central Statistical Office (1992)

Table 16.5 Total consumer expenditure and consumer expenditure on catering (meals and accommodation) at 1985 prices (£000 million)

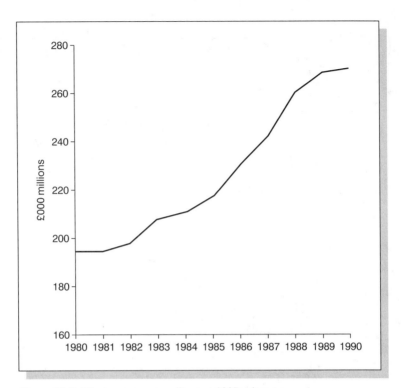

Figure 16.1 All consumer expenditure at 1985 prices

show the growth in graphical form. The amounts shown include accommodation but exclude drink and, as such, are indicative of spending trends on catering services.

The pattern of household spending on food, drink and catering changed significantly during the fifteen years between 1976 and 1991. Over this period there is a clear indication of a change in spending priorities (Table 16.6). Spending on food as a percentage of total expenditure fell by almost seven points. Spending on alcoholic drink declined slightly in importance as an item in the family budget. Within this, however, spending on wine almost doubled while beer suffered a decline in share of spending. At the same time, catering increased its share of spending to more than 8 per cent. Catering spending overtook spending on alcohol in 1987 and continued to climb to 1990 (see Figure 16.3).

There was a remarkable boom in catering during the 1980s and the consumer benefited from a very wide variety of restaurant types, from theme restaurants to the rapidly expanding pizza outlets. Throughout the 1980s, the commercial sector of the industry grew rapidly while staff catering and institutional

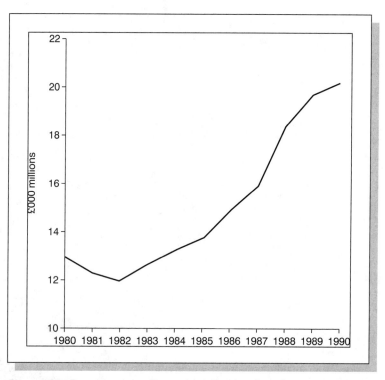

Figure 16.2 Consumer expenditure on catering (meals and accommodation) at 1985 prices

	1976	1981	1985	1986	1990	1991
Food	19.2	16.3	14.47	13.7	12.3	12.4
Alcoholic drink	7.6	7.3	7.3	6.9	6.4	6.6
Catering	5.4	6.3	6.4	6.9	8.0	8.7

Source: Central Statistical Office (1992)

Table 16.6 Pattern of household spending 1976–1991 (percentage of total household expenditure)

provision declined in importance as meal providers – a reflection of an affluent decade. At the same time, contract caterers began to flex their muscles and seek new markets in healthcare and education. One of the triggers for this was the introduction of compulsory competitive tendering for catering services provided by public sector organizations such as schools and hospitals. The

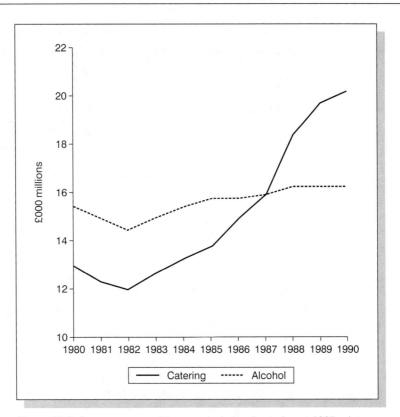

Figure 16.3 Consumer expenditure on alcohol and catering at 1985 prices

leading contract caterers sought to generate growth in their traditional field of staff catering by improving quality and by the acquisition of competitors. Both Compass and Gardner Merchant were bought out by their management from their parent companies.

Another feature of the 1980s was the emergence and establish-ment of mid-market restaurant brands such as Pizza Express and the increasing presence of burger outlets such as McDonald's and Burger King. Pubs became more important as suppliers of catering. Nevertheless, there were dark clouds on the horizon for brewers and licensees of public houses. The general public, in spite, or because of growing affluence, did not wish to drink beer. That most British of drinks, ale, was in decline even faster than beer as a generic commodity including lager. The public demanded wine and got it in abundance from a variety of sources, amongst which supermarkets had grown in strength to the point that they outperformed specialist off-licences. Table 16.7 shows the changing pattern of drinks' expenditure at constant

Percentage change	Beer	Spirits	Wine/cider	All alcohol
1968–1979	+30	+107	+104	+57
1979–1987	−11	−6	+46	0
1968–1987	+15	+95	+199	+57

Source: Slattery (1999), derived from Central Statistical Office.

Table 16.7 Percentage change in drinks expenditure at constant prices in Britain 1968–1987

prices. The figures reveal a big change in drinking habits leading to soaring wine imports. But the wine was not being drunk in pubs so much as in pub-restaurants, wine bars and, increasingly, at home. There was substantial growth in the number of restricted on-licenses to sell alcohol awarded by licensing justices; such on-licences are characteristic of restaurants where the beverage of choice for most customers was wine. It was not a good decade for brewers, but worse was to come.

Towards the end of the millennium: the 1990s

Overview

Industry in general and the catering industry in particular have had mixed fortunes in the 1990s. The boom of the late 1980s stalled and in the early 1990s interest rates rocketed from 7 to 15 per cent. As is well-known, many people were over-mortgaged and found themselves caught in the negative equity trap on their houses. Unemployment rose and house repossessions became the order of the day. Consumer confidence fell as fear of unemployment grew and, inevitably, consumer spending as a whole declined. Table 16.8 shows household consumption expenditure for the period 1989 to 1997 at constant 1995 prices to remove the effect of inflation. This is compared with spending on catering services.

It is clear from Table 16.8 that spending in general fell between 1989 and 1992 and then recovered slowly between 1993 and 1997, showing real growth. The consumption pattern for catering is different: catering was hit harder by the recession and showed virtually nil growth in the period. These are not exactly the characteristics of the growth industry with which caterers tend to believe they are involved. The most recent figures from the Office for National Statistics (1998; 1999a; 1999b) are more encouraging:

	1989	1990	1991	1992	1993	1994	1995	1996	1997
Total	413	416	407	408	420	429	438	454	471
Catering	39	40	37	36	38	37	38	40	41

Source: Office for National Statistics (1998)

Table 16.8 UK household consumption expenditure and catering services expenditure at 1995 prices (1989–1997) £000 million

these show that catering consumption reached £43,000 million in 1998 – an increase of 6.3 per cent on 1997. Even more encouraging is the figure for the first quarter of 1999 which shows a real increase of 9.9 per cent over the first quarter of 1998. The figures reflect a restoration of consumer confidence in an environment of lower interest rates, low inflation and reducing unemployment.

It should be noted that the above figures include meals and accommodation. It is possible to obtain disaggregated figures for the period 1989 to 1997 and these are shown in Table 16.9. This table shows consumption expenditure in restaurants and hotels and is not comparable with Table 16.8.

It is clear from Table 16.9 that the restaurant sector was faring less well than the hotel sector. Restaurants were badly hit by the recession and lost out in the struggle to maintain their share of overall consumer spending. The relationship between consumer spending in general and catering spending broke down. Between 1989 and 1997 the catering services share shrank from 6.9 per cent in 1989 to 5.5 per cent in 1993 and was still 5.5 per cent in 1997.

	1989	1990	1991	1992	1993	1994	1995	1996	1997
Catering	26	26	24	22	23	23	23	25	26
Accommodation	7	7	6	7	7	7	8	8	8
Catering and accommodation total	33	33	30	29	30	30	31	33	34
All UK	413	416	407	408	420	429	438	454	471

Source: Office for National Statistics, 1998
Note: Business expenditure is excluded from the above. Overseas tourist expenditure is included.

Table 16.9 Consumption expenditure of households on restaurants and hotels at 1995 market prices (£000 million)

Hospitality, Leisure & Tourism Series

	1992	1993	1994	1995	1996	1997	1998
Beer	15	14	15	14	14	15	14
Spirits	6	6	6	5	5	6	5
Wine	5	5	5	5	6	6	6
Cider	1	1	1	1	1	1	1
Total alcohol	26	26	27	26	27	27	27

Source: Office for National Statistics (1999a)

Table 16.10 UK household expenditure on alcohol at constant 1995 prices (£000 million)

It appears from this that consumers had re-arranged their priorities for spending in the 1990s and were either eating out less frequently or eating out more cheaply: possibly a combination of the two. Spending on alcoholic drink was also lacking in fizz in the 1990s and beer consumption was decidedly flat while wine drinking was buoyant, a pattern revealed in Table 16.10.

In the period shown wine consumption grew from £4700 million (billion) to £6000 million: a very healthy 27 per cent, or an average 4.5 per cent per year. In 1998 wine had a 22 per cent share of the alcohol market – up from 18 per cent in 1992. Beer's share declined from 57 per cent in 1992 to 53 per cent in 1998. Thus the trend in drinking habits set in the 1970s and 1980s continued throughout the 1990s and has persisted through the recession. Alcohol consumption overall has remained stable in the 1990s but the key thing to note is that it is failing to maintain its share of consumer spending overall. In 1989 alcohol consumption represented 6.9 per cent of total spending while in 1993 the share fell to 6.2 per cent and in 1997 was down to 5.7 per cent. This is indeed a change in spending priorities which is likely to be consolidated further. As evidence for this it is worth examining spending patterns over a longer time scale. Indices are used to indicate the rate of change in Table 16.11.

In the quarter century reviewed above, alcohol spending grew by a third, food by only a quarter while all spending nearly doubled. In the same period, UK tourists quadrupled their spending abroad. Spending by incoming tourists grew less dramatically: by two and a half times. Clearly, spending by UK tourists abroad is growing faster than spending in the UK by overseas tourists, although the gross amounts are roughly equal at about £15 billion for each category. The important thing to bear in mind is that UK consumers have changed the composition of their

	1971	1981	1986	1991	1997
Alcohol	100	127	134	132	135
Food (domestic)	100	104	109	115	127
UK tourists abroad	100	193	229	298	440
Overseas tourists in UK	100	152	197	187	246
All spending	100	121	144	166	193

Source: Office for National Statistics (1998)

Table 16.11 UK household expenditure 1971–1997 at constant 1995 prices (indices: 1971 = 100)

budget so as to spend relatively less on food and alcohol and more on transport, travel and household goods. These changes are not transient and they have profound implications for the hospitality industry. If food and alcohol are regarded as necessities, it is probably not so surprising that once consumers' needs are met demand will level out. By contrast, travel abroad, at least for holidays, is a luxury, the demand for which is growing rapidly.

The case of dining out is different from both holidays and food consumption because it includes necessity and luxury, or discretionary, components. The basic reasons for eating-out may be categorized as follows:

1 *Necessity* – e.g. travel, work or study.
2 *Contingency* – e.g. association with other activities such as shopping, leisure.
3 *Time-saving* – e.g. association with female employment.
4 *Pleasure* – e.g. social, family and friends meeting, celebrations, gastronomy.

To a limited extent the categories do merge into each other and it might be safer to talk about a spectrum of reasons for dining-out with pure pleasure and pure necessity at opposite ends of it. We have seen that during past decades, the share of spending needed for essential goods and services has declined, with a rising share of spending being taken by non-essentials such as leisure and luxury goods. Given that the industry at one end of the spectrum produces essential services, it is reasonable to anticipate that demand will level out – or at least grow slowly. At the non-essential end of the spectrum, there exists potential for real growth provided that incomes and expenditure in general continue to grow. Apart from incomes and consumer spending, there are structural features in British society which are likely to have a positive effect on the demand for eating-out in the future. A marked increase in female employment has led to a growth in demand for pre-prepared foods and for eating-out. There are now roughly equal numbers of men and women in employment. Female employment has grown against a background of decline in male employment. Almost half of women are employed in part-time jobs, but even part-time employment seems to increase the propensity to eat out or purchase a take-away meal. Purcell (1992) surveyed 500 women in England between the ages of 25 and 54. The responses showed that take-away meals were most often bought by households with women in full-time employment and least often when women were not employed. The frequency of eating out was also related to employment – 25 per cent of full-timers ate out once a week or more as against 16 per cent of part-timers and 7 per cent of those not in employment. The indicative evidence is that future growth in female employment will lead to higher consumption of catering services. In effect, people are buying leisure time by saving on the time required for food preparation in the home.

Trends in society cannot readily be slowed or reversed and the desire of married women to seek work and raise family income is not merely dependent on the state of the economy. There is good reason to expect that eating-out will grow further as incomes rise and more women engage in economic activity. Household chores such as routine cooking do not mesh well with the life-style desired in the new millennium. Increases in leisure time are likely to lead to more leisure activity, travel away from home and dining-out associated with this activity and dining-out as a leisure pursuit in itself (O'Connor, 1993). In their latest *Eating-Out Review*, Mintel (1999) observe that while spending on eating-out has increased by an apparent 24 per cent since 1994, the real increase is only 4 per cent. This is roughly in line with the figures shown in Table 16.9 and supports the view that growth in eating-out has been modest since the mid–1990s, at which point it had fallen below 1989 levels. It would be wrong to conclude from this that the catering scene has lacked vigour. In fact, the dining-out market has been in a state of dynamic flux. A tremendous amount of change has been taking place during which some businesses have succeeded and some have been casualties of the change process.

Restaurants

The past decade has been one of the most lively in terms of growth in the supply of mid-market restaurants (Slattery, 1999). There has been a growth in the number of restaurant brands as well as growth in the number of units operating as branded establishments. There has been considerable innovation in the development of theme restaurants and pizza restaurants. Fast-food restaurants and roadside chains have expanded and increased their share of consumer spending. There have also been failures such as the collapse of the Pierre Victoire chain. Some consolidation of ownership has taken place with companies such as Bass and Whitbread purchasing established restaurant chains. According to Mintel (1999) chains have almost doubled the amount they spend on advertising. McDonald's spent over £150 million on advertising and promotion in 1998, while Burger King spent £40 million and Whitbread £20 million. As competition in the market increases, brands and chains seem likely to increase their advertising budgets. If independent restaurants and small chains are to survive and develop they will need to increase their promotional activity, albeit on an appropriately modest scale.

Contract catering

According to the British Hospitality Association (1999) *Contract Catering Survey 1999*, contract catering has been a high growth sector of the hospitality industry. Turnover has increased by over £400 million over a three year period. The substantial growth is attributed to acquisitions from the in-house market and a strong trend towards out-sourcing catering and other support services. Growth in total turnover was 17.4 per cent, while growth in catering turnover was estimated to be 11.2 per cent before inflation was taken into account. The contract catering sector is believed to have a turnover of £3 billion. Catering for people in business and industry is the main area of activity, but education and healthcare are believed to be potential growth areas. A shift in policy from compulsory competitive tendering to the concept of 'best value' may prove to be no obstacle to the development of new contract business in the public sector.

Public houses

The pub trade in Britain has been undergoing rapid transformation since the Monopolies and Mergers Commission's study of beer supply and the tied-house system. Government regulations designed to increase competition and consumer choice in the supply of beer resulted in the Beer Orders. Brewers were limited to ownership of a maximum of 2000 pubs. Where a larger number was owned, they were required to dispose of them within a specified time scale. Brewers have had to decide, where

Hospitality, Leisure & Tourism Series

they owned more than 2000 pubs, whether to remain brewers and sell off some of their pubs or to become specialist retailers by selling off their breweries and running large chains of pubs. As a result of the impact of the Beer Orders, new pub companies have been formed which are not involved in brewing and which have new ideas about how pubs should be run and what they should offer to the public. Licensing laws have been relaxed and much greater flexibility in times of opening is now permitted.

Formerly most pubs were defined by the name of the brewer whose beer they sold. This pattern is changing to one where pubs themselves are carefully branded and designed to satisfy particular segments of a changing leisure market. The new pub companies are growing as they acquire more pubs from large brewers.

The demand for the pub experience is in flux too. As already noted, beer consumption is in long-term decline. Pubs which either do not serve food or provide entertainment are simply not viable. Customers now demand more variety from their pub experiences and are eclectic in their choice of venue as well as being willing to experiment. In order to maintain and develop revenues, many pubs have tried to enhance their food trade and some have become restaurants. Dining-out in pubs has grown considerably and they are increasing their share of the market. Mintel (1999) estimate that pubs have about 22 per cent of the eating-out market. It appears likely that pubs will continue to strive to increase their food revenues.

Other sectors

Meal provision by hotels is to a degree dependent on room occupancy rates, although banqueting, conferences and leisure clubs play a role in providing food and beverage business. A new feature is the move by a few operators to experiment with outsourcing some or all of the food and beverage business. There are some instances where this has been done successfully. It is too early to draw any conclusions from what has been done so far, but it is probable that experiments of this type will continue.

Traditional cafes have been in decline for some years, but a new feature of the catering scene is the coffee bar serving speciality beverages in simple and attractive surroundings. Both the coffee bar and its counterpart the sandwich bar are clearly meeting perceived customer needs and the operators are confident that they can continue to expand successfully.

Catering for the leisure sector is highly diverse, ranging from sports stadia with associated restaurants and banqueting facilities to cafes in museums and galleries. As the range and quality of provision increases customers are choosing to satisfy their desire to eat at the venue they are visiting. An increase in leisure time and growth in participation in leisure activities of all types present opportunities for further development of eating-out at leisure venues.

Lessons for the future

1 While it is true that disposable income and consumer expenditure generally are key factors in driving demand for eating-out, they are not the only factors of importance in assessing demand. Lifestyle, female employment patterns and social composition are also important.

2 There is a need for systematic research to be undertaken on the eating-out market extending over a long period of time. This should be undertaken by an academic establishment so that research outcomes can be widely published and be freely available.

3 Spending on food for home preparation has fallen in relative terms: in 1953 one third of the domestic budget was spent on food compared with one ninth in 1997. At the same time, spending on food prepared by caterers has grown steadily, but is no longer keeping pace with spending generally. Large restaurant companies are increasing their advertising budgets as the catering market gets more competitive.

4 The impact of innovation in restaurants and dining styles is generally positive for the market: whether ethnic, theme, modern or traditional, product innovation is often warmly received. It is easier for the larger companies to experiment and to evaluate outcomes, but they can also make bigger errors.

5 In 1975 expenditure on meals out was £2 billion a year; by 1995 this had expanded to £23 billion. Most of this expansion is no more than inflation. The lesson here is: do not confuse inflation with growth: revenues need to be deflated if real growth is to be assessed.

6 Spending on alcoholic drink and especially on beer has declined in relative terms as an item in household spending, but spending on wine has grown strongly. Pubs could improve their revenues by developing their wine sales as well as their catering.

7 The importance of women as consumers of catering services is growing. Some sectors of the industry are responding positively to this but others have yet to seize the opportunities presented by this.

References

British Hospitality Association (1999) *Contract Catering Survey 1999*, London: British Hospitality Association.

Bryn Jones, M. (1970) *Food Services in Britain 1970–1980*, London: New University Education.

Central Statistical Office (1983) *Family Expenditure Survey*, London: HMSO.

Central Statistical Office (1992) *United Kingdom National Accounts*, London: HMSO.

Central Statistical Office (1993) *Social Trends 23*, London: HMSO: 82–83.

Hammond, R. J. (1954) *Food and Agriculture in Britain 1939–45*, Stanford, California: Stanford University Press.

Hotels and Catering Economic Development Committee (1976) *Trends in Catering*, London: NEDO.

Medlik, S. (1978) *Profile of the Hotel and Catering Industry*, Oxford: Butterworth-Heinemann, 108.

Ministry of Agriculture, Fisheries and Food (1995) *National Food Survey 1994*, London: HMSO.

Mintel (1999) *Eating-Out Review*, London: Mintel.

O'Connor, J. (1993) A Review of Dining-Out Patterns in Britain, *International Journal of Contemporary Hospitality Management*, **5**: 3–9.

Office for National Statistics (1998) *United Kingdom National Accounts (Blue Book)*, London: The Stationery Office, 267–271.

Office for National Statistics (1999a) *Consumer Trends No. 12*: London: The Stationery Office, August: 31 and 63.

Office for National Statistics (1999b) *Social Trends, 29*, London: The Stationery Office: 105–109.

Purcell, K. (1992) Women's Employment and the Management of Food in Households, in *Food and Beverage Europe 1993*, London: Sterling Publications, 145–148.

Slattery, P. (1999) Personal communication.

Smethurst Foods Ltd (1965) *The British Eating Out*, National Catering Inquiry, Smethurst Foods Ltd, London.

Index

Hospitality, Leisure & Tourism Series